THE

INDIGO

PRESS

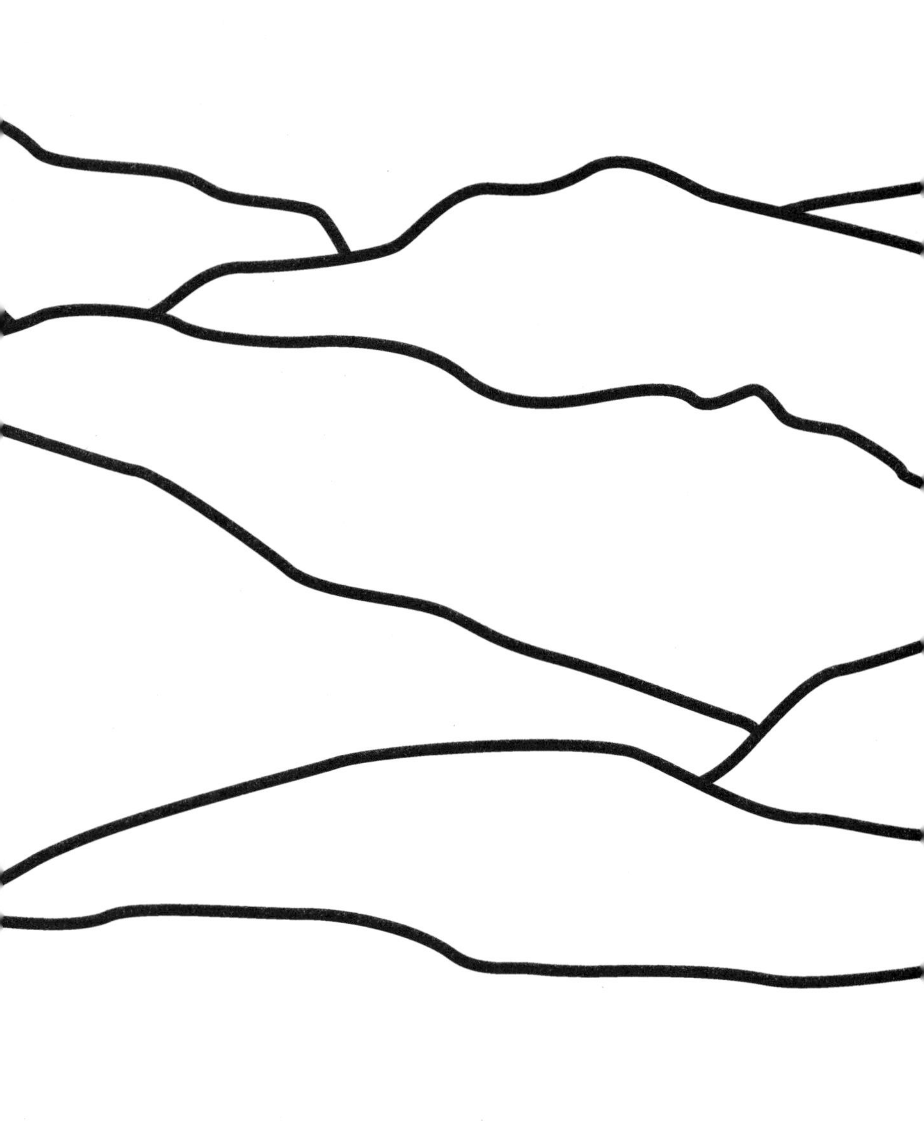

THE TWITTERING MACHINE

THE
INDIGO
PRESS

The Twittering Machine, Paul Klee, 1922

THE TWITTERING MACHINE

RICHARD SEYMOUR

THE
INDIGO
PRESS

THE INDIGO PRESS
50 Albemarle Street
London W1S 4BD
www.theindigopress.com

The Indigo Press Publishing Limited Reg. No. 10995574
Registered Office: Wellesley House, Duke of Wellington Avenue
Royal Arsenal, London SE18 6SS

A CIP catalogue record for this book is available from the British Library

ISBN 978-1-9996833-8-2
eBook ISBN 978-1-911648-03-1

Design by www.salu.io
Typeset in Goudy Old Style by www.beyondwhitespace.com
Printed and bound in Great Britain
by TJ International, Padstow

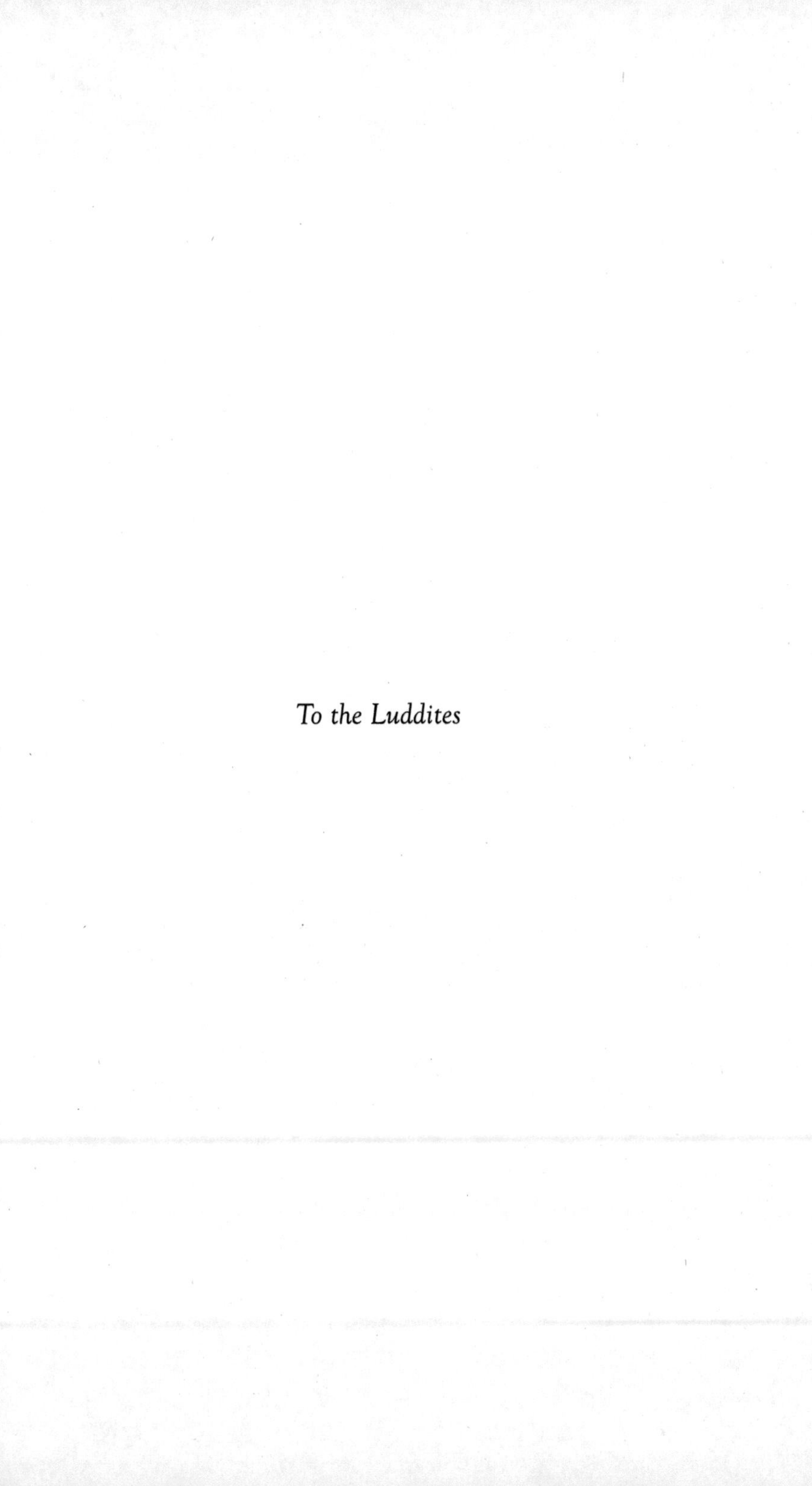

To the Luddites

CONTENTS

AUTHOR'S NOTE

In writing this book, I set out to avoid burdening it with references and scholarship. I want it to be read as an essay, rather than as a polemic or an academic work. But for anyone who wants to know more, or simply finds themselves asking, 'How does he know that?' there are bibliographical notes at the end. If you find yourself itching to research a quote, statistic, or fact, simply skip to the end and search under the page number for the relevant phrase.

FOREWORD

Everything on the computer is writing. Everything on the net is writing in sites, files and protocols.

Sandy Baldwin, *The Internet Unconscious*

The Twittering Machine is a horror story, even though it is about technology that is in itself neither good nor bad. All technology, as the historian Melvin Kranzberg put it, is 'neither good nor bad; nor neutral'.

We tend to ascribe magical powers to technologies: the smartphone is our golden ticket, the tablet our mystic writing pad. In technology, we find our own alienated powers in a moralized form: either a benevolent genie or a tormenting demon. These are paranoid fantasies, whether or not they seem malign, because in them we are at the mercy of the devices. So, if this is a horror story, the horror must partly lie in the user: a category that includes me, and probably most of the people reading this book.

If the Twittering Machine confronts us with a string of calamities – addiction, depression, 'fake news', trolls, online mobs, alt-right subcultures – it is only exploiting and magnifying problems that are already socially pervasive. If we've found ourselves addicted to social media, in spite or because of its frequent nastiness, as I have, then there is something in us that is waiting to be addicted. Something that social media potentiates. And if, with all these problems, we still inhabit the social media platforms – as over half the world's population does – we must be getting something out of it. The dreary moral-panic literature excoriating 'the shallows' and the 'post-truth' society must be missing a vital truth about their subject.

Those who enjoy the social media platforms tend to like the fact that they give them a shot at being heard. It weakens the monopoly on culture and meaning formerly enjoyed by media and entertainment companies. Access isn't equal – reach is bought and paid for by corporate users, PR agencies, celebrities, and so on, who also have better-funded content – but it can still give marginalized voices a chance where previously they had none. And it rewards quickness, wit, cleverness, play, and certain types of creativity – even if it also rewards darker pleasures, such as sadism and spite.

And if the use of social media unsettles political systems, this isn't entirely bad news for those traditionally excluded by those systems. The once-hyped idea of 'Twitter revolutions' vastly exaggerated the role of social media in popular uprisings, and these have since been overtaken by darker forces embedded in social media, from ISIS to Men's Rights Activists (MRA) killers. But there are times when the flow of information between citizens makes all the difference; times when the traditional news media can't be relied on; times when the possibilities of social media can be put to good use. Times, generally, of crisis.

Nonetheless, the crucial part of Kranzberg's observation is that technology is never neutral. And the crucial technology, in this story, is writing. A practice that binds humans and machines in a pattern of relationships, without which most of what we call civilization is impossible. Writing technologies, being foundational to our ways of life, are never socially or politically neutral in their effects. Anyone who has lived through the rise of the internet, the spread of the smartphone and the ascent of social media platforms will have seen a remarkable shift taking place. As writing has morphed from analogue to digital, it has become massively ubiquitous. Never before in human history have people written so much, so frantically: texting, tweeting, thumb-typing on public transport, updating statuses during work breaks, scrolling and clicking in front of glowing screens at 3 a.m. To some extent, this is an extension of changes in the workplace, where computer-mediated communication means that writing takes up an ever-larger share of production. And, indeed, there is an important sense in which the writing we're doing now is work, albeit unpaid. But it is also indicative of new, or unleashed, passions.

We are, abruptly, *scripturient* – possessed by a violent desire to write, incessantly. So, this is a story about desire and violence, as well as writing. It is also a story about what we might be writing ourselves into, culturally and politically. It is not an authoritative account: that is impossible this early in the evolution of a radically new techno-political system. This book is an attempt, as much as anything else, to work out a new language for thinking about what is coming into being. And finally, if we are all going to be writers, it is a story that asks the minimal utopian question: what else could we be doing with writing, if not this?

CHAPTER ONE

WE ARE ALL CONNECTED

There is in our future a TV or Internet populism, in which the emotional response of a selected group of citizens can be presented and accepted as the Voice of the People.

Umberto Eco, 'Ur-Fascism'

In 1922, the surrealist Paul Klee invented the Twittering Machine. In the painting, a row of stick-figure birds clutches an axle, turned by a crank. Below the device where the voices squawk discordantly is a reddened pit. The Museum of Modern Art explains: 'the birds function as bait to lure victims to the pit over which the machine hovers.' Somehow, the holy music of birdsong has been mechanized, deployed as a lure, for the purpose of human damnation.

I.

In the beginning was the knot. Before text, there was textiles.

From about five thousand years ago, the Inca civilization used quipus, coloured strands of knotted string, to store information, usually for accounting purposes. They were sometimes called 'talking knots', and they were read with practised motions of the hand, much as Braille is today. But every beginning is, to some extent, arbitrary. We could just as well start with cave painting.

The 'Chinese Horse' in Dordogne is more than twenty thousand years old. The image is spare. The animal has some objects protruding from it which might be spears or arrows. Hovering above is an abstract design which looks like a square pitchfork. Here, surely, is writing: marks on a surface intended to represent something for someone else. One could also begin with clay engravings, notches on bone or wood, hieroglyphs, or even – if you take a very narrow view of what writing is – the blessed alphabet.

To begin with knots is just to stress that writing is matter, and that the way the texture of our writing materials shapes and contours what can be written makes all the difference in the world.

II.

During the fifteenth century, sheep began to eat people. Thomas More wondered how animals 'that were wont to be so meke and tame, and so smal eaters' could have turned carnivore. He blamed enclosures. The emerging agrarian capitalist class found that they could do better business rearing sheep to sell wool on the international markets, than if they allowed peasants to subsist on the land. Sheep ate; people starved.

In the nineteenth century, the Luddites exhorted against another paradox: the tyranny of machines over human beings. The Luddites were textile workers, who noticed the way the owners were using the machinery to undermine the bargaining position of workers and accelerate their exploitation. A proto-labour movement, they used the only disruptive tactic available to them: they smashed the machines. But to little avail in the long run, as work was more and more automated and taken under managerial control. Machines operated the workers.

Something similar is happening to writing. At first, says historian Warren Chappell, writing and print were one and the same thing: 'They both begin with the leaving of footprints.' As though writing were both the journey and the map, a record of where the mind has been. Printed matter, arguably the first authentically capitalist commodity, has been the dominant format of public writing almost since the invention of the movable-type printing press almost six hundred years ago. Without print capitalism and the 'imagined communities' it helped call into existence, modern nations would not exist. The development of modern bureaucratic states would have been impeded. Most of what we call industrial civilization, and the scientific and technological developments it depends upon, would have come, if at all, far more slowly.

Now, though, like everything else, writing is being restructured around the format of the computer. Billions of people, above all in the world's richest countries, are writing more than ever before, on our phones, tablets, laptops and desktop computers. And we are not so much writing, as being written. This is not really about 'social media'. The term 'social media' is too widely used to be wished away, but we should at least put it in question. It is a form of shorthand propaganda. All media, and all machines, are social. Machines are social before they are technological, as the historian Lewis Mumford wrote. Long before the advent of the digital platforms, the philosopher Gilbert Simondon explored the ways in which tools generate social relationships. A tool is, first, the medium of a relationship between a body and the world. It connects users in a set of relationships with one another and the world around them. Moreover, the conceptual schema from which tools are generated can be transferred to new contexts, thus generating new types of relationship. To talk about technologies is to talk about societies.

This is about a *social industry*. As an industry it is able, through the production and harvesting of data, to objectify and quantify social life in numerical form. As William Davies has argued, its unique innovation is to make social interactions visible and susceptible to data analytics and sentiment analysis. This makes social life eminently susceptible to manipulation on the part of governments, parties and companies who buy data services. But more than that, it produces social life; it *programmes* it. This is what it means when we spend more hours tapping on the screen than talking to anyone face to face; that our social life is governed by algorithm and protocol. When Theodore Adorno wrote of the 'culture industry', arguing that culture was being universally commodified and homogenized, it was arguably an elitist simplification. Even the Hollywood production-line showed more variation than Adorno admitted. The social industry, by contrast, has gone much further, subjecting social life to an invariant written formula.

This is about the industrialization of writing. It is about the code (the writing) which shapes how we use it, the data (another form of writing) which we generate in doing so, and the way in which that data is used to shape (write) us.

III.

We are swimming in writing. Our lives have become, in the words of Shoshana Zuboff, an 'electronic text'. More and more of reality is being brought under the surveillance of the chip.

While some platforms are about enabling industry to make its work processes more legible, more transparent and thus more manageable, data platforms like Google, Twitter and Facebook turn their attention to consumer markets. They intensify surveillance, rendering abruptly visible huge substrata of behaviour and wishes that had been occulted, and making price signals and market research look rather quaint by comparison. Google accumulates data by reading our emails, monitoring our searches, collecting images of our homes and towns on Street View and recording our locations on Google Maps. And, thanks to an agreement with Twitter, it also checks our tweets.

The nuance added by social industry's platforms is that they don't necessarily have to spy on us. They have created a machine for us to write to. The bait is that we are interacting with other people: our friends, professional colleagues, celebrities, politicians, royals, terrorists, porn actors – anyone we like. We are not interacting with them, however, but with the machine. We write to it, and it passes on the message for us, after keeping a record of the data.

The machine benefits from the 'network effect': the more people write to it, the more benefits it can offer, until it becomes a disadvantage not to be part of it. Part of what? The world's first ever public, live, collective, open-ended writing project. A virtual laboratory. An addiction machine, which deploys crude techniques of manipulation redolent of the 'Skinner Box' created by behaviourist B. F. Skinner to control the behaviour of pigeons and rats with rewards and punishments. We are 'users', much as cocaine addicts are 'users'.

What is the incentive to engage in writing like this for hours each day? In a form of mass casualization, writers no longer expect to be paid or given employment contracts. What do the platforms offer us, in lieu of a wage? What gets us hooked? Approval, attention, retweets, shares, likes.

This is the Twittering Machine: not the infrastructure of fibre-optic cables, database servers, storage systems, software and code. It is the machinery of writers, and writing, and the feedback loop they inhabit. The Twittering Machine thrives on its celerity, informality and interactivity. The protocols of the Twitter platform, for example, centred on its 280-character limit on posting length, encourage people to post quickly and often. One study suggests that 92 per cent of all activity and engagement with tweets happens within the first hour of the post being made. The feed has an extremely rapid turnover, so that anything which is posted will, unless it 'goes viral', tend to be quickly forgotten by most followers. The system of 'followers', '@ing' and threading encourages sprawling conversations to develop from initial tweets, favouring constant interaction. This is what people *like* about it, what makes it engaging: it is like texting, but in a public, collective context.

Meanwhile, hashtagging and 'trending topics' underline the extent to which all of these protocols are organized around the massification of individual voices – a phenomenon cheerfully described by users with the science fiction concept of the 'hive mind' – and hype. The regular sweet spot sought after is a brief period of ecstatic collective frenzy around any given topic. It doesn't particularly matter to the platforms what the frenzy is about: the point is to generate data, one of the most profitable raw materials yet discovered. As in the financial markets, volatility adds value. The more chaos, the better.

IV.

From print capitalism to platform capitalism, the apostles of 'big data' see in this story nothing but human progress. The triumph of data heralds the end of ideology, the end of theory and even the end of the scientific method, according to former editor-in-chief of *Wired*, Chris Anderson.

From now on, they say, rather than conducting experiments or generating theories to understand our world, we can learn everything from mammoth data-sets. For those in need of a progressive-sounding pitch, the advantage of making markets massively more legible is that it spells an end to market mysticism. We no longer have to believe, as neo-liberal economist Friedrich Hayek did, that only markets left to their own devices could really know what people want. Now the data platforms know us better than we know ourselves, and they can help companies shape and create markets in real time. A new technocratic order is augured, in which computers will enable corporations and states to anticipate, respond to and mould our desires.

This fantastical, dubious prospectus is only plausible to the extent that we are writing more than we ever have, and under these very novel conditions. Estimates of social platform usage vary wildly but, to take a middling example, one survey found that American teenagers were spending nine hours a day looking at a screen, interacting with all kinds of digital media, composing emails, sending tweets, gaming and viewing clips. Older generations spend more of their time watching television, but they spend a similar amount of time gazing at screens – up to ten hours a day. Ten hours is more time than most people spend asleep. And the number of us checking our phones within five minutes of waking ranges from a fifth in France to two thirds in South Korea.

Writing is not all we are doing. Much of the time is spent consuming video content, for example, or purchasing quirky products. But even here, as we'll see, the logic of algorithms means that we have often, in a sense, written the content, collectively. This is what 'big data' allows: we are writing even when searching, scrolling, hovering, watching and clicking through. In the strange world of algorithm-driven products, videos, images and websites – everything from violent, eroticized, animated fantasies aimed at children on YouTube to 'Keep Calm and Rape' t-shirts – unconscious desires recorded in this way are written into the new universe of commodities. This is the 'modern calculating machine' that Lacan spoke of: a machine 'far more dangerous than the atom bomb' because it can defeat any opponent by calculating, with sufficient data, the unconscious axioms that govern a person's behaviour. We write to the machine, it collects and aggregates our desires and fantasies, segments them by market and demographic and sells them back to us as a commodity experience.

And insofar as we are writing more and more, it has become just another part of our screened existence. To talk about social media is to talk about the fact that our social lives are more and more mediated. Online proxies for friendship and affection – 'likes', and so on – significantly reduce the stakes of interacting, while also making interactions far more volatile.

V.

The social industry giants like to claim that there is nothing wrong with the tech that can't be fixed by the tech. No matter what the problem, there's a tool for that: their equivalent of 'one weird trick'.

Facebook and Google have invested in tools to detect 'fake news', while Reuters has developed its own proprietary algorithm for locating falsehoods. Google has funded a UK start-up, Factmata, to develop tools for automatically checking facts – such as, say, economic growth figures, or the numbers of immigrants arriving in the USA last year. Twitter uses tools created by IBM Watson to target cyberbullying, while a Google project, Conversation AI, promises to detect aggressive users with sophisticated AI technology. And as depression and suicide become more common, Facebook CEO Mark Zuckerberg announced new tools to combat depression, with Zuckerberg even claiming that AI could spot suicidal tendencies in a user before a friend would.

But the social industry giants are increasingly caught out by a growing number of defectors, who have expressed regret over the tools they helped create. Chamath Palihapitiya, a Canadian venture capitalist with philanthropic leanings, is a former Facebook executive with a guilty conscience. Tech capitalists, he says, have 'created tools that are ripping apart the social fabric of how society works'. He blames the 'short-term, dopamine-driven feedback loops' of social industry platforms for promoting 'misinformation, mistruth' and giving manipulators access to an invaluable tool. It's so bad, he says, that his children 'aren't allowed to use that shit'.

You might be tempted to think that whatever dark side the social industry has is an accidental by-product, like a spandrel. You would be wrong. Sean Parker, the Virginia-born billionaire hacker and inventor of the file-sharing site Napster, was an early investor in Facebook and the company's first president. Now he's a 'conscientious objector'. Social media platforms, he explains, rely on a 'social validation feedback loop' to ensure that they monopolize as much of the user's time as possible. This is 'exactly the kind of thing that a hacker like myself would come up with, because you're exploiting a vulnerability in human psychology. The inventors, creators . . . understood this consciously. And we did it anyway.' The social industry has created an addiction machine, not as an accident, but as a logical means to return value to its venture capitalist investors.

It was another former Twitter adviser and Facebook executive, Antonio García Martínez, who explained the potential political ramifications of this. García Martínez, the son of Cuban exiles who made his fortune on Wall Street, was a product manager for Facebook. Like Parker and Palihapitiya, he casts an unflattering light on his former employers. He stresses Facebook's ability to manipulate its users. In May 2017, it emerged, through leaked documents published in *The Australian*, that Facebook executives were discussing with advertisers how they could use their algorithms to identify and manipulate teenagers' moods. Stress, anxiety, feelings of failure were all picked up by Facebook's tools. According to García Martínez, the leaks were not only accurate but had political consequences. With enough data, Facebook could identify a demographic and hammer it with advertising: the 'click-through rate' never lies. But it could also, as a running joke in the company acknowledged, easily 'throw the election' by simply running a reminder to vote in key areas on election day.

This situation is completely without precedent, and it is now evolving so quickly that we can barely keep track of where we are. And the more technology evolves, the more that new layers of hardware and software are added, the harder it is to change. This is handing tech capitalists a unique source of power. As the Silicon Valley guru Jaron Lanier puts it, they don't have to persuade us when they can directly manipulate our experience of the world. Technologists augment our senses with webcams, smartphones and constantly expanding quantities of digital memory. Because of this, a tiny group of engineers can 'shape the entire future of human experience with incredible speed'.

We are writing, and as we write, we are being written. More accurately, as a society we are becoming *hard-written*, so that we cannot press delete without gravely disrupting the system as a whole. But what sort of future are we writing ourselves into?

VI.

In the birthing bloom of the web and instant messaging, we learned that we could all be authors, all published, all with our own public. No one with internet access need be excluded.

And the good news gospel was that this democratisation of writing would be good for democracy. Scripture, text, would save us. We could have a utopia of writing, a new way of life. Almost six hundred years of a stable print culture was ending, and it was going to turn the world upside down.

We would enjoy 'creative autonomy', freed from the monopolies of old media and their one-way traffic of meaning. We would find new forms of political engagement instead of parties, connected by arborescent online networks. Multitudes would suddenly swarm and descend on the powerful, and then dissipate just as quickly, before they could be sanctioned. Anonymity would allow us to form new identities freed from the limits of our everyday lives, and escape surveillance. There were a host of so-called 'Twitter revolutions', misleadingly credited to the ability of educated social industry users to outflank senile dictatorships, and discredit the 'elderly rubbish' they spoke.

And then, somehow, this techno-utopianism returned in an inverted form. The benefits of anonymity became the basis for trolling, ritualized sadism, vicious misogyny, racism and alt-right subcultures. Creative autonomy became 'fake news' and a new form of infotainment. Multitudes became lynch mobs, often turning on themselves. Dictators and other authoritarians learned how to use Twitter and master its seductive language games, as did the so-called Islamic State whose slick online media professionals affect mordant and hyper-aware tones. The

United States elected the world's first 'Twitter president'. Cyber-idealism became cyber-cynicism.

And the silent behemoth lurking behind all this was the network of global corporations, public-relations firms, political parties, media companies, celebrity avatars and others responsible for most of the traffic and attention. They too, rather like the advanced cyborg in *Terminator 2*, have managed pitch-perfect emulation of human voices, insouciant, ironic and intimate. Legal persons according to US law, these corporations also have carefully produced personalities: they miss you, they love you, they just want to make you laugh: please come back.

Meanwhile publicity, taken to the level of a new art form for those with the resources to make the most of it, is a poisoned chalice for almost everyone else. If the social industry is an addiction machine, the addictive behaviour it is closest to is gambling: a rigged lottery. Every gambler trusts in a few abstract symbols – the dots on a dice, numerals, suits, red or black, the graphemes on a fruit machine – to tell them who they are. In most cases, the answer is brutal and swift: you are a loser and you are going home with nothing. The true gambler takes a perverse joy in anteing up, putting their whole being at stake. On social media, you scratch out a few words, a few symbols, and press 'send', rolling the dice. The internet will tell you who you are, and what your destiny is through arithmetic 'likes', 'shares' and 'comments'.

The interesting question is what it is that is so addictive. In principle, anyone can win big; in practice, not everyone is playing with the same odds. Our social industry accounts are set up like enterprises competing for eyeball attention. If we are all authors now, we write, not for money, but for the satisfaction of being read. Going viral, or 'trending', is the equivalent of a windfall. But sometimes, 'winning' is the worst thing that can happen. The temperate climate of 'likes' and approval is apt to break, lightning-quick, into sudden storms of fury and disapproval. And if ordinary users are ill-equipped to make the best of 'going viral', they also have few resources to weather the storms of negative publicity, which can include anything from doxing – maliciously publishing private information – to 'revenge porn'. We may be treated as if we are micro-enterprises, but we are not corporations with public-relations budgets or social industry managers. Even wealthy celebrities can find themselves permanently damaged by tabloid attacks – so how is someone tweeting on the train, and during toilet breaks at work, supposed to cope with the internet's devolved form of tabloid scandal and bottom-feeding culture?

A 2015 study looked into the reasons why people who try to quit the social industry fail. The survey data came from a group of people who had signed up to quit Facebook for just ninety-nine days. Many of these determined quitters couldn't even make the first few days. And many of those who successfully quit had access to another social networking site, like Twitter, so that they had simply displaced their addiction. Those who stayed away, however, were typically in a happier frame of mind, and less interested in controlling how other people thought of them, thus implying that social media addiction is partly a self-medication for depression and partly a way of curating a better self *in the eyes of others*. Indeed, these two factors may not be unrelated.

For those who are curating a self, social media notifications work as a form of clickbait. Notifications light up the 'reward centres' of the brain, so that we *feel bad* if the metrics we accumulate on our different platforms don't express enough approval. The addictive aspect of this is similar to the effect of poker machines or smartphone games, recalling what cultural theorist Byung-Chul Han calls the 'gamification of capitalism'. But it is not only addictive. Whatever we write has to be calibrated for social approval. Not only do we aim for conformity among our peers but, to an extent, we only pay attention to what our peers write insofar as it allows us to write something in reply, for the 'likes'. Perhaps this is what, among other things, gives rise to what is often derided as 'virtue-signalling', not to mention the ferocious rows, overreactions, wounded *amour propre* and grandstanding that often characterize social industry communities.

Yet, we are not Skinner's rats. Even Skinner's rats were not Skinner's rats: the patterns of addictive behaviour displayed by rats in the 'Skinner Box' were only displayed by rats in isolation, outside of their normal sociable habitat. For human beings, addictions have subjective meaning, as does depression. Marcus Gilroy-Ware's study of social media suggests that what we encounter in our feeds is hedonic stimulation, various moods and sources of arousal – from outrage porn to food porn to porn – which enable us to manage our emotions. In addition to that, however, it's also true that we can become attached to the *miseries* of online life, a state of perpetual outrage and antagonism. There is a sense in which our online avatar resembles a 'virtual tooth' in the sense described by the German surrealist artist Hans Bellmer. In the grip of a toothache, a common reflex is to make a fist so tight that the fingernails bite into the skin. This 'confuses' and 'bisects' the pain by creating a 'virtual centre of excitation', a virtual tooth that seems to draw blood and nervous energy away from the real centre of pain.

If we are in pain, this suggests, self-harming can be a way of displacing it so that it appears lessened – even though the pain hasn't really been reduced, and we still have a toothache. So if we get hooked on a machine that purports to tell us, among other things, how other people see us – or a version of ourselves, a delegated online image – that suggests something has already gone wrong in our relationships with others. The global rise in depression – currently the world's most widespread illness, having risen some 18 per cent since 2005 – is worsened for many people by the social industry. There is a particularly strong correlation between depression and the use of Instagram among young people. But social industry platforms didn't invent depression; they exploited it. And to loosen their grip, one would have to explore what has gone wrong elsewhere.

VII.

If the social industry is an attention economy, its payoffs distributed in the manner of a casino, winning can be the worst thing that happens to someone. As many users have found to their cost, not all publicity is good publicity.

In 2013, a forty-eight-year-old bricklayer from Hull in the north of England was found hanging, dead, in a cemetery. Steven Rudderham had been targeted by an anonymous group of vigilantes on Facebook who had decided that he was a paedophile. For no good reason, someone had copied his profile image and made a banner with it, accusing him of being a 'dirty perv'. It took fifteen minutes for it to be shared hundreds of times; and three days of hate mail, and death and castration threats, for Rudderham to kill himself.

Only a few days previously, it emerged, Chad Lesko of Toledo, Ohio had been repeatedly assaulted by police and abused by local residents because they thought he was wanted for the rape of three girls and his young son. The false accusation came from a dummy account set up by his ex-girlfriend. Ironically, Lesko had himself been abused by his father. Such mobbing, increasingly common on the social industry, is not always the result of conscious malice. Garnet Ford of Vancouver, and Triz Jefferies of Philadelphia, were both witch-hunted by social media because they were confused with wanted criminals. Ford lost his job and Jefferies was hounded by a mob at his home.

These examples may be extreme, but they touch on a number of well-known problems exacerbated by the medium, from 'fake news', to trolling and bullying, to depression and suicide. And they raise fundamental questions about how the social industry platforms work. Why, for example, were so many people disposed to believe the 'fake news', as it were? Why was no one able to stop the crowd in their tracks and point out the vindictive lunacy of their actions? What sort of satisfaction did the participants expect to get out of it other than the schadenfreude of watching someone go down, even to their death?

While the social industry is perceived as, and can be, a great leveller, it can also simply invert the usual hierarchies of authority and factual sourcing. Those who joined lynch mobs had nothing to authorize the beliefs they acted on other than someone's say so. The *more anonymous the accusations were, the more effective they were.* Anonymity detaches the accusation from the accuser and any circumstances, contexts, personal histories or relationships that might give anyone a chance to evaluate or investigate it. It allows the logic of collective outrage to take over. It no longer matters, beyond a certain point, whether the individual participants are 'really' outraged. The accusation is outraged on their behalf. It has a life of its own: a rolling, aimless, omnidirectional wrecking ball; a voice, seemingly, without a body; a harassment without a harasser; a virtual Witchfinder General. Standards of veracity are not only inverted, but detached from the traditional notion of the *person* as the source of testimonial truth.

A false accusation is a particular type of 'fake news'. It involves matters of justice, and summons people to take sides. And since most people have no idea what is happening, no one is in a position to mount a defence of the accused. This leaves observers with the choice of maintaining a worried silence, or ducking for cover within the mob thinking, 'there but for the grace of God . . . '. At least, in the latter case, you get some 'likes' for your trouble.

The social industry did not invent the lynch mob, or the show trial. The vigilantes were out looking for alleged paedophiles, rapists and murderers to torment long before the advent of Twitter. People took pleasure in believing untruths before they were able to get them sent directly to their smartphones. Office politics and homes are filled with a version of the whispering campaigns and bullying that we see online. To disarm the online lynch mobs, trolls and bullies would be to work out why these behaviours are so prevalent elsewhere.

What, then, has the social industry changed? It has certainly made it easier for the average person to disseminate falsehoods, for random bullies to swarm on targets and for anonymized misinformation to spread lightning-quick. Above all, however, the Twittering Machine has *collectivized* the problem in a new way.

VIII.

In 2006, a thirteen-year-old boy named Mitchell Henderson killed himself. In the days that followed, his family, friends and relatives congregated on his MySpace page, leaving virtual tributes to the dearly departed.

Within days, they were targeted by a group of trolls. The trolls were at first amused by the fact that Henderson had lost his iPod in the days before he died and began to post messages implying that his suicide was a frivolous, self-indulgent response to consumer frustration: 'first-world problems'. In one post, someone attached an image of the boy's actual gravestone with an iPod resting against it. But what really sent them spiralling into fits of hilarity was the bewildered outrage they could provoke in the unsuspecting family. The more upset the family got in response, the funnier it was.

Over a decade later, an eleven-year-old boy from Tennessee, Keaton Jones, made a heartbreaking video in which, crying, he described the bullying he was subject to in school. His mother, Kimberley Jones, posted it on her personal Facebook page, and it swiftly went viral across various social industry platforms. Celebrities, from Justin Bieber to Snoop Dogg, joined in the wave of support for the child, and a stranger set up a crowdfunding appeal to raise money for Jones's family.

A degree of scepticism about the story would have been entirely warranted. There is already a long tradition of Upworthy[1]-style, emotive, 'compassionate' viral content, much of it manipulative where not downright fabricated. These videos tend to use sentiment to reinforce conventional morality. For example, a well-known viral video featuring a homeless man who spends money donated to him on food for others (rather than on the demon booze) was used to raise $130,000 in donations before it was debunked. Yet there was no such scepticism as far as Keaton Jones's story was concerned, and it seems to have been true.

Nonetheless, almost as fast as Jones was canonized, the tide turned. Social industry detectives had fished around on Kimberley Jones's Facebook account and found photographs of her, smiling, with the confederate flag, and posts where she spoke disobligingly about Colin Kaepernick's NFL protest against racism. Overtly racist comments were attributed to her, based on material found on a fake Instagram account. Rumours, never corroborated, emerged that Jones was bullied because he had used racist epithets in class. Tweets making this claim were retweeted hundreds of thousands of times. A parody account, 'Jeaton Kones', which portrayed Jones in stereotypical Southern 'white trash' colours, went viral.

Jones was, in the idiom of social industry users, 'milkshake-ducked'.

1 A 'viral' content website, specializing in 'uplifting' and 'inspirational' videos and stories.

He had become one of an ever-growing subpopulation of people who, having been adored by 'the internet' for five minutes, are abruptly hated because something unpleasant has been discovered or invented about them. But in this case, and not for the first time, the internet became far more ruthless and cynical with its questionable moral alibi than even the most sadistic school bully. As though there is already something potentially violent and punitive in idealizing someone; as though the whole point of such mawkish idealizations is that they have to fail – you set them up, the better to knock them down.

As this was unfolding, the latest in a string of cyberbullying-related child suicides took place in the United States. Ashawnty Davis, who, her parents say, was subject to bullying at school, found that a smartphone video of herself fighting another girl from the same school had been uploaded to a social industry app, where it went viral. Davis suffered tremendous anxiety over the video. Within two weeks, she was discovered in a closet, hanged. The discomfiting proximity of these events raises alarming thoughts. Would 'the internet' stop, would it even be able to stop, if it had driven Jones to commit suicide? If, rather than simply trolling a grieving family, online swarms had caused their grief in the first place?

A crucial difference between the Henderson story and the Jones story is that the trolls in the first case were marginal, subcultural, self-consciously amoral and easy to revile. In the second case, though trolls were certainly operating, their actions blended into those of millions of other social industry users driven by a mixture of sympathy, identification, emotional voyeurism, the sensation of being part of something important, ultimately souring into resentment, distrust and spite. The trolling was generalized.

One distinction, perhaps, is that trolls, unlike most users, are fully aware of, and exploit the cumulative impact of, hundreds of thousands of small, low-commitment actions, like a tweet or retweet. Most of those who participated in the mobbing of Jones spent at most a few minutes doing so. It was not a concerted campaign: they were just part of the swarm. They were minute decimal points in a 'trending topic'. Individually, their responsibility for the total situation was often homoeopathically slight, and thus this indulgence of their darker side, their more punitive, aggressive tendencies, was minor. Yet, incentivized and aggregated by the Twittering Machine, these petty acts of sadism became monstrous.

As the trolling slogan has it, 'None of us is as cruel as all of us.'

IX.

The risk, in appealing to such outré examples, is that it can legitimize a form of moral panic about the internet, and therefore dignify state censorship. This would be the traditional answer to the Oresteian Furies: domesticate them with the 'rule of law'. It is predicated on upholding a traditional hierarchy of writing, at the top of which is a written constitution or sacred text from which written authority flows. What a society deems acceptable and unacceptable is anchored to an authoritative, venerable text. Of course, the rule of law has never been as good at restraining the Furies as liberals hoped. The McCarthyite witch-hunts of mid-twentieth-century America showed that political paranoia could easily be disseminated through the workings of the liberal state.

What is happening now, however, is that the digitalization of capitalism is disturbing these old written hierarchies, so that the spectacles of witch-hunting and moral panic, and the rituals of punishment and humiliation, are being devolved and decentralized. The spectacle, which the French Situationist Guy Debord defined as the mediation of social reality through an image, is no longer organized by large, centralized bureaucracies. Instead, it has been devolved to advertising, entertainment and, of course, the social industry. This has birthed new ecologies of information, and new forms of the public sphere. It has changed the patterns of public outrage. The social industry hasn't destroyed the power of ancient written authority. What it has added is a unique synthesis of neighbourhood watch, a twenty-four-hour infotainment channel and a stock exchange. It combines the *panopticon effect* with hype, button-pushing, faddishness and the volatility of the financial markets.

However, the record of the liberal state in dealing with the social industry is poor, and there is a tendency for it to fuse with the logic of online outrage, rather than containing it. Cases of legal overreaction to statements made on the internet are well known. The debacle famously known in the UK as the #twitterjoketrial involved the state arresting, trying and convicting twenty-eight-year-old Paul Chambers for making a joke on Twitter. He expressed his irritation with the local airport being closed by 'threatening', in clearly sarcastic tones, to blow it 'sky-high'. Chambers' conviction was quashed after a public campaign, but not before he lost his job. Less well known, but perhaps just as ridiculous, was the case of Azhar Ahmed, who, in a moment of anger about the war in Afghanistan, posted that 'all soldiers should die and go to hell'. Rather than treating it as an emotional outburst to which he was entitled, the courts convicted him for 'sending a grossly offensive communication'.

Perhaps more telling are cases where police action was prompted by social media outrage. This is what happened to Bahar Mustafa, a student at Goldsmiths in southeast London. As an elected officer in her student union, she had organized a meeting for ethnic-minority women and non-binary students. Conservative students, outraged that white men were asked not to attend, mounted a social media campaign to expose her 'reverse racism'. In the furore, she was accused of circulating a tweet with the ironic hashtag #killallwhitemen, as proof of this 'reverse racism'. Mustafa, though insistent that she had never actually sent such a tweet, was arrested. The Crown Prosecution Service, rather than treating this as a bit of internet trivia, tried to prosecute her, only withdrawing the case when it became clear it had little chance of success. But it fuelled an apocalyptic multimedia storm of fury, resulting in racist abuse directed at Mustafa and invitations to 'kill herself' or offer herself to 'gang rape'. These tweets did not result in prosecution. Nor do the vast majority of such posts. Instead, the law was fused to arbitrary patterns of outrage flaring up against individuals deemed to have breached thresholds of taste and propriety on the social industry. The Furies are often magnified by the rule of law, rather than being chastened by it.

This means improvised rituals of public shaming, breaking like a thunderstorm on the medium, can feed into official responses. And because the social industry has created a *panopticon effect*, with anyone being potentially observed at any time, any person can suddenly be isolated and selected for demonstrative punishment. Within online communities, this produces a strong pressure towards conformity with the values and mores of one's peers. But even peer conformity is no safeguard, because anyone can see into it. The potential audience for anything posted on the internet is the entire internet. The only way to conform successfully on the internet is to be unutterably bland and platitudinous. And even if one's whole online life is spent sharing 'empowering' memes, 'uplifting' quotations and viral video clickbait, this is no guarantee against someone, somewhere finding your very existence a fitting target for abuse. Trolls programmatically search for 'exploitability' in their targets, where 'exploitability' means any vulnerability whatsoever, from grieving to posting while female or black. And trolling is a stylized exaggeration of ordinary behaviour, especially on the internet.

Not everyone is programmatic in their commitment to exploiting and punishing vulnerabilities, but many still do so, knowingly or otherwise. And it is compounded by the human propensity to confuse the pleasures of aggression with virtue. The late writer, Mark Fisher, described the progressive version of this through the baroque metaphor of the 'Vampire Castle'. In the Castle, Fisher wrote, well-meaning leftists accede to the pleasures of excommunication, of in-crowd conformity and of rubbing people's faces in their mistakes, in the name of 'calling out' some offence. Political faults, or even just *differences*, become exploitable characteristics. Since no one is pure, and since the condition of being in the social industry is that one reveals oneself constantly, then from a certain perspective our online existence is a list of exploitable traits.

And when a user's exploitable traits become the basis for a new round of collective outrage, they galvanize attention, add to the flow and volatility, and thus economic value, of the social industry platforms.

X.

'Language is mysterious', writes the religious scholar Karen Armstrong. 'When a word is spoken, the ethereal is made flesh; speech requires incarnation – respiration, muscle control, tongue and teeth.'

Writing requires its own incarnation – hand–eye coordination, and some form of technology for making marks on a surface. We take a part of ourselves and turn it into physical inscriptions which outlive us. So that a future reader can breathe, in the words of Seamus Heaney, 'air from another life and time and place'. When we write, we give ourselves a second body.

There is something miraculous about this, the existence of a 'scripturient' animal, barely a dot in the deep time of the planet's history. Early theories of writing could hardly resist seeing it as divine – 'God-breathed', as the Book of Timothy has it. The Sumerians regarded it as a gift from God, alongside woodwork and metalwork – a telling juxtaposition, as if writing was indeed just another craft, another textile, as in Inca civilization. The Egyptian word 'hieroglyph' literally translates as 'writing of the gods'.

The ancient Greeks exhibited an interesting distrust of writing, worrying that it would break the link to sacred oral cultures and, by acting as a mnemonic device, encourage laziness and deceit. Yet they also considered scripture holy in that it retained a link to the voice. The religious historian David Frankfurter writes that the letters of their alphabet, insofar as they denoted sounds, were regarded by ancient Greeks as 'cosmic elements'. Singing them could bring one to a state of perfection. So in addition to writing as mnemonic, accounting device and craft, here was writing as musical notation, divine poetry.

The relationship of writing to the voice has always been confused by historical myths. The Polish-American grammatologist I. J. Gelb was typical of his Cold War contemporaries in arguing that the purpose of writing was ultimately to represent speech, and therefore alphabets were the most advanced form of writing. In the alphabet, each letter represents a sound, or a phonetic element. In other writing systems, elements might include logograms, where a whole word is represented by a single element; ideograms, where a concept is represented without any reference to the vocal sounds involved in saying it; or pictograms, where the written element resembles what it signifies. The assumption of the superiority of alphabets, a progress myth of modernity, is based on the fact that they allow an infinite number of infinitely complex statements to be written down.

Most of the writing we are surrounded by today does not represent speech. Like seismic writing, musical notation, electronic circuit diagrams and knitting patterns, today's computer programs and internet code and script – the *ur*-writing of contemporary civilization – mostly dispense with phonetic elements. What is more, our online writing is increasingly rebus-like, drawing on non-alphabetic elements – emojis, check marks, arrows, pointers, currency symbols, trademarks, road signs, and so on – to convey complex tonal information quickly. Indeed, one of the ironies of writing on the social industry is that it uses non-alphabetic notation in order to represent speech better. The parts of our speech that have to do with tone, pitch and embodiment, and which are conveyed in real time in face-to-face conversation, tend to be lost in alphabetic writing, or expressed only with considerable elaboration and care. The economy of emoticons and memes is about giving the voice a convenient embodiment.

XI.

In 1769 the Austro-Hungarian inventor Wolfgang von Kempelen developed the first model of his *Sprechmaschine* (speaking machine).

It was an attempt to produce a mechanical equivalent of the apparatus – lungs, vocal cords, lips, teeth – which produces the acoustically rich, subtle and varied set of sounds known as the human voice. The inventor struggled, through successive designs using a box, bellows, vibrating reed, stoppers and a leather bag, to make his machine speak. Each time, its idiot leathery mouth yammered, and nothing remotely human came out.

At last, the problem of reproducing speech efficiently was solved with the telephone. Speak into a traditional telephone, and the sound waves hit a diaphragm, making it vibrate. The diaphragm presses on a small cup filled with fine carbon grains which, when pressed together, conduct a low-voltage electrical current. The more the diaphragm presses down, the more densely the grains are packed together, the more the electricity flows. Thus, by means of a mild electrical current, the voice could be separated from the body, uncannily reappearing halfway around the world.

In a way, it was a form of writing. The sound waves inscribed a pattern on the diaphragm and carbon particles, which converted the pattern into an electrical signal for transmission. But it left no permanent trace. The invention of a device which could be programmed with written instructions to carry out a series of logical operations – the computer – changed this, by changing the hierarchy of writing. When you write using an old typewriter, or pen and paper, you leave real, physical inscriptions on a surface. Even when mechanized, the shapes are imperfectly formed, and there are likely to be spelling errors and stray punctuation marks. When you write using a computer, spelling and punctuation errors are usually picked up, and the letters are formed as close to perfectly as possible. But the 'inscription' you see is the virtual, ideal representation of an entirely different system of writing being carried out on complex electronic circuitry, whirring discs, and so on.

Our entire experience with the computer, the smartphone and the tablet is designed to conceal the fact that what we're seeing is writing. According to the software developer Joel Spolsky, what we encounter is a series of 'leaky abstractions': 'a simplification of something much more complicated that is going on under the covers'. So where we see a 'file', 'folder', 'window' or 'document', these are abstractions. They are simplified visual representations of electrical parts performing a series of logical operations according to written commands. When we see 'Notifications' and 'Feed', we are seeing the simplified visual representation of the operations of written software code. These abstractions are 'leaky' because, though they look and feel perfectly formed, the complex processes they represent can and do fail. As in *The Matrix*, the writing programmes an image for our consumption: we don't see the symbols, we see the steak coded by the symbols. The image is the lure. What it obscures is that all media – music, photography, sound, shapes, spaces, moving imagery – has already been translated into the language of written numerical data.

But it is when we begin to write to the Twittering Machine that a new and unexpected wrinkle is introduced into the situation, upending the traditional division between the voice and writing. The Twittering Machine is good at reproducing elements of speech usually lost in writing, in a computer-mediated written format. It is not just that nuances of pacing, tone, pitch and expression are conveyed with some labour-saving economy by means of emoji and other expedients. In ordinary conversation, the participants are all simultaneously present, and the discussion unfolds in real time, not with the usual lag of written correspondence or emails. Because of this, conversation is informal, loose in its use of conventions, and assumes a lot of shared ground between the participants. The social industry aspires to the same celerity, informality, to give the impression of being a conversation. It gives voice to the voice.

However, what the Twittering Machine produces is in fact a new hybrid. The voice is indeed given a new, written embodiment, but it is massified. It becomes uncannily detached from any individual. It acquires a life of its own: immense, impressive, playful, polyphonic, chaotic, demotic, at times dread-inspiring. The holy music of birdsong becomes, not a chorus, but a cyborg roar.

XII.

It is ironic, given this massification, that so much social media talk is obsessed with individual liberation. What the social industry does is *fragment* individuals in new ways – you are so many enterprises, accounts, projects – and routinely reaggregate the pieces as a new, transient collective: call it a swarm, for the purposes of marketing.

The flipside of supposed individual liberation is the idea of a 'new narcissism', of selfie-stick, of navel-gazing status update. In truth, there is always narcissism, and it is hardly a sin. And if writing is about giving yourself a second body, then it is in some ways nothing but sublimated narcissism. However, the 'Skinner Box' structure posits, as its ideal subject, an extremely *fragile* narcissist, someone who must constantly feed on approval cookies, or lapse into depression.

The Twittering Machine invites users to constitute new, inventive identities for themselves, but it does so on a competitive, entrepreneurial basis. It can be empowering for those who have been traditionally marginalized and oppressed, but it also makes the production and maintenance of these identities imperative, exhausting and time-consuming. Social media platforms engage the self as a permanent and ongoing response to stimuli. One is never really able to withhold or delay a response; everything has to happen in this timeline, right now, before it is forgotten.

To inhabit the social industry is to be in a state of constant distractedness, a junkie fixation on keeping in touch with it, knowing where it is and how to get it. But it is also to loop what the psychoanalyst Louis Ormont calls 'the observing ego' into an elaborate panopticon so that *self-surveillance* is redoubled many times over. This is central to the productive side of the social industry. Indeed, in a sense it is nothing but production – of endless writing – more efficient in its way than a sweatshop. Jonathan Beller, the film theorist, has argued that with the internet, 'looking is labouring'. It is more precise to say that looking and being looked at is an irresistible inducement to labour.

What is it that we're labouring on? The birth pangs of a new nation. If print capitalism invented the nation, for many people the platform of their choice is also their country, their imagined community. Education systems, newspapers and television stations still defer to the national state. But when sociologists describe the proliferation of 'lifeworlds' online, it goes without saying that their porous outlines have little to do with national boundaries.

So if a new type of country is being born, what sort of country is it? And why does it seem so continuously primed for explosion?

CHAPTER TWO

WE ARE ALL ADDICTS

The trouble with modern theories of behaviourism is not that they are wrong but that they could become true, that they actually are the best possible conceptualization of certain obvious trends in modern society.

Hannah Arendt

Remember this: The house doesn't beat the player. It just gives him the opportunity to beat himself.

Nick 'The Greek' Dandolos

Oh this is going to be addictive.

First tweet of Dom Sagolla, software engineer and Twitter co-founder

I.

In 2017, Jonathan Rosenstein, one of the developers of Facebook's 'like' button, deleted his Facebook app. He was worried about what he had helped birth. These 'bright dings of pseudo-pleasure' that the button provided, he told the *Guardian*, had 'unintended, negative consequences'. It was supposed to be a happy button, a way for friends to be nice to each other. Instead, it had created addicted, distracted, unhappy users. It was cyber-crack.

Leah Pearlman was a user. Having also helped design the 'like' button, she was drawn to its lure. But the promise of the red notification was never fulfilled. 'I check and I feel bad,' she explained. 'Whether there's a notification or not, it doesn't really feel that good. Whatever we're hoping to see, it never quite meets that bar.' For the sake of her own sanity, she delegated the management of her Facebook account to an employee.

Many social industry and tech executives resist their own technologies. Mark Zuckerberg's Facebook account is run by employees. Apple's Steve Jobs wouldn't let his children near an iPad, while his replacement, Tim Cook, doesn't allow his nephew to use social networking sites. Apple's design strategist Jony Ive warns that 'constant use' of tech is overuse. As always, tech is adept at producing profitable solutions to the problems it creates. Now smartphone users can trade in their addictive devices for a range of minimalist alternatives, with the limited texting and call-making functionality of a very old mobile phone. Indeed, some of them initially sold at a substantially higher price than the smartphones they sought to replace.

But how was the addiction machine invented? The social industry platforms appear, as much as anything, to have stumbled on the techniques, in much the same way that their venture-capitalist funders stumbled on the profit model. But the potential for addiction was always there. Facebook's creator, Mark Zuckerberg, was always attuned to social technologies exploiting the pleasures of prying and social competition. One of his earliest sites, Facemash, exploited Harvard's online facebooks, which displayed photos and information about students. Taking photographs from these sites, he invited users to rate their comparative 'hotness'. Similar to another website, Hot or Not, users were shown two photos at a time and invited to vote for the 'hottest'. The college forced him to take it down for using the photographs without permission. But the site collected 22,000 votes before it was removed.

Zuckerberg returned with thefacebook.com in 2004, which was billed as an 'online directory'. The site combined some of the affordances of Friendster.com with the format of the Harvard facebooks. Its bare user interface and minimalist design suggested that it was to be a community tool, not titillation. Yet, according to David Kirkpatrick's history of the platform, *The Facebook Effect*, early users reported a fascination with the site. 'I can't get off it.' 'I don't study. I'm addicted.' The site wasn't just a directory, but a riveting source of voyeurism and social comparison for the students. One of the site's earliest users, Julia Carrie Wong, wrote for the *Guardian* of the insidious way that it combined 'useful information and prurient entertainment' while transforming social interactions so that 'popularity was easily quantifiable'.

Today, most successful apps and platforms depend on our enthusiastic willingness to share information about ourselves. Zuckerberg initially professed to be mystified by the quantity and detail of data people were willing to give him. He told a friend at Harvard: 'People just submitted it. I don't know why. They "trust me". Dumb fucks.' He had unwittingly tapped into the complex pleasures of self-display. The most obvious and oft-scolded aspects are the narcissistic pleasure of exhibitionism and competitive pleasure of being compared to others. But one of Twitter's early founders, Noah Glass, put his finger on another dimension: people would use social networking to make them feel less alone. Whatever was happening to them – an earthquake, redundancy, divorce, a frightening news item or just boredom – there would always be someone to talk to. Where society was missing, the network would substitute.

These pleasures are redoubled by the 'network effect'. The more people use it, the more valuable it is to each user. Zuckerberg understood, early on, that this was how he would build his site. As he told the university newspaper *The Harvard Crimson*, 'The nature of the site is that each user's experience improves if they can get their friends to join it.' Other colleges quickly signed up. And it took just a year for it to attract the attention of advertisers, thanks to the brute scale and objectivity of its data. By 2005, when Interscope Records launched Gwen Stefani's single 'Hollaback Girl', they approached Facebook. Facebook, unlike advertisers using cookie data, could *guarantee* that Interscope's advertisements would be seen by a specific demographic: college cheerleaders. The result was that 'Hollaback Girl' resounded at football stadiums that autumn. Facebook made two decisions. By the end of 2006, it had opened its service to all, accumulating a total of 12 million users. At the same time, its engineers set about developing algorithms to analyse patterns in their vast gold mine of data. Facebook piously claims that it doesn't sell user data, but the idea was to use the data to quantify, manipulate and sell user attention.

Facebook was catnip for advertisers, but it was also a large-scale public laboratory. By 2007, with 58 million active users on the site, teams of academics from Harvard and the University of California were studying profiles to gather information about the connection between users' tastes and values and how they interacted. Harvard sociology professor Nicholas Christakis, heralding a rebirth of the university's tradition of behavioural science, told the *New York Times* that the sheer scale of the data promised 'a new way of doing social science . . . Our predecessors could only dream of the kind of data we now have.'

As William Davies points out, however, behaviourist analysis only works if 'those participating in experiments do so naively'. The more they know about what is going on, the less reliable the results. The most infamous expression of this was the publication, in 2014, of the results of an experiment conducted on Facebook users. Seven hundred thousand users had been the unwitting subjects of the manipulation of their newsfeeds to enable researchers to explore 'emotional contagion'. The damage to Facebook's reputation was relatively limited, and social industry companies continue to supply masses of data, at cost, to researchers.

The biggest step forward for Facebook also radicalized its 'Skinner Box' propensities: the 'like' button. Facebook did not invent this tool. Reddit already used an 'upvote' button, and Twitter had allowed users to 'favourite' tweets since 2006. In 2007, the social aggregator site, FriendFeed, used a 'like' button for the first time. FriendFeed was purchased by Facebook in 2009, just as it launched its own 'like' button. This was an example of the practices of 'knifing the baby' and 'stealing the oxygen' that Microsoft pioneered in the late 1990s. Facebook was appropriating the work of a smaller rival, a number of whose features it had already built into its own design, and then buying it up to snuff out a market that threatened it.

According to Pearlman, the 'like' button was introduced to change user behaviour. This is what drives many of the innovations on social networking sites. For example, when Instagram introduced an 'Archive' feature for old or unwanted photos, it was to disincentivize users from deleting them and depriving the platform of content. In this case, Facebook had been looking at a 'bomb' button, or an 'awesome' button, which would replace redundant expressions of sentiment in comments threads with low-effort, quantifiable expressions of emotion. Instead of ten messages offering 'congratulations' for a wedding photo, there might be a hundred 'likes'. This would then incentivize people to make more status updates. It also built on Facebook's existing technique of quantifying popularity and allowing quick and objectively measurable social comparisons.

To say that it worked would be an understatement. The 'like' button changed everything on Facebook. User engagement exploded. By May 2012, with one billion active users, Facebook was so rich with profit potential it was able to make an Initial Public Offering for its stock. Other social industry platforms were unable to resist the advantages of the 'like' button. One after another, they followed suit: YouTube and

Instagram in 2010, Google+ in 2011, Twitter in 2015. With the social industry platforms a new industrial model was being born, and the 'like' button was a decisive moment in its consolidation.

The 'like' button is the pivot of the 'Skinner Box' model – the administration of rewards and punishments – in the struggle for the attention economy. It is the economic organization of addiction.

II.

Whether or not we think we are addicted, the machine treats us as addicts. Addiction is, quite deliberately, the template for our relationship to the Twittering Machine. The problem is, no one knows what addiction is.

What is so addictive about a 'like'? Until relatively recently, the medical and psychiatric establishment treated substance abuse as the paradigm for all addictions. Governments, led by the United States, have prosecuted a 'war on drugs' justified by the claim that users are chemical slaves, lacking control over their lives. This perspective was inherited from the temperance movements of the late nineteenth and early twentieth centuries, which saw alcohol as a demon possessing the drinker. It was then expanded to all use of recreational drugs, whether addictive or not.

Drug use, though, accounts for only a fifth of all addictive practices. Over the last few decades, there has been a profusion of treatments for a variety of obsessions – Bloggers Anonymous, Debtors Anonymous, Gamblers Anonymous, and so on. And since the 1990s, there has been a growing concern with something called 'internet addiction', followed by 'social media addiction'. The model for research into social media addiction is gambling addiction. Kimberly Young, a psychologist and founder of the Center for Internet Addiction, was an early pioneer in the field. An established expert in gambling addiction, she noticed similarities between the kinds of people who bet their house on a hand of poker, and the kinds of people betting their lives on a blinking screen. Neither involved a physical drug, yet both showed addictive patterns.

Young looked for a cluster of symptoms pointing to 'excessive' internet use. If users were preoccupied with the medium, if it took up increasing amounts of their time, if cutting down left them feeling restless, moody or irritable, or if they used it to escape from personal problems or feelings of dysphoria: that was addiction. Users were given a score, based on questionnaire answers, showing how severe their addiction was. Subsequent research into social media addiction has been similarly concerned with 'excessive' use of platforms for escapist purposes or mood management, adverse consequences and loss of control.

This has yet to congeal into a stable clinical category. *The Diagnostic and Statistical Manual of Mental Disorders* (DSM), the bible of psychiatrists in the US, has tended to see addiction through the prism of drug use. It has never recognized internet addiction. Even now, while it recognizes 'gambling disorder', it does not speak of gambling addiction. Even if the DSM were to change its approach, there would still be a problem, and it would be the same problem that afflicts most of the DSM's clinical categories. To describe a cluster of behaviours doesn't explain how these behaviours are related or what causes them. We can call something addiction because it resembles other phenomena that have been called addiction. But that still doesn't mean we know *what addiction actually is*. Amid the prevailing conceptual confusion, we need a new language.

III.

Addiction is all about attention. For the social industry bosses, this is axiomatic. We attend to what feels good, to 'rewards'. And, in an attention economy, the social industry platforms are waging a constant battle to manipulate our attention in real time.

Facebook's founding president Sean Parker echoed a raft of research in claiming that social media platforms achieve this by exploiting the craving for a 'dopamine hit'. Their machinery generates regular hits in the form of 'likes', with flashing red notifications administering the same high that a slot-machine addict gets when three bells line up. The anthropologist Natasha Dow Schüll argues, based on her study of gambling, that once these unnaturally large dopamine rewards flood into the brain, 'we lose our willpower.' Our brains, not prepared by evolution for such a flood, 'become overwhelmed and screwed up'. Nora Volkow, director of the US National Institute on Drug Abuse, insists: 'Addiction is all about the dopamine'.

And, whether or not the theory is true, techniques based on the dopamine theory seem to work. Adam Alter, a psychologist who studies online addiction, has sifted through the data collected by the app Moment, which tracks smartphone usage. Some 88 per cent of users spent 'an average of a quarter of their waking lives on their phones'. His own data showed, to his astonishment, that he had spent three hours a day on his phone, picking it up an average of forty times a day. And his behaviour may be relatively moderate: a 2013 study found that the average user checks their phone 150 times a day, which other research suggests includes 2,617 touches, taps or swipes. One recent survey even found that one in ten users has checked their phone during sex. But for Alter, as for most of us, the bait was so subtle and seductive that the catch didn't even notice his mouth clamping around the hook.

Not everyone accepts the dopamine consensus, however. Marc Lewis, a former heroin addict and neuroscientist, has written movingly about his own escape from addiction, and contributed enormously to the science of addiction. In his book, *The Biology of Desire*, he argues that addiction is not about taking this or that substance. It is the 'motivated repetition' of a thought or behaviour. The thought or behaviour might initially be motivated by the prospect of a high, or by the wish to avoid depression. But once it has been repeated often enough, it acquires its own motivation.

This is possible, Lewis says, because of the way the brain works. The billions upon billions of nerve cells that organize thoughts and emotions undergo constant change. Cells die, new cells are born. Some synapses become more efficient through practice, enabling better connections, others less so. By repeating a thought or a behaviour, we ensure the synapses and cells associated with it flourish, while underused cells die or become less effective. We change the 'brain's wiring', the 'neural circuitry' of wanting. The more we repeat an action, the more we train our brains for further repetition. We create an attention tunnel. As Lewis puts it, 'what fires together, wires together'.

At another level, that of meaning, one could say that addiction is a thwarted form of love. It is a passionate attachment to something that, slowly, occupies a larger and larger part of one's mind. It exercises a veto over other loves, aspirations and dreams. It occupies attention, when attention is subject to economic scarcity. It usurps our ingenuity, when the goal in life becomes maintaining access to the object, staying close to it. For the Twittering Machine, this is good: it keeps us writing. In an attention economy, addiction is not so much a scourge as a mode of production.

Anything that so captures our attention must be the object of intense fantasies. In the history of junkie literature, for example, drugs are magical, fairy-tale objects, summoning abundance from nothing, defying the laws of physics. Or so it seems at first. Thomas De Quincey's famous *Confessions of an English Opium-Eater*, for example, stands out for its utopian air. With the first hit, he had discovered 'the secret of happiness', 'a resurrection, from the lowest depth', an 'abyss of divine enjoyment', 'an apocalypse of the world within', 'portable ecstasies . . . corked up in a pint bottle'. He had discovered the magic beans, the goose that laid the golden egg, the flax spun into gold: emotional plenitude. A bounty comparable only to the oceanic bliss in pursuit of which mystics of all faiths have undergone extraordinary physical and mental rigours.

As the high diminishes, however, the fantasies become darker. When the Catholic mystic and poet Francis Thompson sang of 'The Poppy', the source of his 'withered dreams', it was as though he had become a hapless husk for the magical substance:

> The sleep-flower sways in the wheat its head,
> Heavy with dreams, as that with bread.
> [. . .]
> I hang 'mid men my needless head,
> And my fruit is dreams, as theirs is bread.
> [. . .]
> Love! *I* fall into the claws of Time:
> But lasts within a leavèd rhyme
> All that the world of me esteems –
> My wither'd dreams, my wither'd dreams.

His head, the actual source of his dreams, was, just like the flower, a 'needless' drooping cocoon for the opium. He credited his remaining creative power to the drug. Addicts tend to *fetishize* the object of their addiction. They attribute to it their own agency and imagine that it holds great powers that it really doesn't. At the same time, they suffer a profound subjective impoverishment: the addict is as poor as the object is rich.

The Twittering Machine appears to have a similar magical quality. Technology has never been just technology. It is always a world of intense emotional attachments. The Twittering Machine promises to give us access to everything, limitlessly, allowing us to transcend the limitations of mere flesh. This is how the telecommunications firm, MCI, sold the internet two decades ago. People could communicate 'mind to mind'. No race, no gender, no age, no infirmity. 'There are only minds,' the advertising breathlessly suggested. 'Utopia? No . . . The internet. Where minds, doors and lives open up.' This was digital Clintonism, a kind of thin liberal utopianism. Standing in a weak shadow of the opiate sublime, it promised an abundance of being, ageless immortality, protean plasticity beyond the bedrock of the body. The name of this abundance was *connectivity*, a truly magical substance.

The social platforms give concentrated expression to this idea, turning it into a business model and raison d'être. Facebook's first video advertisement reminded us that the universe 'is vast and dark and makes us wonder if we are alone'. We build connections, it said, to 'remind ourselves that we are not'. Connection was the basis for 'a great nation', 'something people build so they can have a place where they belong'. By implication, the platforms would be nation-builders, through the power of connectivity. At the outset of the 'Twitter revolutions', this same magical substance was supposed to outflank the old regimes and engender democratic upheaval.

But as the cyberpunk writer Bruce Sterling points out, connectivity is not necessarily a symbol of affluence and plenty. It is, in a sense, the poor who most prize connectivity. Not in the sense of the old classist stereotype that 'the poor love their cellphones': no powerful group would turn down the opportunities that smartphones and social media offer. The powerful simply engage differently with the machine. But any culture that values connectivity so highly must be as impoverished in its social life as a culture obsessed with happiness is bitterly depressed. What Bruce Alexander calls the state of permanent 'psychosocial dislocation' in late capitalism, with life overrun by the law of markets and competition, is the context for soaring addiction rates. It is as if the addictive relationship stands in for the social relationships that have been upended by the turbulence of capitalism.

The nature of this social poverty can be recognized in a situation typical of a social industry addict. We often use our smartphones to take us away from a social situation, *without actually leaving that situation.* It is as though we are both lonely and threatened by intimacy. We develop ways of simulating conversational awareness while attending to our phones, a technique known as 'phubbing'. We experience this weirdly detached 'uniform distancelessness', as Christopher Bollas calls it. We become nodes in the network, equivalent to 'smart' devices, mere points of relay for fragments of information; as much extensions of the tablet or smartphone as they are of us. We prefer the machine when human relationships have become disappointing.

IV.

Over the last twenty years, a number of apparently discrete social changes have taken place in the richer countries, above all in Europe and North America. First, a sharp decline in all forms of violence, including sexual violence, has been found in most of these societies. Almost simultaneously, these societies have seen a decline, almost a crash, in rates of alcohol and nicotine consumption, which historically have tended to be consumed socially. Finally, young people are having far less sex, something that has been subject to a great deal of mocking prurience. It seems odd, after all, that young people are more sexually liberal than their forebears, while at the same time more likely to avoid sex itself.

One thing that these tendencies have in common, though, is that they all show a decline in sociality. Other data confirms this. Analysis of American post-Millennials by psychologist Jean Twenge finds that they are far less likely than their predecessors to go out, go on dates or have sex. This is one of the reasons for the plummeting teen pregnancy rate. The trend, she says, is strongly correlated with the ubiquity of smartphones prevalent since 2011–12. Cigarettes and alcohol, like the proverbial coffee, have been used as props for social interaction. It is no accident, says the psychoanalyst Darian Leader, that as soon as we abandoned cigarettes, the mobile phone appeared in our hands – as though we can't face one another without some sort of medium. But the smartphone is not a prop for social interaction. It is an escape route, a way to connect with someone who isn't there; or is only there as a written trace, a ghost in the machine.

The fantasy of plenitude, the superabundance of online shit, may allow us to experience our social poverty as affluence, as in the fantasy that the internet and the social industry are 'post-scarcity'. Like many fantasies, this has some basis in reality when not just 'free stuff', but even affection and romantic excitement can be accumulated in an objectified form as 'likes' and 'matches'. But as with so many fairy tales, it is the fantasy, the wish fulfilment, of the poor. Social media are not the *cause* of this social impoverishment, any more than drugs are. They are just a more sophisticated remedy than booze and fags.

But the Twittering Machine is a techno-political regime which in its own way absorbs any nascent desire to challenge these painful conditions. The literary critic Raymond Williams once wrote of certain technologies which promoted 'mobile privatization'. While electrification and railway-building were public affairs, cars and personal stereos were simultaneously mobile and bound to the self-sufficient individual or family home. Silicon Valley has taken this logic much further, extending privatization into the most public of spaces, soliciting our participation on a solitary basis. At the same time, it has taken the place of previous forms of self-medication. Just as the pharmaceutical giants are losing ground with their 'one weird trick' pill-shaped remedies for social distress, tech says 'there's an app for that'. The psychoanalyst Colette Soler has written of 'the unprecedented development of techniques of listening targeting solitary voices in distress rather than really finding help for them'. The Twittering Machine is a technique for listening to solitary voices on a giant scale – shout at a politician, denounce a celebrity, rant at a CEO – the possibilities are endless.

Rather than reducing addiction to a chemical experience, then, we have to look at what problems addiction might be solving. In an arresting image, Marcus Gilroy-Ware compares social media to a fridge which has something new in it every time we look. It might only be a half-empty tube of tomato paste, an out-of-date yoghurt or last night's scraps. And we might not really be hungry. But at least we understand hunger, in a way that we don't necessarily understand the obscure feelings of dissatisfaction that sent us to the fridge in the first place. We have the option of treating this opaque wanting as if it *were* hunger, to be satisfied with a feed. But what is it that we're eating?

V.

Why is addiction such a useful economic model for social industry giants – indeed, for so many businesses? How does it work with the informational politics of the machine? And what does it say about the relationship of this machine to its users? Part of the answer lies in the mid-twentieth-century behaviourist revolt against free will. A revolt with a strange utopian dimension.

This is paradoxical, since the idea of free will is central to the liberal market-based system we inhabit. We're supposed to be able to decide what we prefer within the rules – rules which English philosopher Thomas Hobbes, in a pregnant metaphor, compared to the 'laws of gaming'. We may not decide the rules, but we decide where to place our bets and when to ante up. And on the face of it, that surely is what we do on the social industry. No one forces us to be there, and no one tells us what to post, 'like' or click. And yet our interactions with the machine are *conditioned*. Critics of social media like Jaron Lanier argue that the user experience is designed much like the famous 'Skinner Box' or 'operant conditioning chamber' invented by the pioneering behaviourist B. F. Skinner. In this chamber, the behaviour of laboratory rats was conditioned by stimuli – lights, noises and food. Each of these stimuli constituted a 'reinforcement', either positive or negative, which would reward some forms of behaviour and discourage others. In the Skinner Box, test subjects are *taught how to behave* through conditioning. And if this model has found its way into the mobile apps, gaming and social industries, it might reflect the way that behaviourist ideas have achieved a surprising renaissance among businessmen and policymakers in recent decades.

B. F. Skinner was not just a behavioural scientist, alongside peers, such as Pavlov, Thorndike and Watson. He was also a radical social reformer. For him, abandoning the myth of free will, and reorganizing society as an elaborate laboratory in which behaviour was carefully moulded by stimuli, was a utopian pursuit. This made him slightly different from the policymakers and academics of his era, for whom behavioural science was supposed to secure the social order and help the US win the Cold War against Russia. The behavioural scientists at Harvard were closely linked to the US Military, and Skinner himself had cooperated with the military during the Second World War. One of his major experiments was Project Pelican, where he deployed his theory of 'operant conditioning' to train pigeons to fly planes and drop lethal missiles while keeping pilots out of harm's way. The programme was surprisingly successful, but was never implemented. In the Cold War years, however, Skinner was sceptical about the widespread anti-communism of the time, and was suspected by the authorities because he opposed nuclear testing. He was far more interested in reforming American society than Russian society.

To reform American society, Skinner had to destroy what he thought were its ruinous myths of 'freedom' and 'will'. These concepts, he claimed, were literally nonsense: they described no observable reality. The same was true for other terms used to define mental states. In *Science and Human Behavior*, Skinner insisted that emotions were 'fictional causes' of, and an unscientific way of describing, behaviour. All of these states could be redescribed as behaviour produced by a good stimulus or a bad stimulus: a 'positive' or 'negative' reinforcement. Frustration, for example, was the behaviour emitted by a test subject not receiving an accustomed reinforcement. Loneliness was just a special form of frustration. It was not that Skinner didn't believe in mental states. He was, like most behaviourists, agnostic about them. As long as he had the means to observe behaviour up close, he didn't need to infer anything about mental states.

The utopian undercurrent of this approach was the belief that human behaviour could be regulated to avoid unnecessary harm. This was first fully outlined in Skinner's bestselling science-fiction utopian novel, *Walden Two*. The title evoked the libertine philosophy of Henry David Thoreau, and Skinner even expressed some interest in nineteenth-century anarchism. But the utopian community of the book is closer to the 'Bensalem' of Francis Bacon's *New Atlantis*, a New World colony ruled by a scientific caste dedicated to enlightenment. Rather than being run by scientists directly, however, Walden Two is ruled by behavioural engineering: a sort of algorithm, manipulating the environment to produce good citizens. The algorithm could go on being updated to account for the latest scientific research, and it would be free of the moralism and bullying associated with doctrines of 'free will'. Since choices were determined by reinforcements, bad behaviour reflected a failure in the system. Punishment was abandoned, restrictions on sexual love dropped and the workload radically reduced to give workers more time for creativity.

Skinner tried, repeatedly, to develop technologies that would implement his ideas. For example, in the post-war era he developed and marketed a teaching machine to eliminate failure in the classroom. The machine would pose quick questions or supply sentences with blanks to be filled in. The students would mark the answer on a strip of paper that the machine would read and assess. This was a perfect behaviourist technology, because it treated its users as learning machines. It varied the pace and pattern of stimuli to keep users attentive, much as Facebook algorithms engage users, effectively 'teaching' them how to behave on the machine by varying the content of their feed. For Skinner, the machine would remove the arbitrariness and inefficiencies of human teachers. And it would change student behaviour by *teaching them to be right*.

One obvious problem with this is that quite a lot of what there is to teach can't be quickly tested. You can test knowledge of historical dates, mathematical equations and capital cities. Anything more complex, like critical analysis, is beyond the ken of a machine. When there is no right answer, *students have to learn how to be wrong*. They have to give up and mourn their mistaken belief that they know everything. Another problem is that we are not learning machines. So what can a teaching machine do with the part of us that never learns anything? How to educate the part of us that stubbornly entertains unrealistic fantasies and unreasonable passions, regardless of reality, cleaving to self-destruction in the face of all warning? Behaviourism blithely overlooks this everyday reality, or treats it as an inconvenience to work around. Yet arguably it is this irrational kernel, this human oddity, that gives us the desire to learn anything in the first place.

The most important problem with teaching machines, though, is political. In *Walden Two*, the community is overseen by a benign tyrant, Frazier. In defending his techniques, Frazier argues that the alternative is to leave them in the hands of wicked movements like the Nazis. This comparison only serves to illustrate his authoritarianism. The fantasy is that it is possible to know, through scientific research, what is good and how people ought to live. It is a fantasy in which meaning is replaced by technique, and all that is contrary, disputatious and unpleasant in social life is replaced by a smooth surface and flow. (Perhaps it is no coincidence that the aesthetic of late capitalism, and particularly of smartphones and apps, is so obsessed with smoothness and flow.) This requires relentless intrusive surveillance and laboratory-like manipulation of the entire population. But the secret of the good life is not something that *can* be known, it being different for everyone. So, behind the rule of science and technology, there has to be a tyranny somewhere making these decisions. A small number of real-world communities attempted to emulate Walden Two, with varying degrees of success, one of the main drawbacks being that leaders often identified with the benevolent authoritarianism of Frazier.

Radical behaviourism produced bad utopias and bad theory. Beginning in the 1970s, it was overtaken in the field of psychology by cognitive approaches which were more interested in analysing mental states. Nonetheless, bad theory sometimes produces useful techniques. For example, a teaching machine might not know anything about human desires, but a highly sophisticated machine with enough data could learn to manipulate them. By picking up on regular behavioural patterns, it could learn how to 'teach' minds, to train the brain's attention in particular ways. Sure enough, behaviourist ideas have gained traction. Having lost ground in psychology, they filtered into neuroscience, which was taking an aggressively reductive turn. By the early 1990s, brain scientists had come to believe that mental states could be explained by the physical structure of the brain, which in turn could be explained by genetics and environment. Rather than wrestle with the complexities of mind, meaning and motivation, it was sufficient to study the brain as an organism. This belief was not only congruent with behaviourist ideas about conditioning, but was strongly influenced by behaviourism. And it was extremely useful for the pharmaceutical giants. For example, if mental states like depression or anxiety could be understood as chemical states, they could be treated with 'happy' pills.

Behaviourism also inspired the enormously influential discipline of behavioural economics, which extends its reach into the heart of government as well into highly profitable industries such as amusement, gambling and tech. Nir Eyal, a businessman and behavioural economist, argues that successful businesses use these techniques to get customers addicted: the 'Hook Model' of business. The idea is to use 'rewards' to plant an 'internal trigger' in the customer's mind. If, for example, the slightest pang of loneliness, boredom or frustration makes us pick up our phones without thinking, that is an internal trigger: we're hooked. Strikingly, Eyal's theory rests on the radical contention that 'there is no such thing as a "self". You are just a collection of your past experiences and habits.' The best way for a company to make a continuous profit is to be first in the queue in defining those experiences and habits.

Skinner's utopia shadows the Twittering Machine. Although, like all corporations, the social industy giants claim to be giving people what they want, their techniques assume that we can't know what we want. Nor, even if they thought we did know, would they have any reason to give it to us. The machine is not a democracy, and it isn't even a market; we are neither customers nor voters. We are digital 'serfs', says Jaron Lanier, the 'livestock of a feudal demesne', according to Bruce Sterling.

We inhabit a laboratory, a real-life operant conditioning chamber, into which we have been lured by the promise of democratized luxury. In the early days of the internet, the promise was that we could 'Ask Jeeves'; now we are offered 'tools' and 'virtual assistants'. On that basis, millions of us have entered a web of surveillance in which we are the servants, providing endless hours of free labour. We are even subtly assigned 'microtasks' without noticing. Every time we fill in a Captcha, where we are asked to transcribe some letters and numbers to 'prove we are human' and get access to our emails, we may be helping a commercial firm digitize an archive. In the emerging world, free labour is extracted from customers under the guise of 'participation' and 'feedback'.

From the point of view of freedom, says Shoshana Zuboff, this new 'surveillance capitalism' is worse than the panopticon. The panopticon teaches us to conform with dominant norms. But that sort of power at least acknowledges that we might not conform. In surveillance capitalism, by contrast, the mechanisms of observation and manipulation are designed without any assumption of psychological self-determination. Conformity disappears into the machinery, an order of stimulus–response, cause and effect.

Skinner's techniques, coupled with the post-Cold War scientific world view, armed corporations and governments with a form of subtle, micro-level social engineering, backed up with decades of scientific research and, now, big data. In the social industry, the teaching machine became an addiction machine. And, as it transpires, it is not the classroom for which operant conditioning is best suited, but the casino.

VI.

What if one were to store up all the energy and passion . . . which every year is squandered . . . at the gaming tables of Europe?

Ludwig Börne

The analogy between the gambler and the social media junkie is hard to avoid. Tristan Harris, Google's former design ethicist, calls your smartphone 'The Slot Machine in Your Pocket'. Most smartphone apps use 'intermittent variable rewards' to keep users hooked. Because rewards are variable, they are uncertain: you have to pull the lever to see what you're going to get. Adam Alter adds that with the invention of the 'like' button, users are gambling every time they post. Natasha Schüll, based on her work on machine-gambling, agrees.

Today's casinos are very different from the macho dice and card play organized by old-school crime bosses. At the roulette table, the gambler could justify his perverse pleasure in risk-taking as a matter of honour in competition with peers. In recent decades, however, the favoured form has moved from the table to the slot machine. And the slot machines, digital and complex, have come a long way from the days of the one-armed bandit. Now the gambler experiences no macho showdowns, just an interactive screen offering multiple permutations of odds and stakes, deploying user-experience design techniques similar to video-gaming to induce pleasure. The machines have a range of devices to give users the appearance of regular wins to keep them playing. These are often 'losses disguised as wins', insofar as the pay-off is less than the cost of playing. But the wins are not even the goal of playing. When we're on the machine, Schüll finds, our goal is to stay connected. As one addict explains, she is not playing to win but to 'stay in that machine zone where nothing else matters'. The gambling industry recognizes this desire to avoid social reality. It is called 'time on device', and everything about the machine is designed to cultivate it.

'Time on device' pinpoints something crucial about addiction. Traditionally, casinos have blocked out daylight and banned anything that conveys the sense of time passing: no windows, no clocks, and a constant supply of refreshments rather than timed meals. Some gambling-machine addicts today prefer to urinate in a paper cup rather than leave the device. Pubs and opium dens also have a history of blotting out daylight to allow users to enjoy themselves without the intrusion of time. The sense of dropping out of time is common to many addictions. As one former gambling addict puts it, 'All I can remember is living in a trance for four years.' Schüll calls it the 'machine zone' where ordinary reality is 'suspended in the mechanical rhythm of a repeating process'. For many addicts, the idea of facing the normal flow of time is unbearably depressing. Marc Lewis describes how even after kicking junk he couldn't face 'a day without a change of state'.

The Twittering Machine, as a wholly designed operant conditioning chamber, needs none of the expedients of the casino or opium den. The user has already dropped out of work, a boring lunch, an anxious social situation or bad sex, to enter into a different, timeless, time zone. What we do on the Twittering Machine has as much to do with what we're *avoiding* as what we find when we log in – which, after all, is often not that exciting. There is no need to block out the windows because that is what the screen is already doing: screening out daylight.

And it manages time differently. For gamblers, the only temporal rhythm that matters is the sequence of encounters with destiny, the run of luck. For drug users, what matters is the rhythms of the high, whether it is the 'stationary' effect of opium or the build, crescendo and crash of alcohol. The experience of platform users, on the other hand, is organized in a trance-like flow. The user is plunged into a stream of real-time information and disciplined to stay constantly ahead of it. Twitter highlights not the time and date of posts, but their age and thus *currency*: 4m, or 12h, as the case may be.

The ensuing trance-like state, according to digital theorist David Berry, is remarkably similar to what in early stock markets was called the 'ticker trance'. Financial speculators would become absorbed in watching the signals conveyed on stock market ticker tape, vigilant to every minute variation in a real-time flow. That is to say the timestamp, like the coded information on the ticker tape, is information about the state of the game. It enables users to place an informed bet.

If social industry platforms are like casinos, then they build on the existing extension of gambling in the neo-liberal era. Whereas gambling was controlled in a paternalistic way in the post-war era, laws have been increasingly liberalized over the past forty years. In the UK, this change was heralded by Lord Rothschild's Royal Commission on Gambling, and culminated in nearly wholesale liberalization with the Gambling Review Body's recommendations in 2001. Today, the majority of Britons gamble in some form, most commonly through the National Lottery. Similar transformations have taken place in the United States and Canada, and the European Commission has pressured holdouts like Italy, Austria and France to liberalize.

All of this has taken place concurrently with waves of *financial* liberalization, wherein capitalist dynamism was increasingly dependent on the bets and derivative bets of the stock market. And there is a logical convergence between financialization and tech. The financial sector is the most computerized sector of capitalism, and the use of software for trading has resulted in numerous efforts to 'game the system' – as in May 2010, when a trader's use of algorithms to repeatedly 'spoof' bets against the market some nineteen thousand times, briefly caused a trillion-dollar crash.

Culturally, the idea of life as a lottery, which only a few magical adepts know how to 'work', has gained widespread traction both as a folk social theory and as an explanation for human misfortune. This links gambling to destiny and divine judgement in a way that reaches back to its earliest expressions. As the late literary scholar Bettina Knapp explained, the use of gambling as a divinatory device, as a way to work out what the Supreme Being wants of us, has been found in Shintoism, Hinduism, Christianity and the *I Ching*. At several points in the Bible, the drawing or casting of lots is used to discern divine will. In essence, the lot or die is a question about fate, posed to a superpower. Something similar happens when we post a tweet or a status or an image, where we have little control over the context in which it will be seen and understood. It's a gamble.

The cliché holds that the social industry platforms administer 'social approval' in metrically precise doses. But that's like treating gambling as though it were only about the pay-offs. Every post is a lot cast for the contemporary equivalent of the God of Everything. What we're really asking for when we post a status is a verdict. In telling the machine something about ourselves, whatever else we're trying to achieve, we are asking for *judgement*. And everyone who places a bet expects to lose.

VII.

Losing, and anteing up until you lose everything, is a normal part of addiction. Yet this self-destructive aspect is strangely foreclosed by the prevalent 'dopamine' model of addiction. In that theory, behaviourism is fused with the fruits of neuroscience to argue that addiction is a result of behaviour followed by positive reinforcement: a rush of dopamine and adrenaline, for example, causing the behaviour to be repeated. Repetition is then further negatively reinforced by physically unpleasant withdrawal symptoms.

It is true that addiction has definite physiological effects. A study of 'internet addiction' found that withdrawal symptoms are very similar to those for drug addiction: elevated heart rate, blood pressure and anxiety. But dopamine doesn't work quite the way it was assumed to work. According to the neuroscientist Robert Sapolsky, the latest research finds that it is linked not to pleasure, but to *appetite and anticipation*. It makes us hanker for something but doesn't give us a high. Dopamine, as the anthropologist Helen Fisher puts it, travels down the 'neurochemical pathways for wanting'. It is not about pleasure, but desire. Addiction is something that is done with wanting, by those who are done with wanting.

So far, though, even this is perfectly congruent with behaviourist assumptions. But physiological patterns are not an explanation for addiction; they are what needs to be explained. The chemical pathways created by the motivated repetition of behaviour are not, at the same time, its sufficient cause. If addiction is a passion, a form of love gone awry, then the medical model of addiction misses the point as surely as does the medical model of love. All experience has a biochemical signature, so it is legitimate to describe it at that level. To *reduce* experience to chemistry, however, is to bypass what is essential to it: its meaning.

The psychologist Stanton Peele and psychiatrist Archie Brodsky argue that to be addicted is to form an emotional dependency where another emotional relationship has failed. And whether you become dependent on another person, a set of beliefs or a substance is an accident of circumstance. Social class, culture and childhood experiences dispose you to different types of dependence. Your route out of a damaging addiction might be to discover a better dependence, a new consuming passion. This is to treat recovery not so much as a lucky escape from a disease, but as a creative act. Addicts who quit, says Marc Lewis, do so 'uniquely and inventively'. They don't merely plot a path to abstinence; they learn an entirely new way of being.

It is not an accident that so many recovering from a drug addiction make their way to religion, the ultimate consuming passion. (And for the gambler, as Pascal suggested, the ultimate wager.) The Latin root word, *addicere*, has its origins as a technical term in Roman law. To be addicted was to be given over, delivered. But by the early modern period, it had come to mean something else: to addict was to devote, consecrate or sacrifice. To be addicted was to be dedicated, usually to a vocation or calling. Paradoxically, it involved the free surrender of choice, just as any calling does. This is far from the image of the addict as a pathetic, chemically enslaved wreck, their moral autonomy in tatters. And it suggests that the psychologist Jeffrey Schaler is right to argue that the problem is we have chosen the wrong addictions. What we call addictions are misplaced devotions: we love the wrong things. But what sort of *vocation* could the Twittering Machine be? How can we be *devoted* to a technology that is marketed as *our* servant?

VIII.

To an extent, our devotion to the machine has taken place without our informed consent. After all, what is the distinction between addiction and ordinary use? The more the Twittering Machine expands and colonizes our daily lives, the more the lines between 'excessive' and 'normal' behaviour are blurred.

The more society becomes dependent on the social industry to achieve everyday goals, such as socializing, entertainment, job-seeking and romance, the more it becomes logical, not pathological, to use them often and to become anxious when cut off. Think of the smartphone, the technological basis for platform interaction that, in a few short years, has taken over our lives. Since the popularization of the BlackBerry, dubbed the 'CrackBerry' by compulsive users, the smartphone has been associated with addictive behaviour. As we did before with mobile phones and personal computers, we have crossed an invisible techno-cultural threshold beyond which there is no return.

The smartphone is our portal to the world, our golden ticket out of here. It holds our credit cards, music, magazines, audiobooks, maps, movies, games, tickets and keys. It is our wayfinder. It connects us to family members, workmates and irresistible internet bullies. We use it to get dates, to get dinner. It breaks up our day, as Adam Greenfield puts it, into 'jittery, schizoid intervals' with constant updates. We keep it close, charged, at all times. It is as though, one day, it's going to bring us the message we've been waiting for.

All of this rests not so much on unconscious substructures, as on layers of hard material infrastructure. What we refer to with such abstractions as 'the cloud' began with the laying of underground fibre-optic cables along the pathways of the railroad system all over the continental United States. The construction of this system was undertaken not in response to consumer demand, but as part of a digital modernization drive that Clintonite administrative elites believed was essential to future capitalist development. We were, in a sense, addicted to this emerging system before we even knew it existed.

Increasingly, these abstractions are linked to an emerging web of ubiquitous computing technologies which Greenfield has presciently called 'everyware'. Ostensibly designed to smooth the edges of life, this network connects smartphones, sensors, data collectors, cookies and platforms in a constant flow of information. In so doing, it quietly outsources important decisions. When you ask Alexa or Siri for a nearby restaurant or shoe shop, it will be Apple or Google or Amazon that determines your path of movement through the urban space on the basis of their commercial needs. Naturally, these structures can be used by political authority to promote governing norms, but they can also work as more insidious forms of control.

The emerging ideal of the 'smart city', where sensors and data collectors determine the allocation of resources and assets, is a case in point. Such cities are already being built in Canada, China and India. While the Chinese government wants to use the technology to promote a 'social credit' scheme rewarding good behaviour, Google's plans in Toronto are seemingly driven by human need. To be called Quayside, Google's 'smart city' will use data collection and sensors to monitor traffic, weather, pollution and noise, to adjust the roads, paving and architecture in response to emerging issues. This has met stiff local opposition, for fear of what will be done with the data.

However, the *benevolent* face of the 'smart city', the way it seems to make life easier, is also its dark side. It closely resembles French philosopher Gilles Deleuze's idea of a 'control society'. In the society of control, no one tells you what to do, whom to worship, or what is good and bad. You are simply presented with a range of tolerable options. Your reality is rewritten to exclude behaviours that the system finds intolerable. In the same way that online spending habits and clicking activities can determine how much debt you are allowed, or which advertisements you are likely to see, or what shops you will be pointed towards, your activity can be kept within a manageable bandwidth. This bandwidth is necessarily the upshot of political and ideological decisions at various stages, but it becomes submerged in the 'given' structure of things.

And lodged in this web is the social platform, the engine of constant, frantic, distracted writing. It is in this matrix that our passions, our desires, are accumulated as data, the better to manipulate and manage them. We confess to the machine while we walk, offering little ambulatory prayers. In doing so, we become cyborg beings: an assemblage of organic and inorganic materials, bits of technology, flesh and teeth, pieces of media, snippets of code holding it all together. The connections between the parts as simple and fluid as the fingers skating with practised precision over a glassy surface. As Donna Haraway once wrote, our bodies don't stop at the skin. Their very physical infrastructures now extend halfway round the world.

If what is meant by addiction is being unable to do without something, it is increasingly hard to imagine life with any other kind of body. And bodies *think*; there being, of course, nothing else to think with. Whether we're walking or writing, we are always experiencing what the phenomenologists call 'embodied cognition'. This is one of the things Freud adverted to when he claimed in a late, oracular note that the psyche is 'extended'. By claiming that the mind is extended in space, he was identifying it with the body. Adding that the mind 'knows nothing about' its extension, he also linked the body to the unconscious. As though the body thinks without the mind's noticing.

So what happens if bits of us, what the philosopher Brian Rotman calls our 'distributed selves', run in parallel on different processors? It is naive to suppose that these technologies simply expand the powers of our organic bodies. They create *dependencies*; they change us. To use them at all, Lydia Liu argues, we must 'serve these objects . . . as gods or minor religions'. As our lives are rewritten by digital languages, a new theology begins to surface. An emerging dispensation of some 'post-human singularity' theorists is that the universe is fundamentally digital, and that reality is in some very real sense generated by a Universal Computer. This, the digital equivalent of praying to a sun god, gives cosmic dignity to the presuppositions of a transient way of life. It is an extreme expression of the way in which our attitudes to technology have always been religious.

IX.

Addicts administer death in small doses. We are devoted to what kills us. In this respect, it is very *un*like sun worship. For all the obsession with gratification, the most obvious attribute of addiction in its negative sense is that it kills. And nor is this a purely physical death. The drug addicts of Vancouver's Hastings Corridor, described by Bruce Alexander, suffer symbolic death, 'sodden misery', before their biological death from overdose, suicide, Aids or hepatitis. Compulsive gamblers administer death in a symbolic sense, too, building up unpayable debts to the point where they lose everything they have lived for. If their bet poses a question about destiny, the addiction specialist Rik Loose argues, death is the radical answer.

Social media addiction is rarely understood in this extreme light. Nonetheless, users often describe it wrecking their careers and relationships. The complaints are almost always the same: users end up constantly distracted, unproductive, anxious, needy and depressed – yet also curiously susceptible to advertising. Patrick Garratt wrote of his social media addiction causing a 'desperate, hollow pressure of waste' in his working life as a journalist. Social media addiction has been linked, repeatedly, to increased depression: interaction with the platforms correlates with a major decline in mental health, while increased screen time (or 'time on device') may be contributing to a recent surge in teen suicides. Facebook's own guileful way of presenting the issue was to claim that while 'passive' consumption of social media content could pose mental health risks, more engagement could 'improve wellbeing'. This claim, while not supported by the research, would mean more profitable data for the site.

The dominant view of these self-destructive propensities was vividly explained by addiction entrepreneur, the late Allen Carr. In a macabre image, he compared addiction to a carnivorous pitcher plant. The plant lures insects and small animals to their death with the fragrant smell of nectar. Once the creature is inside, gazing down at that delicious pool of sugary liquid, he finds the walls slippery and waxy, then slides down, with growing speed, falling into what he discovers is his watery grave. By the time he realizes that the pleasure is a mirage, it is too late to escape. He is consumed by digestive enzymes. This was Carr's hard sell, one of a range of powerful suggestion techniques he used to break his clients' addictions. But it also condenses how we mostly tend to think of the dark side of addiction – as something that ambushes the user, lured by a simple promise of pleasure.

The problem is, widespread knowledge of the dangers of addiction doesn't stop it from happening. Likewise, we know by now that if social industry platforms get us addicted, they are *working well*. The more they wreck our lives, the better they're functioning. Yet we persist. Some of this can be explained away by the manner in which addiction organizes our attention. The platforms, like gambling machines, are experts at disguising losses as wins. These work thanks to an effect similar to that exploited by practitioners of cold reading and 'psychic' tricks: we attend to the pleasurable 'hits' and ignore the disappointing 'misses'. We focus on the buzz of winning, not the cost of playing the game, and not the opportunities lost by playing. And if occasionally the habit threatens to crush us, we can fantasize that one day a big win will save us. But to explain away behaviour is not really to explain it. It is to collude in the rationalization of behaviour that may not be rational.

The prevalence of addiction might be attributable in general to 'psychosocial dislocation', but as an adaptive strategy it sucks. It quite visibly destroys people. Which raises the troubling question: is self-destruction, in some perverse way, the *yield?* What if we dive into the pitcher plant in part because we expect a slow death? What if, for example, the images of death and disease on the cigarette packet are an advertisement? Of course, it is not what is consciously sought. Heroin users are always trying to rediscover the bliss of the first hit. Compulsive gamblers live for those manic moments when their strategy seems to have paid off with a big win. But if it was really all about dopamine loops keeping us fixated on the next hit, it would be difficult to explain why random hits of *un*pleasure would make social media even *more* gripping. The platforms treat us mean and keep us keen.

One metric for this experience is known as 'The Ratio'. On Twitter, if the replies to your tweet vastly outnumber the 'likes' and retweets, you've gambled and lost. Whatever you have written is so outrageous, so horrible, that you are now in the zone of the shitstorm. The notorious examples of this involve corporate CEOs, politicians and celebrities, ostensibly on the medium for professional purposes, pushing the self-destruct button with an awful post. But the telling examples are not those tweets where there is a momentary lapse in good public relations, but those where intelligent users become embroiled in horrendous, undignified, self-destructive fights with their followers.

Consider, for example, Mary Beard, a Cambridge historian who maintains a profile on Twitter filled with amiable selfies, centre-left views and chat with fans. Beard's downfall came as she mused publicly about the horrendous allegations of Oxfam aid workers gang-raping and sexually exploiting children in Haiti. While stipulating that it couldn't be condoned, she wondered aloud how easy it would be to 'sustain "civilized" values in a disaster zone'. Beard's progressive followers were horrified. She seemed to be relativizing the behaviour of rapists. Would she be saying this, people wondered, if the victims were white? Beard was presumably unaware of any racist implication of her argument, but it was striking that she chose *this* medium as the place to make it. And perhaps just as significant was how ordinary that decision was. Twitter is good for witty banter; the lapidary concision of a tweet makes any put-down seem brutally decisive. Exactly for that reason, it's a terrible place to idly propose provocative theses.

In the ensuing shitstorm, blizzards of concise, lethal replies were launched in her direction. Disappointed followers declared their disaffection. Beyond a certain critical mass, it stopped mattering how accurate the criticisms were. The shitstorm is not a form of accountability. Nor is it political pedagogy, regardless of the high-minded intentions, or sadism, of the participants. No one is learning anything, except how to remain connected to the machine. It is a punishment beating, its ecstasies sanctioned by virtue. Twitter has, as part of its addictive repertoire, democratized punishment.

Rather than backing away from the medium in open-mouthed horror and reconsidering her whole approach to the issue, Beard remained entranced by the flow. As so many users have done, she spent hours upping the ante, trying to rebut, engage and manage the emotional fallout from the attack. She ended the day by posting a tearful photograph of herself, pleading with the medium that 'I am not really not the nasty colonialist you say I am'. This, predictably, egged the medium on, adding 'white tears' and 'white fragility' to the indictment. Hurt feelings, trivial in the scale of human woe, were being used to evade political accountability. (Besides, sotto voce, hurt feelings are *delicious, but not enough.*)

Still, Beard kept returning. It was, in its own way, a form of digital self-harm. The mirror that had told her how awesome she was now called her a scumbag, and it was clearly *irresistible*. Many online self-harmers must set up anonymous accounts to bully themselves, a practice which among the 'incel' (involuntarily-celibate) community is known as 'blackpilling'. On the Twittering Machine, no such efforts are needed. You just have to keep playing and wait for it. Come for the nectar of approval, stay for the frisson of virtual death.

X.

Part of what keeps us hooked is the so-called variability of 'rewards': what Jaron Lanier calls 'carrot and shtick'. The Twittering Machine gives us both positive and negative reinforcements, and the unpredictable variation of its feedback is what makes it so compulsive. Routine rewards might begin to bore us, but volatility, the way the medium suddenly turns on us, makes it more intriguing.

Like a mercurial lover, the machine keeps us needy and guessing; we can never be sure how to stay in its good graces. Indeed, the app manufacturers increasingly build in artificial-intelligence machine-learning systems so that they can learn from us how to randomize rewards and punishments more effectively. This sounds like an abusive relationship. Indeed, much as we describe relationships as having gone 'toxic', it is common to hear of 'Twitter toxicity'.

Toxicity is a useful starting point for understanding a machine that hooks us with unpleasure, because it indexes both the pleasure of intoxication and the danger of having too much – hence the clinical term for the administration of toxic substances, 'toxicomania'. The Renaissance natural philosopher Paracelsus is credited with a major insight of modern toxicology: the dose, not the substance, makes the poison. 'Every food and drink, if taken beyond its dose, is poison,' he said.

If toxicity is having the wrong dose, what are we overdosing on? Even with drugs, the answer is not straightforward. As Rik Loose points out, similar quantities of the same drug administered to different individuals have widely varying effects. The real experience of the drug – the subject-effect, as it's called – partly depends on something other than the drug itself, namely something in the user. The happy pills have no more magic than magic beans. They have a blunt somatic force, but there has to be something else to act on. And if 'psychosocial dislocation' was a sufficient cause, then there would be far more addicts. Beyond a certain point, addiction must act on, and be caused by, the psychic world of the user.

With social media addiction, there are many more variables than with drugs, so it is hard to know where to begin. The designers of the smartphone or tablet interface, for example, have made sure that it is pleasurable to engage with, hold, even just to look at. The urge to reach, irritably, for the device during meals, conversations, parties and upon awakening, can partly be attributed to lust for the object and the soft, nacreous glow of the screen. Once we've navigated to the app, it is the platform designers who take control. For the duration of our visit, life is briefly streamlined, as with a video game, into a single visual flow, a set of soluble challenges, some dangled rewards and a game of chance. But the variety of possible experiences include voyeurism, approval and disapproval, gaming, news, nostalgia, socializing and regular social comparisons. If we're addicted, we might just be addicted to the activities that the platforms enable, from gambling to shopping to spying on 'friends'.

The platforms don't organize our experience according to a master plan. As the sociologist Benjamin Bratton puts it, the mechanism is 'strict and invariable', but within that 'autocracy of means', the user is granted a relative 'liberty of ends'. The protocols of the platform standardize and order the interactions of users. They use incentives and choke points to keep people committed to the machine. They manipulate ends for the benefit of their real clients – other firms. They bombard us with stimuli, learning from our responses, the better to teach us how to be the market demographic we've been identified as. But they don't force us to stay there, or tell us what to do with the hours spent on the platform. Even more so than in the case of drugs, then, the toxicity is something we as users bring to the game.

There is no evidence that this toxicity is chemical. To locate it, we may have to go, as Freud put it, 'beyond the pleasure principle'. The name for our compulsion to pursue that which we know will give us unpleasure is 'death drive'.

CHAPTER THREE

WE ARE ALL CELEBRITIES

Show me someone without an ego, and I'll show you a loser.

Donald Trump, Twitter.com

The ideological function of celebrity (and lottery systems) is clear – like a modern 'wheel of fortune' the message is 'all is luck; some are rich, some are poor, that is the way the world is. . . it could be you!'

Guy Debord, *The Society of the Spectacle*

I.

No one kneads us again out of earth and clay/no one incants our dust. No one.

Paul Celan, 'Psalm'

A swannish-grey June day in Égly, an ugly banlieue on the outskirts of Paris, and Océane was about to do something with celebrity. The ration of celebrity, even less than the famous fifteen minutes, afforded every random stranger on the internet. Speaking to followers on the Twitter-owned live-streaming app, Periscope, she was enigmatically calm. Her eyes, almost as dark as her wavy black hair, betrayed no hint of disturbance. Even when some of her followers tried to troll her, calling her a 'dirty whore', a 'retard', or demanding to see her tits, she remained impassive. She told them: just wait, you'll see, you'll understand.

After a while, and having asked minors not to watch, she stopped talking. At half past four in the afternoon, she walked to the nearby railway station, carrying her smartphone with her, still recording – and threw herself in front of a high-speed train. The broadcast, viewed by 1,208 people, was ended when a rescue worker discovered the phone. Absurdly, many reactions to this suicide blamed the medium. Justine Atlan, a campaigner for online child protection, suggested, 'it's like putting a Ferrari in the hands of a five-year-old. Obviously it's going to slam into a wall.' It would have made just as much sense to blame the existence of public transport, or French national culture, in a society with suicide rates far higher than the European average. By reducing Océane to a child, such think-of-the-children reactions evaded her message.

Freud, in 'Mourning and Melancholia', argues that suicide is always a turning back on the self of a murder meant for someone else. It's always a suicide attack, and it's always, by the same token, a message. In the act of suicide, Lacan said, one becomes an 'eternal sign for others'. This is what Océane wanted. Her death was a protest: in part against the ex-boyfriend whom she said had beaten and raped her; in part against her remote father, a profiteer in the sex industry; and in part against a society which, she felt, lacked empathy, especially on the internet.

Rana Dasgupta, in a powerful essay about the suicide for *Granta*, sees in it a case of celebrity gone horribly awry. Océane was 'wired like everyone else'. She had tried to fit in with online celebrity culture, to 'make her image conform to that of the triumphal media funster'. But confronted with the 'online pageant' of self-promotion, users, like all celebrities, are left with the hollow feeling that only they, in a cold world, have real thoughts and emotions. As in the world of Salinger's Holden Caulfield, everyone else is a fake. What if, Dasgupta asked, 'it was not just celebrity that was seen unfurling in Océane, but that hidden core of celebrity, which is *always-about-to-die?*'

What is it about celebrity that is always about to die? By now, thanks in part to Kenneth Anger's classic account of Hollywood, the suicides, breakdowns and addictions of past-it Hollywood stars are well known. But this isn't just a phenomenon of those who have fallen off their perch. Research finds that suicide among celebrities is anything from seven times to several thousand times that of the general population. There seems to be something about celebrity that horrifies, degrades and diminishes the star, as though the means of exaltation were also the means of their humiliation.

II.

For the first time, we have a generation growing up in the glare of ubiquitous publicity. Everyone can fight for a pittance of fame. 'The people formerly known as the audience', as media critic Jay Rosen calls us, are bidding for stardom. In the attention economy, we are all attention-seekers.

The attention economy is not new. Writing before the advent of the social industry, Jonathan Crary described a concerted effort since the nineteenth century to get individuals to shape themselves in terms of their ability to pay attention. Life became, thanks to changes in audiovisual culture, a patchwork of jagged, broken states of attending, of being riveted by a sequence of stimuli. Advertising, movies, news cycles, all relied on their growing ability to force attention.

Today, the platforms use a number of forcing techniques. These might be compared to the techniques used by mentalists and magicians, which are designed to give the impression of a free and fair choice being made. They are not limited to variable rewards and the 'like' hack. 'Read receipts' give us an anxious prompt to reply to messages, keeping the churn going. Default settings, where the preferred settings are more visually appealing than the alternatives, reward acquiescence and put friction in the way of change. Defaults are often linked to a confirming prompt like a tick, further encouraging compliance. Infinite scrolling makes your social media feed a kind of force-feeding; you never get to the end. Autoplay means that audiovisual parts of your feed stand out more and encourage you to pause.

The ideological power of our interactions with the machine derives from the way that the conditioned choice, be it the compulsive selfie spiral or the angry 3 a.m. thread argument, is experienced as freely and pleasurably chosen. From games to feeds, our capacity for reverie is riveted to a wholly designed dream space, our free-floating attention guided down channels strewn with reinforcements that we often don't even notice.

And the capacity to attend is subject to scarcity. Neuroscientists tell us that, physically, the brain cannot focus on more than one 'attention-rich input' at a time. The state of being distracted, as when one is constantly 'notified' about new messages – new emails, updates, software alerts, app alerts, news alerts – is not a state of magnificently keeping several balls in the air. It is a state of continuous, time- and energy-consuming shifts from one object of focus to another. It can take over half an hour to recover full attention once distracted. The state of distraction that we idealize as 'multitasking' is a form of squandering. To pay attention is to diminish the attention that one has available; to pay attention in this distracted fashion is to waste it.

What sounds like a problem may be the yield. The opportunity to waste attention, or to dispose of spare attention, may be what we seek. The psychoanalyst Adam Phillips speaks of 'vacancies of attention'. If attention is economized, the condition of attention is inattention. To attend to this, we must ignore that, where 'that' is something we may be deliberately avoiding. The vacancies of attention that we must fill appear during public transport journeys, on lunch and toilet breaks, during impasses in dinner conversation, or in those frequent interludes in working life where there is nothing to do but the employee is obliged to look busy. If we didn't have somewhere to put excess attention, who knows what dreams would come?

The stars are a magnet for excess attention: attention-sinks. And they are made, not born. This has been obvious since the nineteenth century when, according to historian Daniel Boorstin, we learned 'the processes by which fame is manufactured'. In a secular, democratic era, fame has been stripped of its mystique, its mechanism exposed. Stars are now 'pseudo-events' accommodating the market demand for a greatness no one believes in. Celebrity, detached from any context beyond itself, has become, in the words of Leo Braudy, 'a virtually unparalleled *fame without a city*'.

Modern celebrity economies, built on this recognition, have devolved into an ever-greater complexity of production. To the existing repertoire of A- , B- and C-list celebs, news eyewitnesses, vox pops, have-a-go heroes, beauty queens and those who regularly write 'letters to the editor', the internet has added camgirls, microcelebrities and the 'Rich Kids of Instagram', some of whom have become even richer and better known than legacy media peers. The platforms have made stars like Justin

Bieber, Chance the Rapper and Charlotte D'Alessio. And everyone gets a taste. Not everyone wants celebrity, but every user is involved. Just by having an account, one has a public image. Just by posting a status, or answering a comment, one has a public-relations strategy.

Instagram users, in addition to collecting likes and followers, can participate in Insta-beauty pageants. Hundreds of thousands of children on YouTube, mostly girls, post videos of themselves asking if they're pretty or ugly. Snapchat users keep tabs on the scores collected by friends, to see who is receiving the most views. Only a bare few are successful enough to monetize their activity by becoming corporate-sponsored 'influencers'. For example, the *Guardian* reports that to become a 'micro-influencer', capable of making $5,000 per sponsored post, one must have at least 100,000 followers on one of the social industry platforms. The vast majority of people don't have more than a thousand followers on any platform. For most people, the likes have to be sufficient reward.

Some are better at working this system than others, but no one knows for sure how stars are made. Too much is contingent on fortune. Where online platforms exist to commodify bits of everyday experience, anything can 'go viral'. Even a brush with disaster can make you an insta-celebrity. For example, Michelle Dobyne of Oklahoma was made an online celebrity in 2016 by escaping from a burning building with her children. Local news cameras recorded her reaction to the event: 'I got my three kids and we bounced out . . . nuh-uh, we ain't gonna be in no fire. Not today.' Witty, charismatic, unruffled, she went viral, an instant meme. YouTube remixes proliferated. Online companies used her image to sell merchandise. News and entertainment channels gained a surge of viewer traffic. This didn't necessarily help Dobyne, who continued to live out of her car until a supporter set up a GoFundMe page. There was even a whiff of racism in her portrayal as an exotic caricature whose plight was funny. The professed admiration for her was therefore complicated, exploitative on the part of the media and, sometimes, tacitly dehumanizing.

The randomness, misfortune and complexity of cultural wants that led to Dobyne's celebrity is typical of the way stars are made. The anthropologist Hortense Powdermaker, in her classic study of

Hollywood, noticed that the randomness of success led to a tendency towards magical thinking in the movie industry. Hollywood formulae were like spells, their market research like divination, executive decisions justified by pseudo-telepathic 'instinct'. These were magical techniques in aid of compelling Lady Luck. In the emerging field of micro-celebrities and insta-fame, there is a cottage industry of such talismanic formulae. News articles, YouTube videos and Instagram coaches offer would-be online celebrities tips, listicles, the magic remedy, for success. Books promise to help users make celebrities of babies or cats. These guides generally state the glaringly obvious – use captions and hashtags, post at peak traffic times, repeat whatever gets most likes, and so on. But their content is less important than *how* they make their case. By generalizing from the practices of those who are successful, they make it appear as though celebrities succeed by virtue of cleverness and tactical nous. For Powdermaker, tellingly, those chasing fame were more like compulsive gamblers than clever strategists.

III.

Even if you win, it's often a poisoned chalice. In 2015, the Instagram model Essena O'Neill smashed her own virtual image. She quit the medium, explaining that the dozens of carefully staged, well-lit, glamorous shots of her smiling blonde self which she had posted were corporate-sponsored. It was all a fake. Beneath each photo, she exposed the burden of painful work and emotional turmoil involved in every shot, from 5 a.m. wake-ups to anxiety and depression. The image, concealing a distressing, excluded reality, had become a tyrant, exhausting to maintain and impossible to live up to. Self-love in this sense was shadowed by bitter self-hate. She committed digital suicide. For O'Neill, letting the self-hate win for once was a liberation.

This split between private and public selves, characteristic of celebrity, is an increasingly ordinary experience of social industry users. A generation is growing up with publicity, not as remote dream but as coercive norm. Donna Freitas' research into young social industry users finds them tyrannized by their obsession with 'likes' and comparison with others. Under constant surveillance, they must give the impression of living their best life, of being 'blissful, enraptured, even inspiring'. It is hard work, with diminishing returns. It generates the feeling of being alone among fakes, a desperate situation. If celebrities often spiral into public displays of self-degradation, Chris Rojek suggests, it is to 'alert the public to the horror, shame and encroaching helplessness' of the private self, faced with its metastasizing public rival.

What hooks us is also what kills us. Increased 'screen time' corresponds to more depression and suicide, particularly for female users. The rise of the platforms and the smartphone corresponds to rising self-harm, with hospital admissions for related injuries among girls soaring by a fifth in the US and over two thirds in England. The effect is much stronger when users spend their 'screen time' engaged in social comparisons: the most addictive part of the medium. In every game of social comparison, we pay most attention to those above us. We lose every time; we fall short. As Alain Ehrenberg put it, 'the depressed individual is unable to measure up; he is tired of having to become himself.'

Correlation, as the cliché goes, is not causation. Indeed, the sprawling complexity of the systems we live in makes it hard to identify direct cause–effect situations. It would be difficult to prove, for example, that seeing an advertisement on public transport made you buy new shoes. All that can be said is that your choice is *conditioned* by the advertising. The social industry platforms hardly invented all the social miseries, insecurities and conflicts of life in the decade or so in which they have come to the fore. Indeed, they may have been taken up as a solution to some of these problems. It is noticeable, for example, that social industry use became ubiquitous in the aftermath of a global financial crash, with devastating effects for billions of people. As opportunities declined and wages stagnated, smartphone ownership, giving users ready access to whole online worlds, may have offered some compensation. And revenues for social industry firms began to take off in the period 2010–11, in a time of severe breakdown in the legitimacy of political institutions, as well as of mass media: the Egyptian uprising, the riots in England, 'Indignados' in Europe and 'Occupy' protests elsewhere. Facebook, Twitter and YouTube all benefited from these events, as they gave ordinary users the means to set the news agenda and to associate with one another in low-cost ways. Scapegoating the social industry evades the question of why people are drawn to it in their billions. What problems does it appear to solve?

Nonetheless, there remains the stubborn and alarming fact that more contact with the social industry platforms corresponds to more misery, more self-harm, more suicide. Which raises urgent questions about how these platforms are conditioning us.

IV.

One of the things we're being conditioned for is ubiquitous publicity itself. The comedian Stewart Lee compares Twitter to 'a state surveillance agency run by gullible volunteers. A Stasi for the Angry Birds generation.' Ironically, this mass-surveillance apparatus, with the social industry harnessing over three billion pairs of eyeballs, was elevated amid a crisis for traditional media over *its* invasions of privacy.

In the UK, the Murdoch-owned press was at the centre of 'Hackgate', after *News of the World* journalists were caught tapping the voicemail of missing teenager Milly Dowler. This unearthed a vast machinery of spying, with private investigators illegally obtaining information about celebrities and politicians. At the height of the scandal, veteran *News of the World* hack, Paul McMullan, justified his practices on the jaw-dropping grounds that 'privacy is for paedos'. Through years of 'invading people's privacy', he said, 'I've never found anybody doing any good.'

Nothing to hide, nothing to worry about: it is no accident that this sinister, cynical credo is shared by bin-hoking journalists and state securitarians. The *News of the World* was a Cold War-era print monopoly that had built up its power through an alliance with Margaret Thatcher's government and the police. That alliance helped the paper's bosses break the print unions and gave them access to privileged information. Yet the motto of authoritarian snoopers is always hypocritical. The *News of the World*, its crooked police informants, and corrupt ex-cops working as private investigators, were up to their necks in criminal behaviour which they kept secret. Jonathan Rees, boss of Southern Investigations, who was paid £150,000 a year by the paper in return for illegally gained information, was jailed for conspiracy to plant evidence. Sid Fillery, an ex-officer and Rees's associate, was jailed for child pornography. Tom Kingston, another ex-cop turned investigator, was convicted of stealing amphetamines. Glenn Mulcaire, a private investigator who worked for the paper, was jailed alongside its royal editor for hacking voicemails. He was also suspected to have attempted to hack the voicemail of a police officer investigating the murder of Daniel Morgan. Morgan was an associate of Rees who was killed in 1987, allegedly by corrupt officers and with Rees's knowledge, when he was working to expose police corruption.

And while the paper depended on a criminal infrastructure, it sanctimoniously used its power to hound people over private moral choices, often to their deaths. Even so jaded a hack as McMullan admits that his paper's articles about Jennifer Elliott, daughter of the actor Denholm Elliott, may have contributed to her suicide. Nor is it just celebrities who have been targeted. Ben Stronge, a chef 'exposed' for swinging, had begged the paper not to publish, as he would never see his children again if they did. They published, and he killed himself. Arnold Lewis, a teacher caught in a similar sting, pleaded with the reporter not to publish. He said he would kill himself. They published, and his suicide followed. The reporter, having been read Lewis's suicide note at the inquest, was asked if it upset her. 'No,' she replied, 'not really.'

The economy of surveillance, converting private experience into profitable information, predates the Twittering Machine. The tabloids represent the most egregious version of it, but on the same continuum is the public confessional that is reality television, 'behind-the-scenes' documentaries, *Oprah*, *Jerry Springer* and 'shrink'-themed celebrity interview formats. *News of the World* was driven out of business, but the social industry has normalized unprecedented surveillance. They have universalized the confessional format. Today, in addition to hacking voicemails, investigators can trawl through vast archives of items posted willingly and publicly on the platforms. And journalists needn't lift a finger. Enterprising users with a grudge will often work to bring decontextualized snippets of controversy to public light. For example, the one-minute celebrity Ken Bone gained admiration for his demeanour while asking a question during a 2016 US presidential debate. But he was brought low by online busybodies turning up a few offensive comments he had made on Reddit. It was trivial, but headlines, hot takes, think pieces and trending flows of attention followed a familiar pattern.

If the pursuit of celebrity poses dangers for would-be stars, the growing fixation of public attention on stars has consequences for the well-being of their 'followers'. The rising profile of 'celebrity-worship syndrome' suggests that constant consumption of the raw material of the lives of others is not just invasive, but also doing something disturbing to the worshippers. Anxiety, stress, physical illnesses and increased body dysmorphia have all been correlated with celebrity obsession. This may help explain why worshippers can suddenly turn on their heroes, should they be caught in the glare of scandal, taking incongruous joy in their destruction. The generalization of this kind of star–follower relationship, based on intimate self-exposure, threatens to spread abroad its most harmful symptoms. To put it another way, if the Twittering Machine seems to offer us the best of both worlds as far as celebrity is concerned, it also gives us the worst.

V.

Consolation comes in the form of 'subversion'. The growing Instagram trend of 'no filter' posts, and hashtags such as #uglyselfie, #fatacceptance, #bodypositivity, #epicfail and #nomakeup, apparently show users ironically playing with and challenging the aesthetic conventions of the medium.

Newspapers, working to the woke dollar, alert readers to trends in 'radical body love' online, and direct them to 'incredible body-positive people to follow'. This challenges oppressive cultural codes, but it is not the subversive strategy it appears to be. The internet may be experienced as a flow of images, but its visual appearance obscures how it really works: behind it all is a written system of protocols and controls. For anything to become content, it has to adhere to these controls. For it to be content on the platforms, it has to be part of an addiction mechanism: it has to be useful for keeping users connected to the machine. One may as well try to subvert a smartphone by changing the wallpaper image.

This refusal of conventional beauty standards fuses with the rising stock of 'authenticity' in attention economies. Since the democratization of celebrity in the nineteenth century, the 'common touch', 'naturalness' and 'authenticity' have been esteemed characteristics of the famous. Today's fascination with catching celebrities in real, 'unfiltered' moments of intimate disorganization, with plastic surgery gone wrong, make-up melting in the heat, tantrums, rows and bad deeds has its roots in this urge to tear away layers of illusion and expose the horror beneath.

In the social industry, this desire for authenticity has become much more urgent. The language of the internet is built around the fear of the fake: usernames, passwords and user-response tests encode the desire that each user account should represent a person who can fulfil contractual obligations. 'Fake Accounts are Not Our Friends', Facebook's advertising campaign asserts. In a terrain where people are acutely aware of being manipulated all the time, the worst thing one can be is 'fake'. One website even allows users to detect when a post tagged #nofilter is discreetly using a filter, so that 'fakers' can be caught out.

Social industry platforms are, moreover, very well suited to gratifying the yearning for authenticity, by allowing fans seemingly direct contact with celebrities. Direct fan management replaces the controlled, centralized regulation of interactions through public relations agencies. The traditional celebrities who adapt best to the medium appear to offer 'backstage' access, albeit in a contrived way that meets fan expectations while observing status differentiation. They generally don't follow back, or engage in prolonged exchanges, and they expect a degree of deference from followers. Micro-celebrities emulate these practices of contrived intimacy. Instagrammers and YouTubers, for example, disclose private parts of their lives, relationships and feelings as part of a consumable performance.

This performance of authenticity is also becoming a necessity for marketing. By 2015, social advertising, based on 'authentic', personalized relationships with consumers, occupied more than a tenth of digital ad spending. We can vary our tactics on the medium, use it to promote images and ideas that contest those that gained consent in legacy media. But each time we do, we confirm, corroborate and consolidate the machine's power over us.

VI.

Aokigahara, the 'sea of trees', is a hauntingly beautiful forest growing out of cooled lava on the northwest flank of Mount Fuji. In Japanese mythology, Aokigahara is roamed by *yurei*, the spirits of those left there to die. It is dense, vast and silent, the volcanic rock and trees absorbing sound. Today, it is where dozens of people commit suicide every year. The bodies turn up dangling from boughs or lying on the forest floor among the tangled roots.

In December 2017, a bleach-blond Hollywood surfer dude stood in the thick of the woods, gawping at a corpse, long dead, spinning at the end of a rope. The surfer dude, wearing a lurid green *Futurama* 'brain slug' hat, looked slightly frantic, panicked. Staring death in the face, he cracked nervous jokes. Logan Paul is a hugely successful YouTube vlogger, and had intended to make a video while camping out in the forest with his friends, when he stumbled on destiny. The camp-out was cancelled. The authorities were called. And the video was posted on YouTube.

Why not? This was authentic, riveting content. Paul had kept his viewers hooked by sharing stylized bits of his life with them. It had proven wildly profitable, winning him over a million dollars a month in Google Preferred ad revenues, starring roles in several YouTube series and his own line of clothing. And here was an undeniably compelling story from his life, the sort of story that should reverberate in excited ripples of attention and reaction. Social industry giants are not moral arbiters. They are agnostic about what users post because their trade is in attention – an abstract commodity – not content. With two billion people ceaselessly churning out content, the platform is so designed as to automatically convert the stuff of everyday life into economically valuable informatics. Content stimulates users to produce more content in a virtuous, or vicious, circle.

But this time, Paul crossed a barely legible threshold of taste and decency. Handled more sensitively, it might have been a gold mine. Instead, the backlash was swift and brutal. Politicians and celebrities lined up to denounce his insensitive display of the corpse. A petition demanding that his channel be pulled gained tens of thousands of signatures. YouTube condemned his actions, suspended him from the Google Preferred revenue stream and cancelled his series appearances. Fellow YouTuber Japanese-American internet celebrity Reina Scully scolded him, 'Get out of my beautiful motherland.' Paul's success brought social responsibilities, he was told. He had disrespected the dead person's family, and risked triggering further suicides. Precisely because suicide is a symbolic act, it can be contagious.

Paul, being a savvy entrepreneur, pivoted quickly. His gamble having failed, he took down the video, delivered a well-scripted, emotional apology, and followed it up with a new segment in which he interviewed suicide experts. He had got 'caught up in the moment'. All he had ever wanted to do was 'raise awareness for suicide and suicide prevention'. He now understood that 'with great power comes great responsibility'. It was a deft turn, converting a scandal into a tacit tribute to his own ongoing importance. This showed he understood how the medium worked. Paul's gamble had worked out badly for him, but not for the social industry: it still generated floods of new content and new flows of attention. If he played it well, he could still benefit from the attention flows he had created.

It is instructive, in this context, to note how the growing niche of live-streamed suicides have fuelled the machine. Jared McLemore from Memphis, Tennessee, set himself on fire. James Jeffrey, from Alabama, shot himself in the head. Erdogan Ceren, from southern Turkey, shot himself in the stomach. Naika Venant, a fourteen-year-old girl from Miami, hanged herself, leaving frantic users to bombard her mother with messages and screenshots. Katelyn Nicole Davis, a twelve-year-old from Georgia, broadcast her own death by hanging after disclosing that she was being sexually abused. In every single one of these cases, the suicide produced floods of monetizable attention. Sequences of footage, screenshots, likes, statuses and comments linked to these broadcasts, entered seamlessly into the flow of the attention economy. The images of people in the moments before their suicide made newspaper and webpage headlines even more dramatic. Desperate faces, on the brink of desperate acts, displaying, as Hungarian poet Béla Bálazs said of the actor's face, the 'silent monologue of the solitary human soul'. Riveting material for the news cycle, tried and tested, drawing valuable attention both to legacy media and to the platform itself.

It is for cultural reasons, external to the logic of the platform, that such content can pose a threat, by inviting government regulation or encouraging users to disconnect. Even then, there is little the platforms can do without upsetting the ecologies of attention and data creation. For example, Facebook's efforts to demonstrate conscientious engagement include changing the content of someone's feed if the machine's sentiment analysis discloses that they might be at risk of suicide. A page offering help for suicidal people might appear in the feed. Friends of the possible suicide might see an enlarged 'report post' button. But what if there are perverse incentives that arise from features that are intrinsic to the profit model? What if Conrad's 'demon of perverse inspiration' now works by algorithm?

In 2017, for example, a young woman from Ohio was sent to prison for nine months, after she live-streamed the rape of her friend by an older man. Marina Lonina was eighteen years old, her friend was seventeen and the rapist, Raymond Gates, was twenty-nine. They had met Gates the previous day, at a mall, and decided to meet him for drinks. He was interested in the victim because he wanted to take her virginity. He brought a bottle of vodka, they drank together, and when she was properly intoxicated, he pushed her onto the bed, held her down and violently raped her. Lonina grabbed her phone and started the broadcast. As the rape proceeded, Lonina was heard giggling in the background while the victim screamed, 'No, it hurts so much.'

About Gates's actions there was no mystery: he was a predator, who by his own account was turned on by reluctant 'virgins'. Lonina's behaviour was more bewildering. According to the prosecutor, Lonina told police that she had started the live stream in the hope that filming it would somehow stop the attack, but – astonishingly – 'got caught up in the likes'. Later, she told a Netflix documentary, *Hot Girls Wanted*, that she hadn't initially realized what was going on but that, 'All these guys on Periscope started writing "Film it! Film it! I want to watch it!" And it wasn't just one, two or three people. There were dozens of people following us. I was in an excited state.'

This claim is astonishing on its own terms, but the mere existence of these 'likes' is also arresting. Most viewers presumably had no reason to expect to see a rape, let alone egg it on. The 'bystander effect' is notoriously worse in the case of witnessed sexual assault than for other crimes, but these were no bystanders. The 'like' button seems to have facilitated a form of detached involvement in spectacular cruelty. And it's plausible that the feedback made a difference. By her own account, for Lonina the approval of a watching public was decisive: she was abruptly making a hit, a box-office success, and it was thrilling enough to override any concern she could have had for her friend. If Lonina came to regret this short burst of celebrity, it is now perpetuated in algorithmic form. Google searches for her name now return pornography websites offering pages titled 'Marina Lonina Periscope Porn' and 'Marina Lonina Rape Video'.

This dark side of celebrity is not in itself new. Josef Fritzel, Ted Bundy, Timothy McVeigh and Jeffrey Dahmer are among the murderers and rapists who have become overnight celebrities, receiving dozens or hundreds of love letters in prison. What is new is that, as celebrity is rewritten by algorithm, all can participate in the darkness.

VII.

Celebrity has always been an efficient means of focusing attention; the best attention hack money can buy. If the addiction machine guides attention by harnessing the pathways of wanting, celebrities are an efficient package for our wants.

Daniel Boorstin called celebrity the condition of being well known for being well known. Another way to put this is to say that people draw attention because they draw attention. There is something spellbinding about what other people are attending to: this is the 'viral' aspect of fame. By 'making the web more social', as Mark Zuckerberg boasted, the platforms have converted ordinary social interactions into potential celebrity pseudo-events: quantifiable, and easily reproduced pieces of information, or memes. On the addiction machine, celebrity is reduced to the barest mechanism of *orchestrating attention*.

This suggests, though, that when we now talk about celebrity, popularity or 'liking', these terms no longer mean exactly what they used to. Far from having an adequate language for what we're going through, we may need to invent a new one. The easy solution is to tell a clichéd story about what's happening, which enables a form of cultural policing. The inventory of moral panic about the internet revolves around young people and sexuality, beginning with *Time* magazine in 1995 warning: 'On a Screen Near You: Cyberporn'. From MySpace to Snapchat, the platforms have been accused of creating hunting grounds for predators. But a more subtle and pervasive worry is that the platforms are begetting a new narcissism. Social media, on this view, is an elaborate hall of mirrors in which we can't stop looking at ourselves.

Complaints about narcissism are almost always, as Kristin Dombek writes, about the 'selfishness of others'. It is always *other people* whose too-hot selfies, too-glamorous dinners, too-happy relationship photographs, too-charming holiday snaps, evince narcissism. Narcissism in this sense is, as Wilde said of wickedness, a myth invented by good people to account for the curious attractiveness of others.

The morally charged language of the backlash against insta-celebrity is, indeed, evidence of a kind of thwarted attraction. Young people are 'obsessed with the superficial', the *New York Post* laments. Young people have taken 'the desire for self-admiration too far', according to psychologists Jean Twenge and Keith Campbell. A swelling library of head-shaking academic papers, articles and surveys detailing the descent into online narcissism adds to the chorus. Young people, the refrain implies, are *so fake*.

The popular cultural lament about narcissism is not totally wrong. Most of what there is to do in the social industry involves continually procuring a self-portrait to admire. It fuses narcissism to a digital mirror, a self-image made out of the quantified 'reactions' of other users. And we all fake it, whether by filter, camera angle, or the carefully edited sentiments and observations with which we build our digital selves. Our smartphone gives us the means to do so. But how far is too far to take self-admiration? At what point does self-love become toxic? And how, practically, do we want people to respond when we call them narcissists?

Historically, we only scold people like this when we suspect them of having a really good time. And lurking in the backlash literature is the extraordinary idea that young people are really enjoying themselves and their bodies. Campbell and Twenge complain that young people have become exhibitionists, entitled materialists, 'aggressive when insulted, and uninterested in emotional closeness'. They reject the comforting idea that narcissism conceals insecurity: in fact, the new breed of narcissists unconsciously think 'they're awesome'. The idea of a generational boom in narcissism is widespread. Zoe Williams worries that selfies, cosmetic surgery and digital oversharing indicate a 'narcissism epidemic'.

The problem with such claims is that the survey evidence is contradictory. For every study claiming to find surging narcissism, another survey finds the opposite. Jeffrey Arnett at Clark University goes so far as to claim that Millennials are 'an exceptionally generous generation'. Perhaps the biggest difficulty is that there is little agreement on what narcissism really is. This is demonstrated in the public rows between psychiatrists over whether Trump, the bombastic quintessence of Twitter celebrity, qualifies as a narcissist. Many researchers try to get round this by comparing long-term shifts in measurable attitudes to the criteria for narcissism listed by the Diagnostic and Statistical Manual of Mental Disorders, or the Narcissistic Personality Inventory. But these are open-ended to the point of being vacuous. And an uptick in people agreeing with statements like 'I am a very important person' or 'I can live my life any way I want to' can mean any number of things. If I claim to be able to live my life any way I want to, for example, I may be expressing a wish, defying religious and secular authoritarians, or declaring a preference for constitutional liberalism or free markets. Or it may have a deeply personal meaning. It would be hard to know without in-depth interviews, which would regularly throw up material that was not amenable to quantitative analysis.

This isn't to dismiss the issue. If, over time, people become more willing to endorse attitudes that seem to resonate with individualist or competitive values, that may tell us something important about the culture. Is it significant, for example, if more people feel they have to be important? Twenge's work with 'Generation Z' finds some of the biggest shifts occurring around 2011, when smartphone ownership became ubiquitous among adolescents. And no one who uses social media for very long can have missed the compulsory 'awesomeness' of everything. A status I agree with is 'awesome', a person I like 'slays' and a sentiment I find congenial has to be quote-tweeted with orgasmic squees of 'THIS. ALL OF THIS.' And if I can induce such charmingly ridiculous outbursts among my followers, I've hit the jackpot. The platforms, being structured as a game of competitive like-hunts, a form of rivalrous attention-seeking, are perfectly well suited to magnifying the existing cultural drift towards compulsory awesomeness.

But narcissism is always ambivalent. The image that satisfies us can also frustrate us. We may love the image, but, as Narcissus discovered, it doesn't love us back. And it is munified at our expense, accumulating all the approval and love we were seeking for ourselves. In our devotion, in our addiction to it, we are belittled.

VIII.

The epitome of modern narcissism is the selfie. But the selfie is a paradox. It supposedly represents a unique person, living her best life, from the best angle, in the best light. But it does so using a technology that, as Adam Greenfield puts it, distributes and smudges the self across 'a global mesh of nodes and links'. This hard infrastructure, from sensors in the smartphone to cellular base stations, undersea cables, microwave relays and networks of users, organizes from end to end a person's experience of the world, her selfhood. In addition to breaking up the self into digitalized components, the technologies of the selfie also have the alarming effect of making everyone look the same.

Some of the repetitive banality of selfies can be blamed on the conventions of selfie-taking. Some of it can be blamed on the pursuit of 'likes' which incentivizes the repetition of popular images. But the platforms, from Snapchat to Instagram, and apps like Meitu, also offer a form of memetic enchantment. Selfies are worked through a limited range of reality-enhancers, called filters. Snapchat filters make us look cartoonish, with cute puppy ears and noses, while Instagram filters were at first notoriously nostalgic, casting a spell of *mal du pays.* Filters soften the features and flaws of the face, making us appear polished, perfect, almost mythical. Through these, photographer Brooke Wendt suggests, we are encouraged to 'act as though under a magic spell for the benefit of the cameras'.

Modern consumers, said William Burroughs, are image junkies. And our selfie-spirals epitomize this junkie craving. For most of human history, selfies were a prerogative of the powerful. As such, they portrayed either majesty or artistic genius. The democratic and industrial revolutions of the eighteenth and nineteenth centuries triggered an explosion of new visibilities: print technologies spread to the poor, the photograph and film were invented, and new forms of self-portrait emerged. From Toulouse-Lautrec's *Self-Portrait Before a Mirror* to Duchamp's *Self-Portrait Before a Five-Way Mirror*, the new selves portrayed were often disabled, injured, distressed, fractured. They portrayed the universal limitations and susceptibilities of all human beings.

With the selfie, we seem to have returned to the ideal of majesty, albeit on an individual scale. Selfies tend to eschew any visible sign of injury, distress or weakness. They portray flawless desirability, heroic self-fulfilment. This portrayal is not only a lie, but it is a very telling kind of lie. It says something about the very brittle form of modern narcissism. When Christopher Lasch diagnosed an emerging culture of narcissism in the 1970s, he insisted on the fragility of this narcissism. The individual was being overvalued at just the point that individuality was disappearing. The 'sovereign individual' of the market was just an ephemeral consumer, trapped in a state of fugue-like enchantment with a flow of easy but transient satisfactions. The template of all satisfactions was the commodity-image: what appeared on television, the silver screen or advertising billboards. Now, the self is the commodity. Doubly so, because at the same time as we are producing a commodity-image version of ourselves, we are also busy producing the data about ourselves that enables the social industry platforms to sell us to advertisers. We truly are the product.

And a product is not a living thing. Looking at a selfie is like looking back on a finished object, on what is no longer alive. In our selfies we look, says Wendt, as though we were already dead. We are not so much living our best life as dying our best death, a good-looking corpse in both senses: looking and looked at. The apparent subject of the selfie is in fact its effect. The image is a techno-social precipitate, a petrification, a product of the way the technology organizes our self-perception.

A feed filled with topless mirror shots, gym photos, new hair, and so on, might be seen as a peculiar form of idolatry. But it is less a tribute to the user than to the power that the machine has over the user. A power which, without prescribing anything, results in a very narrow account of what a self, a life, is really like. It orchestrates a paradoxically distracted, alienated form of attention. To be distracted is to be beside oneself, even as the self is the glorified centre of attention. In that sense, the question is not how much self-love is communally acceptable, but whether we can attend to something more satisfying.

IX.

The massive expansion of online visibility is paradoxical. It is, after all, a virtual space. The self that achieves celebrity is a virtual self, an avatar. To inhabit the social industry is to live in an elaborate panopticon, so that self-surveillance is redoubled many times over. But what is actually being seen?

In its origin in ancient Sanskrit, the term 'avatar' referred to the descent of a deity to earth in carnal form. In computing language, it has come to refer to the making concrete of something abstract. At first glance, this seems exactly the wrong way round, if it is supposed to refer to our online representatives. Surely, what is happening is that our concrete selves are being represented by abstract information?

However, it only appears that way because we still like to think we are at the centre of the process, the little godheads from whom everything on the internet flows. 'As if I wrote the Internet,' Sandy Baldwin writes, 'on my iPhone, wrote the entire thing, texted it, 140 characters at a time.' User experience is designed to feel that way but, as in the operant conditioning chamber, protocol rules. The algorithm rules. The online image is the visual representation, not of us, but of abstract algorithmic processes. We have some say in the materials acted on by the algorithms, in that we select a name, profile picture, banner image, biographical description and the content of posts. But in doing so, we are working for the algorithms, in conditions not under our control. We attend to the image, in the etymological sense of stretching towards it, but it tends to slip out of our reach.

Our status as virtual stars is necessarily fragile. Celebrity is already virtual, in that the stars are idealized representations who attract fantasies and emotional identifications. Identification can quickly turn to loathing. It is always ambivalent, both eroticized and necrotized. We are both attracted and repelled, always striving for, and never finding, the 'right distance' from the moving object of our identifications. The phenomenon of the 'milkshake duck', the viral celebrity who is swiftly brought low, is an online version of this. If anyone can be a celebrity, anyone can fall short of the unrealistic ideals to which celebrities are held. Even if you don't have a record of racist Reddit comments or bigoted tweets, no one's online activity is pure enough to evade criticism. The same applies to the tempestuous rows within internet communities, where the toxic pulsions of identification and dis-identification generate passionate solidarities and sudden explosions of hostility. Every such community has its stars, and these stars are always one step away from perdition.

The rise of fragility-talk betrays a certain anxiety about this point. The racist, sexist alt-right denounces 'snowflake' fragility (you can't take a joke), while the identitarian Left scolds white male fragility (you can't take the critique). As if everyone is suddenly more vulnerable, might start falling to pieces at any moment, but only notices it in others. And if the language of fragility mainly comes up in relation to identity politics, of the Right or Left, this might tell us something about what online celebrity is doing to identity.

Identity seems like a simple idea. 'I am what I am', as Shirley Bassey sang. But one reason why internet discussions of identity become so ferocious is that it is never that simple. The cultural critic Marie Moran cites three historic uses of the term. In the legal sense, identity is what you prove with passports, identity papers and your username and password. It guarantees that you're a legal person who can enter into contracts. In the personal sense, identity pertains to what is uniquely you, often assumed to go to one's core, even though modern markets sell us identities as consumable items. In the social and political sense, identity is how the world has classified you, on the basis of a characteristic you are assumed to have. From a certain point of view, identity in all three senses is necrological, an obituary notice. It overwrites you, in lapidary fashion, with the deposit of history. Here lies the user: account details, turn-ons, preferences, search history, sex, race, class, nation.

The irony of the internet is that it was supposed to free us from identitarian constraints, to enable us to live beyond the diktat of ascription and belonging. Instead, it seems to compound the importance of identity in all three dimensions. Online security discourses show a terror of identity theft. Online celebrity involves obsessively curating a personal self, which may include mobilizing elements of one's ascriptive identity. Online politics is often a struggle over the thresholds of 'cultural appropriation' and identitarian belonging. The social justice warrior's injunction, #stayinyourlane, suggests we can never transcend identitarian boxes. The era of the platforms has witnessed an explosion in identity-talk.

There are some good reasons for this. Much of what is described as identity politics addresses long-standing injustices, impacting on people precisely because of how they're identified, from Black Lives Matter to #MeToo. Beyond this, however, the internal politics of the medium is itself a politics of identity, because it compels us to dedicate more and more of our time to performing an identity. The self that the social industry engages is ephemeral in the sense described by Lasch: trapped in a continuous, distracted response to stimuli. The compensation and incentive is that we can also be the stimuli. We can carefully brand ourselves, producing an identity as a consumable good, an attention magnet, an image for image junkies.

There is death in this. Twenge and Campbell are getting at something when they urge people to worry less about their identities and more about their lives. Between life and the self, there is a choice. This is implicit in the idea of an attention economy. The more compulsively we curate the self, the less we live. We may find it helpful to forget ourselves from time to time. We may need, that is, a form of 'anti-identity' politics, a resistance to all trends which force one to spend too much time on the self, or on a particularly narrow, depressing and ultimately coercive idea of what a person can be. It would treat all the labour spent on the self as wasted potential. It would cultivate forgetting and disconnection.

X.

I had forgot myself; am I not king?

William Shakespeare, *Richard II*

To remember that one is king is also to be apprised that one is living under a tyranny. To value oneself too highly is to live under a one-person dictatorship, with a dissenting remainder that yearns for its overthrow.

From the beginning of life, the image in the mirror is not just a lover, but a rival. As soon as the infant is captivated by a mirror image, it lords it over him like a monarch – 'His Majesty the Baby', as Freud described this primary narcissism. The image is too perfect, in contrast with experience. The infant's sensory-motor system isn't working yet, and he can barely speak. Yet he finds a completely coherent image of himself, confirmed by his parents' gaze, to identify with. And in identifying with the image, he also identifies with the gaze that looks at it. He is not just seeing, but seen. That is what makes the image so tyrannical. The fascination with bodily disintegration, dismemberment, castration and slaughter that Freud associated with the death drive can be seen, in this sense, as auto-iconoclasm. The death drive is a regicide plot.

Life in the Twittering Machine isn't exactly like gazing into the mirror with mother. Mirrors, like the nuclear family, are an old and almost superseded technology. The Freudian theory underpinning Lasch's analysis of narcissism bears the hallmarks of its genesis, by emphasizing the role of a tiny number of adults in the child's emotional universe. The infant's body, in classic Freudian theory, was libidinized through identification with its parents. But the nuclear family structure has loosened, and the enclosed family home is now permeated by new communications technologies.

It is now the screen, not the mirror, in which the child finds not only the image, but the gaze. As the psychoanalyst Alessandra Lemma argues, whatever self-love and self-hate there is, is engendered by a new link between the body and technologies. If there is a death drive, or indeed any drive at all, it is insinuated into this virtual world. But what does that mean? In a sense, drives are already virtual. Freud used the term 'virtual' to describe the space of mental life, of fantasies, dreams and desires. He defined drives, not as physical instincts, but as the mental representation of bodily impulses, which is to say that they virtualize physical realities. Meatspace was already virtual reality. All that we have added, first with the invention of writing, then with print and finally with digital writing, are new layers of virtualization.

It is for this reason that Lacan defined all drives as potential death drives. If a drive is virtual, then, unlike an instinct, it can't be satisfied. It spins on eternally, immortally, indifferent to decency, pleasure or organic survival. And it wages asymmetric war against all constraints, including the deathly constraints of identification. So there is a sense in which the death drive is on the side of life. Given the chance, it would smash the idol we call a self, or a selfie; it would commit digital suicide. Indeed, the perplexing public meltdowns and shitstorms to which online celebrity is beset may be, just as much as the drugs and alcohol benders of traditional Hollywood stars, a thwarted attempt at auto-iconoclasm.

The social industry platforms are far more worried about the prospect of digital suicide, of disconnection, than they are about any purported 'subversive' use of their means. In the supposedly halcyon days of social media, shortly after the global financial crash, the idea of a mass virtual suicide risked going viral, as is always the risk with suicide. The artist Sean Dockray's 'Facebook Suicide Bomb Manifesto' urged users to commit online hara-kiri. Websites offered users a quick and stylish exit from their accounts. Seppukoo.com allowed users to create 'last words', which would be automatically sent to their friends, and created a memorial page in their name before permanently deleting their account. Suicidemachine.org deleted all friends and information, replaced the user's profile picture with a noose icon and added the user to a group called 'Social Media Suiciders'.

Since the platforms benefit from the 'network effect' – the more people are connected, the more valuable it is – this would have been a catastrophic reversal. Both websites were subject to cease and desist letters from Facebook's lawyers, and were duly forced to stop offering the service to Facebook's users. Social industry platform protocols are carefully designed to discourage disconnection, since it is a threat to their very existence. Facebook's own options for permanent deletion are carefully hidden, appearing nowhere in any menu or settings option. Users must instead fill in a form reached through the Facebook Help Center, and wait through a 'reconsideration period'. Meanwhile, Facebook tugs on the heartstrings by displaying photos of friends who will 'miss you' – leveraging its control over uploaded content for commercial purposes.

There is evidence that the existing platforms are reaching their peak. Facebook, Twitter and Snapchat have all seen declining user numbers, especially during 2018. Ironically, Snapchat's fall may have been precipitated by its dependence on celebrity, as a single tweet from Kylie Jenner announcing to her 25 million followers that she didn't 'open Snapchat anymore' instantly wiped $1.3 billion off the company's value. But the trend is universal. Facebook's announcement that it had lost a million users across Europe in one year has cost it $120 billion worth of value, as teens drop out. Twitter, beset by fake posts and cyberbullying, lost a million users and saw its share price plummet.

Yet, at least 40 per cent of the world's entire population still uses the social industry. This remains a massive synchronization of attention, with over six billion eyeballs rapt. The platforms may recede or mutate, but they are unlikely to disappear. They have become monopolies, giants with immense political and ideological power. Their system is never a finished object, but always a work in progress, reacting to the latest trends to keep users hooked. The likelihood is that, in the absence of alternatives, they will work with existing fusions of venture capital, entertainment and amusement complexes, and news media, to produce new technologies for the production of distraction.

However, the platforms only work on the raw material of social trends. They work because competitive individualism was already culturally and politically incentivized, and the rise of mass celebrity ecologies was already under way. And they work, in part, because they address legitimate wants: they offer opportunities for recognition, for creative self-styling, for interruptions to monotony, for reverie or thinking-as-leisure-time. But they only do so on the basis that these activities are economically productive. Far from being a break from overwork, they work us harder than ever.

The platforms have shown us that our attention is valuable. What would happen if we took the suggestion of writer Matthew Crawford, and treated our attention as being too valuable to waste? What if we asserted a right not to be constantly addressed, and not to be continuously servicing an image whose fortunes are as volatile as the platforms' stock market values? The platforms have demonstrated that our everyday lives can be commodified, provided we consent to their darkest corners being flooded with light. What if, as the psychoanalyst Josh Cohen proposes, we deem this intrusion, this obliteration of the 'mute spot' in our being, 'whose natural elements are darkness and silence', to be 'the most profound violation a person can experience'? What if there are great works, vocations, adventures, awaiting us if we can work out what it is our inattentions are for, and find something else to attend to?

CHAPTER FOUR

WE ARE ALL TROLLS

Lulz is engaged in by Internet users who have witnessed one major economic/environmental/political disaster too many, and who thus view a state of voluntary, gleeful sociopathy over the world's current apocalyptic state, as superior to being continually emo.

Encyclopedia Dramatica

Life is unfair
kill yourself or get over it

Black Box Recorder, 'Child Psychology'

I.

Trolls are the anti-celebrities. They are propagandists of human failure. Far from extolling awesomeness, they ruthlessly exploit and show up weakness: for the lulz.[2] They remind you that there's always a point of view from which you don't matter, and from which your pain is hilarious.

In February 2011, schoolgirl Natasha MacBryde went out to kill. She was not unlike many teenagers: driven to anguished despair by school, friends and teachers, bullied by a clique, 'friend-zoned' by a boy she fancied and tormented by a string of abusive, anonymous messages on a social networking site. MacBryde, at the end of her tether, reached a decision. Having researched the method on the internet, she slipped out of her house after dark, climbed a steep embankment, stood on a railway track and waited. The next day, Valentine's Day, her body was found less than 150 metres from her house. The coroner determined that she had killed herself: a vehicular attack on her own body. MacBryde's heartbroken older brother created a Facebook tribute page in her memory.

Spotting an opportunity, a twenty-five-year-old 'RIP troll' from Reading, Sean Duffy, commenced a trolling campaign. He blitzed the page with comments and meme images with MacBryde's face: 'I fell asleep on the track lolz', 'I caught the train to heaven lol', 'I committed

2 'Lulz' is a trolling idiom: a corruption of 'lol', meaning 'laugh out loud'.

suicide for the lulz', 'Natasha wasn't bullied, she was just a whore' and 'Train late and bloody? My bad'. He posted an image from *The Simpsons*, of a Valentine's card given to Ralph Wiggum by Lisa Simpson, with a train belching out the slogan: 'I Choo-Choo-Choose You'. He made a YouTube video called 'Tasha the Tank Engine'. Duffy was a veteran of several such campaigns. He seemed to be particularly fascinated with taunting the grieving parents of dead teenagers. In a stroke of irony that would delight his online confederates, his campaign resulted in another teenager, wrongly accused of making the posts, attempting to commit suicide.

In court, in a meagre effort to mitigate his actions, Duffy's solicitor explained that he had Asperger's and didn't understand the effects of his actions. Yet his campaigns showed an extraordinary sensitivity to pain thresholds. For example, he chose Mother's Day to taunt the grieving mother of teenager Lauren Drew by sending her an image of a coffin with the words 'Happy Mother's Day' on it. He posted on Drew's memorial page, 'Help me mummy, it's hot in hell'. If anything, far from being oblivious, he seemed enthralled by the pain he could cause. It is precisely because trolls know what hurts that they find it so hilarious.

It is perhaps telling that his messages so closely resembled the campaign waged by the Westboro Baptist Church against the murdered Wyoming student, Matthew Shepard. In October 1998, Shepard had been beaten, tortured and left to die. The defence claimed that his killers only intended to rob him, but were driven to homicidal rage by his making a sexual pass at them: the notorious 'gay panic' defence. Amid this controversy, the Westboro Baptist Church picketed Shepard's funeral and set up a website gloating that Shepard was 'burning in hell'. They continue to maintain an online 'memorial' to Shepard featuring a crude gif of Shepard's head being consumed by flames, and a sound file purported to be him screaming 'from hell'. That their cackling, sadistic, relishing of hellfire was overtly linked to a sexually repressive morality might suggest something about the origins of Duffy's nastiness towards dead teenage girls.

Nor was Duffy's an isolated case. One of the first major exercises in RIP trolling, without any overt moral rationale, occurred in 2006.

Trolls from the 4chan message board descended on a MySpace page memorializing the twelve-year-old Mitchell Henderson, who had committed suicide. It emerged that he had lost his iPod days before his death, and trolls posted messages implying that his suicide was a frivolous act driven by consumerist frustration: 'first-world problems'. One post contained an image of the boy's gravestone with an iPod resting against it. A year after Duffy appeared in court, the Facebook page of Matthew Kocher, a fifteen-year-old who drowned in Lake Michigan, was defaced by trolling messages, such as 'LOL u drowned you fail at being a fish'.

When the seventeen-year-old Chelsea King was raped and murdered in southern Chicago in 2010, King's father was astounded to be attacked by trolls: 'I can't for the life of me understand why somebody would want to hurt somebody that's so broken and so grieving.' That brokenness is exactly what the trolls were seeking to punish. 'We are a mass of vulnerabilities', Jon Ronson writes in his book on public shaming, 'and who knows what will trigger them?' Trolls know. They are experts on vulnerability.

Yet members of the trolling subculture are for the most part not unusual. Academics studying trolling as a form of 'online deviancy' have engaged in a sophisticated form of the moral panic that pervades the press. Trolls are monstered, allegedly defined by a 'Dark Tetrad' of personality traits such as Machiavellianism, narcissism, psychopathy and sadism. These stories, dull and predicate-begging, merely redescribe trolling behaviour in morally excitable language without giving any account of it. Whitney Phillips, author of *This Is Why We Can't Have Nice Things*, found that, far from being deviant, trolls tended to be quite ordinary young men – with the emphasis on young men. Their 'gleeful sociopathy', as the trolling bible Encyclopedia Dramatica calls it, was enabled by forms of emotional detachment only available in online anonymity. Wearing the 'mask of trolling', they could treat any complex human situation, no matter how tragic, as exploitable material for lulz.

Their detached humour was epitomized by a blizzard of 9/11 jokes and memes, ranging from images of wrestlers demolishing the World Trade Center, to Kanye West addressing the towers with a remix of his bizarre 2009 interruption of Taylor Swift: 'Yo al Qaeda, I'm a really happy for you, I'm a let you finish. . . but the war of 1812 was the best attack on US soil of all time!' But for Phillips, this pervasive detached cynicism was part of the media and political landscape. 'Now watch this drive,' Bush said, returning to his golf swing after delivering a sober message on resisting terrorism. 'Stuff happens,' Rumsfeld said with sociopathic cheer among scenes of destruction in occupied Iraq. On television, fifteen-second snippets of horror and atrocity were sandwiched into prolonged vacuity in such a way as to provoke ironic detachment. Trolls did not invent this affective gap. And just as they fed on existing cultural trends, their sensation-mongering thrives in a 'click-based web economy'.

As the platforms have quantified attention, trolling has broken out of its subcultural bounds. What began as a tactic in a seemingly purposeless, directionless war, purely for the lulz, has gone universal. Most trolls are not RIP trolls, lulz trolls, government sock puppets or the misogynists whom Karla Mantilla dubs 'gendertrolls'. Most trolls are just average users. Everyone has an inner troll, researchers have found. What makes the difference is the environment the user is placed in. Those who see trolling on their feed are more likely to troll. In the recursive stimulus–response chamber of the social industry, trolling expands: the more trolling there is, the more trolling there will be. Trolling has gone mainstream. We are all practised experts in 'triggering' vulnerabilities.

II.

We are all trolls. The internet may have inflamed cultural tendencies already in gestation. From the first trolls on the Arpanet 'TALK' system used by university employees in the 1980s, to the message boards launched on the commercialized web of the late 1990s, it may have enabled new subcultures and magnified their consequences. But we were all trolling before trolling was 'a thing'.

The controlled cruelty of the wind-up is familiar fun, from Bart Simpson prank-calling bartender Moe, to Tom Green or Ashton Kutcher duping hapless members of the public. If trolls are 'gleefully sociopathic', delighting in deceiving, taunting and playing games with their foils, they aren't unlike a lot of pop culture heroes, from Eric Cartman to Dr House. On YouTube, prank videos – often grim or verging on sociopathic – have monetized trolling. This includes a skit by YouTuber Sam Pepper, in which he kidnapped a young man and forced him to watch as a masked man set about 'murdering' his friend. No one was killed in the production. Michael and Heather Martin repeatedly trolled their children by yelling at them or breaking their toys until they went bright red and erupted into sobs, racking up millions of views. As Heather Martin later mournfully admitted, they 'would get excited' when they got 'a lot of views'.

Trolling is popular entertainment, even if it sometimes runs afoul of barely legible cultural thresholds. The bafflement and ungovernable rages of the victim are always funny, and there is always sadistic detachment in the humour. When internet users are 'rickrolled'[3] the reactions are often funny. When 4chan trolls called video game stores to enquire about the non-existent sequel to an outdated game, the explosions of exasperated fury were funny. When a hapless internet troll went on Fox News representing the bogus group Forsake the Troops, Sean Hannity's credulous outrage was funny. Most people, at some time or other, have been trolls.

But the widespread popular appeal of trolling begs one to ask, what is so funny about it? 'Every joke', Freud wrote, 'calls for a public of its own and laughing at the same jokes is evidence of far-reaching psychical conformity.' For Henri Bergson, comedy 'dreams. . . but it conjures up, in its dreams, visions that are at once accepted and understood by the whole of a social group'. To understand a joke, to 'get it', is to be part of a culture, to share in a dream. And since jokes are usually tendentious, at someone's expense, to enjoy a joke is to take sides. If trolls are archetypal jokers, whose side are we taking when we see the funny side? Whose side are we on, when the joke is that someone's weaknesses make them pathetic and worthy of punishment? As Adam Kotsko has written,

3 A form of bait-and-switch trolling where users access a link pointing to seemingly interesting content, only to be confronted with the music video of Rick Astley's 1980s hit, 'Never Gonna Give You Up'.

the popular fascination with the sociopath rests on a fantasy of social mastery. If I was a sociopath, I wouldn't be so awkward, so gullible, so inhibitively moral: in a word, so vulnerable.

There is also something enjoyably nihilistic about trolling. Trolls, inhabiting a culture that is as illogical as it is cruel, delight in nonsense and detritus: calculated unreason, deliberate misspellings, the ironic recycling of cultural nostalgia and the effluent of celebrity, the sedimented layers of opaque references and in-jokes, id-streams of racism, misogyny, gore and outlandish porn. Trolling, to borrow a phrase from Phillips, is the 'latrinalia' of popular culture: the writing on the toilet wall. It's the coprolalia of End Times.

André Breton, who invented the term 'black humour', defined the 'simplest Surrealist act' as 'dashing down the street, pistol in hand, and firing blindly, as fast as you can pull the trigger, into the crowd'. Trolls, modern surrealists, take joy in the sheer random illogicality of their attacks, the nonsense they alight on for lulz, the pointlessness of the suffering they inflict. But they aren't firing as blindly as they like to think.

III.

Trolls are even more attention-hungry than their celebrity counterparts. An early guide to flaming (the practice of saying things to make other users upset) on the Arpanet 'Bulletin Board System' contended that it was the only way that 'people will read your opinions', since a net-wide flame war is impossible to ignore. Yet, over the years, especially once the internet was commercialized, trolls became attention-shy. They form a community of sadists, but only on the condition that it consists of people with no identifying characteristics: from 'anons' to sock puppets.

Trolling anonymity has its roots in the way the 4chan message board, on which the trolling subculture germinated, was set up. Founder Christopher Poole ensured that each user would have a default identity of 'anon' because, as he told *Rolling Stone*, it 'enables people to share things they wouldn't otherwise do'. And it was on the site's '/b/' message board that the trolls, calling themselves '/b/tards', gathered. The site deleted child porn and criminal material, including photographs of a murder victim posted by the killer. However, of course, this left in place a cornucopia of grotesquery, from stretched anuses to anti-Semitic jokes. Trolls took anonymity to another level. They were not simply evading surveillance. A troll who gave away personal information, or let slip a private conviction, would risk being trolled by the community. The only way to get by as a troll was to identify fully with the collective, and its value of detachment. The laughter of the individual troll was secondary to that of the hive mind. 'None of us', their motto had it, 'is as cruel as all of us.'

In this sense, trolls appear to be the only social industry users who are genuinely liberated from the constraints of identity, enacting in their perverse way the utopian promise of the internet. The mask they don is not so much an identity as an anti-identity. The idea of a mask that liberates someone from their prohibitions is culturally resonant. In the Jim Carrey film, *The Mask*, we are given a version of this story in which the hero is transformed from a neurotic loner into a charismatic trickster and acquires the power to turn reality into a cartoon at will. In this way he thwarts his enemies, who invariably take themselves too seriously. The 'mask of trolling' does something similar. Seeing the world through the mask, Phillips remarks, obscures the real lives and personal struggles behind every story, so that all one sees are the 'absurd, exploitable details'. Reality becomes a cartoon.

On the face of it, then, trolling is different from everyday wind-ups because trolls recognize no limitation, no criterion other than the lulz. As the 'Rules of the Internet' on 4chan's notorious '/b/' message board state, 'nothing is to be taken seriously', there are 'no real limits of any kind' and 'nothing is sacred'. This makes trolls profoundly antisocial. For community to exist, at some point the joke has to stop and the victim let in on the laughter. Otherwise, the fear of ridicule tends to make people clam up. Trolls don't care. Their only community is an anonymous, networked swarm. They check their identity at the door when they login, and with it their normal ethics. Their only attachment is to detachment.

The case of Jason Fortuny, one of the most well-known internet trolls of the 2000s, shows that this detachment is not as straightforward as it seems. He first made his name by sexually humiliating random men. He lured strangers with a fake Craigslist ad in which he pretended to be a woman looking for a 'str8 brutal dom muscular male'. He was inundated with queries, revealing messages, contact details, even photographs – all of which he posted on his blog, causing chaos and even job losses for his victims.

As far as he was concerned, it was their fault for being stupid: trolling was a kind of toughening pedagogy. Interviewed by the *New York Times* in 2008, he said trolling was 'like a pitcher telling a batter to put on his helmet by beaning him from the mound'. In the same way, Fortuny claimed, people needed to get over being hurt by words. Deciding to be hurt made one complicit. About his own trolling, he pleaded: 'Am I the bad guy?. . . No! This is life. Welcome to life. Everyone goes through it.' What, the journalist wondered, did he go through? Sexual abuse. The five-year-old Fortuny had been sexually assaulted by his grandfather, and a number of other relatives, and was estranged from his family. He knew all about sexual humiliation.

Detachment is a survival strategy in a world where one can expect to be abused. Trolls, having ostensibly purged themselves of attachment, express disgust at the attachments of their victims. RIP trolls are most aroused and incensed by the suicides of seemingly privileged white people, which they mock as self-indulgent. Public displays of grief are regarded as a facade for, as one troll put it, 'boredom and a pathological need for attention'. Yet if they were as detached as all that, their repetitiveness would be hard to explain. Duffy's campaigns, for example, despite their malicious inventiveness, were weirdly determined to make the point that dead teenagers were idiots, useless, burning in hell and, if female, sluts and whores. It was as if he was telling the same joke over and over. And a joke repeated too many times starts to look like an obsession, an empty, shell-shocked ritual, or repetition compulsion. It reeks of circling around the void.

The supposed detachment of RIP trolls looks suspiciously like emotional involvement. They are laughing in the face of death, as if they have mastered it. Their mirth resembles what Hobbes called the 'sudden glory' of the laughing animal, the pleasure you get when you abruptly and unexpectedly perceive your superiority. Yet you have to 'get' pain in order to know how best to inflict it. If RIP trolls are magnetically drawn to grief, it might be because they can already imagine how they might feel about loss, how grief might affect them. If they have been compared to 'grief tourists', it is because they can't stay away from the cemetery. The ferocious aggression directed towards mourners is implicitly, pre-emptively directed at the one who trolls. Waging war on mourners is a way of rebelling against one's own susceptibility.

IV.

In August 2012, the Australian television host Charlotte Dawson tweeted what she thought would be her last words: 'You win x'.

A campaign of trolling had exhorted her to 'hang yourself' and 'kill yourself you fucking whore'. The hashtags of the trolling campaign included #diecharlotte and #9gagarmy in reference to a meme site, 9GAG, where trolls congregated. Dawson, a judge on *Australia's Next Top Model*, swallowed a handful of pills.

Just months before, Dawson had been the victim of online paranoia, put at the centre of a media storm for jokingly calling for someone to 'please kill' the Filipino fashion blogger Bryan Grey Yambao, and pouring scabrous insults on a few others. Dawson's joke was in questionable taste. But, with precious piety and a great deal of faux naivety, many users took it as a literal death threat. Dawson laughed it off. But one day in August, she was subjected to abuse by a random Twitter user, apparently displeased with her television persona, who exhorted her to 'please GO HANG YOURSELF!!!'.

Dawson did not take it as a joke. Unable to identify her interlocutor, she tracked down someone else on the ensuing thread, and wrote to her employer, Monash University. The woman, Tanya Heti, was suspended. This infuriated trolls, who portrayed it as an attack on free speech. From Project Chanology, wherein 4chan users targeted the Church of Scientology, to the trolling of the US National Security Agency, trolls tend to be exercised by the abuse and suppression of information. And as far as they were concerned, Dawson was a hypocrite and a bully. This was enough to justify days of ferocious misogyny and incitements to suicide, all the more alarming given that Dawson had been openly struggling with depression for years.

Dawson survived, after being sped to an emergency ward, and subsequently received psychiatric treatment. Rather than take the well-intentioned advice that she should not feed the trolls, she embarked on a campaign of vigilantism. Just as before her suicide attempt, when she had retweeted her trolls in an effort to expose them, she decided to 'out' her trolls and publicly confront them. She became an anti-bullying campaigner. Trolling was just one particularly toxic aspect of her celebrity that Dawson found difficult to bear. Two years later, amid the glare of publicity as her ex-husband was interviewed on *60 Minutes*, she experienced a breakdown, and was found dead, hanged in her home. How much of her depression and ultimate death can be attributed to trolling is not clear: indeed, it could never be clear. What is clear is that the trolls either relished Dawson's agony, or didn't particularly care.

This puts a different perspective on the lauded amorality of trolls. They were not, in this case, doing it for the lulz. Their punishment had a purpose. Many analysts identify trolls as subversive 'tricksters', waging indiscriminate war on social norms. The troll is a 'self-appointed cultural critic', as Benjamin Radford puts it. Gabriella Coleman, basing her analysis on Lewis Hyde's classic analysis of the trickster as a 'boundary crosser' and spirit of 'mischief', sees trolls as embodying the archetype. Even the white-supremacist incitements of the neo-Nazi troll Andrew Auernheimer, known as 'weev', are of the same transgressive type. Whitney Phillips is more critical, but still sees the troll as someone who is out to destroy good and evil as a set of ontological premises. She describes the troll's mission as being to 'subvert, or at the very least tinker with, the existing moral order' – as if the difference between collapsing the moral order, subverting it and tinkering with it was not very great. Trolls like this image of themselves. It allows them to claim that, even if they're sociopaths, they are at least refreshingly free of hypocrisy. They may never tell the truth, but they are more honest than the culture that produced them.

If this were true, however, it would make trolls bizarre and incomprehensible. If they truly attack their victims on the basis of no discernible norm or value, then they have distilled punishment to its purest, pointless essence: you are punished because you are punishable. This would be the height of superego irrationality. Yet, to the extent that the yield of trolling is the outcry of the aggrieved, trolls need there to be some sort of moral order. There have to be just enough people 'taking things too seriously' to keep going. An indifferent shrug means the troll has failed. The death of moral value, the supposed aim of trolls, would be the death of lulz. Further, campaigns like that against Dawson make the troll look a lot like a closeted moralist, or a vigilante. To put it another way, the troll tries to have it both ways, claiming to be both magnificently indifferent to social norms, which he transgresses for the lulz, and often at the same time a vengeful punisher: in his fantasies, both the Joker and Batman.

The ways in which trolling and vigilantism resemble one another are not incidental. When *Stranger Things* actor Millie Bobby Brown quit Twitter, it followed months of harassment under the hashtag, #TakeDownMillieBobbyBrown. The attack began with a tweet by a user making a spurious and unsubstantiated claim of having been victimized by Brown. The user claimed that she had encountered Brown in an airport and asked for a photograph. She claimed that Brown said, 'Only if you remove the hijab,' and then aggressively pulled it off her head and stamped on it. There is no evidence this ever happened, and the user's profile picture showed a white woman without a hijab. Yet the hashtag was used to spread outrageous stories about Brown, often linking the LGBT advocate to homophobic or racist ideas. The story is complicated further still by the fact that some of the misattribution of homophobic sentiment started out as a satire by gay users, whose joke was that it was wildly implausible that Brown would be homophobic. Somehow, on the Twittering Machine, the transition from pure irony to zero irony is fast and frictionless.

It would be literally impossible to disaggregate this toxic combination of banter, punitive spite, misinformed outrage and sheer glee at someone being 'taken down'. On the Twittering Machine, they quickly become indistinguishable. And this ambiguity, this family resemblance between trolling and witch-hunting, is part of what makes it so viral, and so deadly as weapon.

V.

Trolls have become the main folk devil of the internet, the monstrous metaphor for everything that is wrong with it. Perhaps it's telling that this happened around 2010–11, just when the social industry platforms went stratospheric. Thanks in part to the spread of smartphone ownership, Twitter gained a hundred million active monthly users for the first time, whereas Facebook was close to gaining a billion monthly users.

Since then, trolls have been blamed for everything from hate crime to sharing leaked nude images on the internet, the term metastasizing so that there can now be everything from 'gendertrolls' to 'patent trolls'. Politicians often use the term to deride their social media critics, which at its most cynical works to deprive the criticism of its political substance. Previously, the role of internet folk devil was occupied by spammers, stereotypically represented as a Nigerian man trying to con a little old lady out of her savings, despite the fact that most spamming came out of the United States. Anti-spammer vigilantes often targeted Nigerian men for sexual humiliation in ways that were classically racist. Fittingly, since it is also a tactic of war, trolling is represented instead through reheated Cold War stereotypes about meddling Russians, in a way that serves Washington's traditional self-image as a defender of a liberal and open internet.

If trolling has generalized on the Twittering Machine, it is probably due to an elective affinity: that is, the practice coheres with the social patterns encouraged by the protocols of the machine. Trolling, like all manipulative communication, from marketing to military propaganda, reduces language to its effects. That is to say, it uses language in the way it does, not to persuade you of an idea but to change your behaviour. The social industry platforms have invented a form of teaching machine that uses reinforcements to induce users to respond accurately to marketing signals. In so doing, they've created an apparatus that can easily be gamed by trolls, who simply use it as it was designed to be used.

This is one reason the social industry bosses, despite noisy protestations of good intentions, seem unable to do much about trolling. The machine is perfectly congruent with the tendency that Raymond Williams described, wherein the New Right sought to rebuild societies to resemble the brutal struggle for survival among states. These societies were nihilistic, he said, their goal 'a willed and deliberate unknown, in which the only defining factor is advantage'. The platforms have distilled the idea of advantage into perfectly abstract metrics of attention and acclaim. Attention that is wrested most efficiently through manipulation, from the 'thirst trap' to 'fake news'.

In a way, the social industry platforms have turned John Forbes Nash's 'fuck you buddy' game into a principle of interaction. In Nash's game, played with chips and cards, each player tries to win all the chips. To win, however, they have to make temporary agreements with other players, which they ultimately go back on. They have to screw each other over. On social media, there are incentives towards short-term cooperation, 'signal boosting', the better to win more 'chips' (likes and followers). But these same incentives lead to users treating one another as raw material for their own success, and turn on one another with startling ease. They also lend themselves to a kind of hypervigilance – to what Eve Kosofsky Sedgwick calls 'paranoid reading'. One of the by-products of trolling anonymity is that it is often hard to tell whether or not one is being trolled. Friendly criticism appears as flaming, queries as concern trolling, a mild joke as an attack. Trolls have always relished their ability to trigger chain reactions, and as trolling goes viral, it flows seamlessly into online vigilantism, from which it is often indistinguishable. Trolling has become generalized because a directionless war-of-all-against-all is exactly what the machine is designed for.

But while a war against vulnerability is by definition a war against anybody, not everyone is equally vulnerable. The logic of online social Darwinism favours the dominance of the least vulnerable. When the irony-Nazi and celebrity troll Andrew Auernheimer, or 'weev', bombastically declared that 'trolling is basically internet eugenics', a way of driving the 'filth' and 'retards' off the internet and into the 'oven', he was giving a programmatic expression to tendencies already present in trolling. There is no clear correlation between trolling and support for right-wing politics. If anything, many right-wingers seem to have adapted the cultural style of trolls for their own purposes. But even among the majority of trolls who claim to be 'equal opportunity offenders', their victim choice betrays a tacit morality.

Trolls, in the subcultural sense, are overwhelmingly white men from anglophone and Nordic countries, who disproportionately attack women, queer and transgender people, black people and the poor. Their vaunted detachment performs a familiar white-male fantasy of ironclad superiority. When Anonymous trolls first donned *V for Vendetta* masks for their campaign against the Scientologists, they could hardly have better demonstrated this fantasy. On the trolling message boards, it doesn't pay to admit to being a woman, unless one is prepared to post naked photographs or 'camwhore'. As Jamie Bartlett describes, one woman who did agree to 'camwhore' for the '/b/ tards' inadvertently supplied enough information to enable the trolls to track her down. While she watched helplessly, they found her location, contact details, Facebook and Twitter accounts and university. They doxed her and shared her nude images with her relatives. One of the trolls called her and reported that she was crying 'like a sad sad sobbing whale', but the '/b/ tards' didn't give a shit: it was her fault for being stupid, and she deserved the consequences.

Trolling for the lulz thus segues into 'gendertrolling', wherein the aim is to silence vocal women through swarm-like harassment, rape threats, epithets like 'cunt' and 'whore', and the threat of 'doxing'. Faced with an actual, committed 'gendertroll', most trolls would see it as an opportunity for some countertrolling. Anyone who took the issue that seriously would be asking for it. Nonetheless, the spontaneous ideology of trolling is masculinist, and it's often impossible to tell the difference between a 'real' sexist attack and something said to provoke, for the lulz. Pew Research found that a quarter of young women have been sexually harassed, and another quarter stalked, on the internet. Danielle Citron's study of online hate crime finds that 53 per cent of non-white women, and 45 per cent of white women, have suffered harassment. Everyday sexism is everyday psychological warfare.

VI.

A Talmudic saying has it that to 'shame another in public' is a sin 'akin to murder'. As if shame was something like a death sentence. Jon Ronson mentions the startling finding that 91 per cent of men and 84 per cent of women can recall at least one vivid fantasy of murdering someone. Almost all of these fantasies were driven by the experience of humiliation, as if the worst thing you could do to someone is to destroy their idea of themselves. Most find a way to sublimate the desire. Some people murder themselves.

In 2006, a thirty-one-year-old Neapolitan woman, Tiziana Cantone, committed suicide by hanging. This, the last of several suicide attempts, followed years of public shaming over a leaked sex tape. The tape went viral and became the basis for mocking memes, sometimes printed on t-shirts or mobile phone covers. This was 'revenge porn', a malign form of internet celebrity. Cantone had sent the footage of herself having sex to an ex-boyfriend and some other friends on WhatsApp. And it was her ex who decided to troll her by posting the footage online. The devastating shaming visited on Cantone forced her to leave her job, change her name, move to Tuscany and fight in the courts to get the footage removed from the internet. Recognized everywhere, she was subjected to mocking skits by Italian footballers, turned into a joke by radio hosts and even denounced in smarmy terms by a politician from the Democratic Party. She was doing everything to erase all trace of herself, short of suicide. Until she committed suicide.

Whether or not the uploading of the footage began as an attempt at trolling, the subsequent campaign of moralistic spite, the fetishistic, detached nature of the mockery and the rapidly commodified memes, quickly came to resemble trolling. As Ronson points out, this kind of lethal shaming is hardly new to the platforms. News media have often hounded people to misery or death with exuberant public shaming campaigns.

In recent years, this included the smearing of the so-called 'poverty hoaxster', blogger Linda Tirado, the public humiliation of Australian Duncan Storrar for asking a question inconvenient to the government, and the journalist Richard Littlejohn's hounding of trans woman Lucy Meadows until she committed suicide. Many others have been taken apart with cheerful amorality, usually without the elan or wit of the better trolls, or with a scintilla more justification. But the social industry has now greatly expanded the potential ranks of previously anonymous individuals who are susceptible to this kind of predation, as well as the ranks of potential predators. Not only that, but the way in which social media mobs form to shame an individual can provide legacy media corporations with a prefabricated story which they can quickly monetize.

The monstering of Justine Sacco over a tasteless joke is one of Ronson's most telling case studies. Sacco had tweeted ahead of a flight to South Africa, with what she says was deliberate dark irony, 'Going to Africa. Hope I don't get AIDS. Just kidding. I'm white!' With only 170 followers, she had no reason to expect widespread attention. But during her flight, Twitter exploded with rage over what was seen as an intentional and literal racist provocation rather than, as she intended, a commentary on white ignorance. The paranoid reading prevailed. As soon as she landed, Sacco was submerged by angry tweets and concerned messages from friends. The furore was then taken up by newspapers and broadcasters. The Rupert Murdoch-owned *New York Post* sent journalists to follow her around. Her old tweets, often deliberately tasteless, were mined by BuzzFeed. For a badly worded joke – or worded all too well, hitting its mark too surely – she lost her job and spent years in misery – tormented, perhaps above all, by how happy everyone seemed to be by her ruin.

The schadenfreude of those looking forward to Sacco's devastation upon landing is recognizable. Ronson sees in it his own initial 'happy little "Oh, wow, someone is fucked."' But he also draws attention to the necessary detachment of this punitive glee: 'Whatever that pleasurable rush that overwhelms us is – group madness or whatever – nobody wants to ruin it by facing the fact that it comes with a cost.' Whatever it is that enables social industry users and journalists to overlook the cost of their buzz-driven show trials, to refuse context with a certain invested glee and wilful philistinism, to refuse the slightest scrap of interpretative generosity, it is just as much a fetish as the 'mask of trolling'. From one perspective, it looks like hypocrisy: you can have outrage or gleeful schadenfreude, but not both. From another perspective, just as the laughter of anons is secondary to that of the collective, the outrage of individual tweeters is secondary and vicarious. The main job of participants is to fuel the outrage of the anonymous collective. In that case, the main difference between trolls and shamers is one of emphasis. The former often mistakenly think they don't have a moral commitment; the latter often mistakenly think they do.

Sacco was, in a way, a small-scale troll who inadvertently provoked, in response, a mass trolling campaign. Her victimization, the fusion of trolling and vigilantism, was extraordinarily lucrative for media firms. Ronson estimates that Google alone may have made $120,000. Perhaps this collusion between troll and witch-hunter proves so extraordinarily volatile because it plays out something we already do to ourselves, intra-psychically. As if the Freudian slip or gaffe is just a way of trolling ourselves, inciting and enjoying the rage of our own internal Witchfinder General. Or, as if trolls operate on our existing unconscious dissent towards the identities and ideas we take too seriously, while online witch-hunters magnify to gigantic proportions the ways in which we are already punishing ourselves for our dissent.

Popular internet wisdom warns, 'Don't feed the trolls'. A logical corollary might be, 'Don't feed the moralists'. They are both part of the same spiral.

VII.

Trolling, and the backlash against trolling, is for the most part good money. But even when it starts to cost them business, the social industry giants are consistently bad at dealing with trolls. 'We suck at dealing with abuse and trolls on the platform,' then Twitter CEO Dick Costolo lamented in 2015, 'and we've sucked at it for years.'

This is an understatement: it is difficult to suck at something you're barely trying to accomplish. Twitter's Trust & Safety Council, responsible for protecting users, says the company should not get involved in distinguishing between good and bad speech. Twitter is 'the free speech wing of the free speech party', exclaimed then vice president Tony Wang. The 'marketplace of ideas' should sort it out, argues its user-safety chief, Del Harvey. Bad speech, she insists, is best countered with more good speech. Of course, since Twitter can't distinguish good speech from bad, it can't know that the 'marketplace of ideas' will promote good speech. But whatever the problem, more monetizable content is the answer.

Still, by 2015 Twitter's share values began to suffer as user growth stagnated in response to the nastiness of the medium. Under Costolo's successor, Jack Dorsey, the company responded to the problem by taking an idea from Facebook. Rather than lose profitable content, they used algorithms to change user experience. Rather than seeing tweets in the order that they were posted, users would see tweets aligned to their tastes. Subsequently, harassment has been addressed by means of tweaks to the algorithm. It was an optimal solution. Even if it didn't reduce bullying, it shifted the conversation and it mitigated Twitter's long-term problem with user engagement.

Intriguingly, this solution paid no attention to user demand. The social industry bosses don't trust that users know what they want. As Facebook's former chief technical officer, Ben Taylor, explained: 'Algorithmic feed was always the thing people said they didn't want, but demonstrated they did via every conceivable metric.' The metrics in question are those of user engagement, which fuel the mobile advertising business. Even if users complain bitterly about being trolled and abused, as long as we stay hooked, then the metrics will say we love the system. And if trolling provokes us to engage more intensely with the machine, typing out angry replies until the early hours of the morning, that still looks like pleasurable engagement in the metrics.

The doctrine of 'free speech' on the platforms is both a business doctrine and the assertion of a kind of sovereign power. When Reddit was used to circulate leaked celebrity nude images, then CEO Yishan Wong rallied strongly to 'the ideal of free speech'. Reddit was not just another corporation, he insisted, but more like 'the government of a new type of community'. And a government should exercise 'restraint' in its powers. But Reddit is not a constitutional republic, and Wong was misappropriating the language of 'free speech'. On Reddit, as on almost every platform, speech is controlled. It is subject to user-engagement protocols determined by the commercial aims of the owners. In defending the 'free speech' of users, Wong was asserting a state-like monopoly over speech on his platform. He was defending the company's sovereignty against challenges from governments, rival companies and citizens. The only successful challenge to this monopoly comes in the form of property law. When Reddit finally deleted the threads containing leaked celebrity nude images, it was under threat of copyright suits. But this strategy only works for those with resources. For most of us, it is completely ineffectual.

To the extent that the social industry platforms admit to controlling user speech, they tend to hide behind 'community standards'. The phrase itself is propaganda: there is no 'community' involvement in creating these standards. And these standards have long been a debacle, leading to bizarre decisions. For example, Facebook once ironically censored the ACLU's (American Civil Liberties Union) page over a post about censorship, deleting an iconic, Pulitzer Prize-winning photograph from the Vietnam War for violating its standards. It has often seemed perverse in its handling of 'hate speech'. Though eager to align itself with Black Lives Matter in its publicity, it suspended Shaun King, the Black Lives Matter activist, for sharing an experience of racist abuse. Yet its moderators regularly allow obvious racist abuse to stand. Often, social industry platforms are gulled into acting against a user by 'report trolling' – in which trolls submit false reports about their targets and incite others to do the same. They also act under pressure from governments to curtail opposition content. Facebook, for example, has cooperated with the Turkish and Israeli governments to remove Kurdish or Palestinian pages. Nor did 'free speech' prevent Facebook from sharing data with police surveillance programmes tracking protesters in Ferguson and Baltimore.

Facebook, responding to criticism, has developed a convoluted set of moderating guidelines. Yet this could not conceivably solve the problem. Every banned item has to be, and is, hedged with exceptions.

Sexual content is not permitted, for example – unless it is satirical. This meant, as Sarah Jeong pointed out, that anuses are banned unless photoshopped onto a politician's face. Racist terms are banned – unless they're self-referential, empowering or humorous. This means that racist content that a moderator thinks is funny could be allowed to stand, while someone angrily responding to it could be deemed abusive and their posts removed. Much depends on how teams of reviewers, hired on a casual basis in low-wage economies, interpret the morass.

The issue is not moderating guidelines. Any platform will have controls, and often they will be used unfairly. The issue is who determines the controls, and whether we want these commercial giants to have a monopoly over speech rights. The issue is whether they are even capable, given their overriding commitment to user addiction, and given their cooperation with governments, of controlling speech in a fair and accountable way.

VIII.

In recent years, trolls have allegedly taken over politics, as the traditional Right became the dark Right. Trump, the trolling pachyderm of the Twitter right, is the meet exemplar of this trend. Amanda Marcotte traces the emergence of a dark Right to the moment that trolls were recognized by a louche young reactionary, the journalist Milo Yiannopoulos, as the potential substrate for a hard-right youth movement. It only needed to be whipped into shape by a little leadership.

Beyond the trolling grass roots, moreover, governments have joined the fray. The Russian Federation has been singled out by US intelligence for allegedly using paid trolls to subvert the US presidential election. There is indeed some evidence that Russia uses trolls to disseminate false and inflammatory stories, even if there is little to suggest that it made a decisive impact on the 2016 presidential election. But Russia is hardly unique. A total of twenty-eight governments, that we know of, maintain troll armies. The US Military has run an online sock-puppet operation since 2011, dubbed 'Operation Earnest Voice', to spread pro-American propaganda overseas. Since 2016, it has authorized and funded what it calls 'counter-propaganda', targeting US citizens. The UK's Joint Threat Research Intelligence Group runs an extensive programme of trolling and false flags to undermine and smear individuals and companies that the government has a problem with.

The relationship between trolling and far-right politics is unclear. To blame it on trolling can be a way of depoliticizing a problem, as when popular Norwegian media reacted to Anders Behring Breivik's massacre of Labour Party members in Oslo and Utøya by stressing the need to engage right-wing activists more in the media. They invoked the adage: 'Trolls burst in the sun'. Moreover, it risks playing into the self-image of the alt-right as bold tricksters and subversives. The alt-right clearly enjoys the association. As one activist told the *Guardian*: 'We're the troll army! We're here to win. We're savage!'

What is true is that online alt-right politics has found a convivial home in trolling subcultures, and has often adopted the tactics of trolling, in its dissimulation and harassment campaigns. For example, the alt-right has appropriated the trolling icon Pepe the Frog. Pepe had long been a 'react' meme on 4chan message boards but, when it went viral on other sites, trolls attempted to 'reclaim' it by deliberately associating it with white-supremacist ideology, such that no one would want to touch it. The success of that operation meant that it was easily appropriated by neo-Nazis and other rightists. More generally, trolling as a tactic of war suits the alt-right's agenda – 'absolute idealism must be couched in irony in order to be taken seriously' according to Nazi blogger Andrew Anglin – and its self-image as a combative insurgency.

This has given the platforms some trouble. Eruptions of viral frenzy don't just benefit the social industry platforms. They have volatilized politics, as Bruce Sterling argues, much as financial speculation unsettles industry. And the alt-right have been quick to take advantage. To this extent, the interests of the incipient far right and of the platforms converge. In 2017, one analysis found that Trump alone was worth about $2.5 billion to Twitter, a fifth of its share value at the time. But even if the social industry firms can't afford to lose the alt-right, it causes them an image problem. They have, ever since the Green Movement in Iran and the Arab Spring, prized their nebulous public image of wokeness.

And, as 'responsible' corporations, they do not wish to be associated with 'bad behaviour'.

In July 2016, Twitter took the symbolic step of banning Milo Yiannopoulos. At this point, Yiannopoulos was still on his upward swing. He was a regular guest on news programmes and talk shows, with a highly marketable brand of controversy. He claimed to be 'the most fabulous supervillain on the internet'. He was kicked off Twitter for having spearheaded a trolling campaign against the *Ghostbusters* actor, Leslie Jones. Jones had been bombarded with racist spite by these trolls ever since the movie's release. It was easy to make an example of Yiannopoulos because of his high profile, and the prominence of the woman he was attacking. But if anything, the ban just fuelled interest in Yiannopoulos. And this interest came not just from far-right college activists, but from American liberals fascinated by his ambiguous darkness and charming sociopathy. The comedian Bill Maher even invited Yiannopoulos on to his late-night chat show to spout bigotry about trans people, and intended to have him back on. It was only when Yiannopoulos made comments appearing to justify adult men having sex with teenage boys that his career collapsed: one of those telling moments when we learn what the thresholds of free speech really are.

Yiannopoulos was in some respects a typical product and exemplar of the alt-right: self-consciously both a troll and an ideological vigilante. He was both joking and deadly serious. His reaction to being banned by Twitter was to bristle, with ill-concealed delight, at the 'emotional children of the left' for being unable to cope with disagreeable statements. 'All I did', he told *Business Insider*, 'was crack a few jokes.' Likewise, when challenged about sexist statements by Cathy Newman on Channel 4 News, he grinned and said: 'And you don't see the humour in that?' The far-right troll 'weev' takes a similar approach in claiming that, when he told reporters he was a 'neo-Nazi white supremacist', he was making fun of them, as it was 'obviously' a ridiculous statement – despite the large swastika tattoo on his body. He followed this up by insisting that the Left end its 'tyrannical campaigns of censorship', on pain of looming bloodshed: and 'my team has all the guns and combat training'. This cultivated ambiguity, this hedging of a serious political agenda with statements ostensibly made just for the lulz, indicates where trolling could fit into the psychic and political economy of the alt-right.

Breitbart, the far-right website which subsequently became Yiannopoulos's regular outlet until his downfall, was also annexed to the Trump campaign. Steve Bannon, then chair of Breitbart News, signed up to the campaign after former Fox executive Roger Ailes became a Trump adviser. And it arguably pioneered a form of in-real-life trolling that serves its reactionary purposes, with its two best-known scoops: the sting against the liberal civil society organization, ACORN, and the framing of African-American Department of Agriculture employee Shirley Sherrod. In the first instance, far-right activists visited ACORN offices claiming to be looking for housing and welfare assistance. The activists spun a yarn about their rough circumstances to elicit compassion from junior ACORN employees, then successfully goaded some of them into making statements that appeared to condone underage prostitution and criminal activity. These exchanges were then spliced together and packaged as an 'exposé'. In the case of Shirley Sherrod, they disseminated a drastically edited clip of a speech made to the liberal anti-racist organization, the NAACP. They made it appear as if she was gloating over her refusal to help a white man, whereas the speech had the completely opposite message. In both cases, Breitbart used heavily edited footage to depict black people as enemies of white society. In both cases, the liberal establishment was provoked into panicked overreaction, prompting sackings, resignations and, in the case of ACORN, its effective termination, only to realize it had been had.

In their ideological framing of the ACORN sting, the conservative activists involved claimed that ACORN inhabited a 'revolutionary, socialistic, atheistic world, where all means are justifiable', thus licensing all means employed by the Right to combat them. In a vivid and telling stroke, they called for conservative activists to 'create chaos for glory'. Andrew Breitbart, discussing the Sherrod case, asserted that her 'racist' speech showed that the NAACP had no right to judge Tea Party members as racist, and indeed was 'a perfect rationalization for why the Tea Party needs to exist'. Rationalization was the key word here.

Notably, while much alt-right trolling reheats anti-communist paranoia along with traditional fascist ideas, pro-Trump trolling campaigns are often aimed at conservatives who are critical of the alt-right. When *The Daily Beast* reported that Breitbart incited 'hate mobs' to threaten and dox critics on the Right, then editor Steve Bannon disavowed any responsibility. Trolling is an effective weapon precisely because responsibility for it is diffuse and ambiguous. Nonetheless, Bannon gloried in the site's reputation for thuggishness. When an insider described Andrew Breitbart as 'the kind of people who, if you accidentally brushed against their shopping cart in the supermarket, their response is to burn down your house', Bannon was delighted. He explained: 'If a guy comes after our audience. . . we're going to leave a mark. We're not shy about it at all. We've got some lads that like to mix it up.'

This relishing of chaos even while scolding it, playing the part of both troll and witch-hunter, insider and outsider, became part of the affective basis for Trumpism. Social industry platforms prize their self-image as a technology of freedom. And they have at times been used for progressive ends, helped marginalized groups gain attention, or enabled demonized figures to outmanoeuvre the legacy media. But in generalizing the troll–vigilante dialectic, they have also provided an ideal tool for the convocation of new, reactionary masses.

IX.

What happens when trolling appears in meatspace? In its subcultural origins, trolling insisted on a sharp differentiation between online and offline behaviour. On the internet, nothing mattered; nothing was to be taken seriously. It was, ostensibly, performance art.

But, as trolling became generalized, the already tenuous gap between the real and the performed tended to collapse. Trolls have always been adept at manipulating bits of culture. They turned Pepe the Frog into a repulsive symbol of fascism. They transformed the music video for Rick Astley's 'Never Gonna Give You Up' into a cruel joke. They turned the *V for Vendetta* mask into a protest icon. And they have often justified their use of racist, sexist or homophobic language as a tricksterish attempt to deflate the terms and make fun of them. But 'irony' isn't as subversive as this implies. Irony made Rick Astley's records start selling again. It handed a popular icon to the alt-right. Irony makes unappetizing ideologies digestible. And while it offers an easy rationalization for trolls engaging in sexist or racist attacks – 'I did it for the lulz' – the effect of these attacks is the same as if they were sincere.

And it started to spill out into the 'real world', with lethal effects. An example of this was the 'Gamergate' scandal. This began when video-game developer, Zoë Quinn, discovered that her ex-boyfriend, Eron Gjoni, had posted a long article about their relationship on the internet. In it, he accused her of cheating and blamed her professional success on her trading of sexual favours for good press. The accusation, which became known as 'Gamergate', was nonsense. It was revenge porn. But it tapped into male resentment over the growing feminist voice in the gaming industry. Men rallied to 'Gamergate', believing not only that a woman had gained from sexual favours, but that this somehow diminished them. It was somehow 'typical' of an injustice they were going through, an injustice signalled by the growing profile of women in the gaming industry. Gjoni wanted the post to trigger storms of harassment, and openly appealed to Quinn's haters on 4chan and Reddit message boards to target her. He succeeded. Quinn faced swarms of trolling anons, death threats, doxing and abuse. She saved copies of the abuse on her computer. By the time she stopped keeping records, the saved abuse took up a total of sixteen gigabytes of computer memory. This was trolling for a cause, even if it wasn't clear what the cause was: none of Gamergate's advocates ever explained what, practically, would allay their collective outrage.

As Sarah Jeong points out, however, the harassment of Quinn was one of only a small number of unambiguous, 'documentable' examples of online harassment. And in the context of Gamergate, as the storms of viral fever spread, dragging journalists, developers and onlookers into the vortex, the accusations of harassment were less clear. Paranoia reigned, understandably in the circumstances. Every opinion was a threat, or a harassment, or a manipulation, or a troll, necessitating belligerent vigilance. It was a classic shitstorm. And it was impossible to change one's opinion without provoking attack. The worst bile, naturally, was reserved for women, especially those who defected from the Gamergate cause. When Grace Lynn, a supporter of Gamergate, had a change of heart, she was subject to waves of harassment culminating in a 'SWATting', where the target's home address is used to make a false emergency call resulting in armed police raiding the property. Lynn defused the situation, but previous 'SWATtings' have resulted in police killing unwitting victims.

The consequences of a major cultural shift were being filtered through the Twittering Machine in the worst way. Instead of amplifying women's demands for equality, or even just clarifying the issues, Gamergate empowered sadists and sexist provocateurs. It became a defining moment in the emergence of a new subcultural style of right-wing activism predicated on male resentment fused with trolling culture. Joining other subcultural streams, from 'pick-up artists' to 'incels' (the 'involuntary celibate'), and adopting a reboot of 1970s anti-feminist activism, many Gamergaters became Men's Rights Activists (MRAs). It is the MRAs, more than anyone else, who have taken their trolling into the real world with bloody consequences. Trolling, having been filtered through the machine, entered meatspace with a vengeance.

In April 2018, at a busy intersection in Toronto, a man drove a rented van into a crowd of pedestrians, killing ten and injuring sixteen. The mode of attack directly echoed the methods of the so-called Islamic State. But the suspect, Alek Minassian, was not a member of any known network and had no criminal record. He had even briefly enrolled in the Canadian Armed Forces. He was an incel partisan. Incels, a subculture within a subculture, a bleak fraction of MRAs, share with their confederates a *Planet of the Apes* vision of female sexuality in which women have evolved to prefer physically dominant men. They think their unwilling celibacy, far from being a normal state of affairs, is a special punishment inflicted by fate. That their sexual frustration derives from genetic deficit. Before his attack, Minassian had declared on Facebook: 'The Incel Rebellion has already begun! We will overthrow all the Chads and Stacys! All hail the Supreme Gentleman Elliot Rodger!'

The Chads referred to by Minassian are stereotypical alpha males, and Stacys are their stereotypically attractive female counterparts. Chad and Stacy are football jock and cheerleader, an American success story: and the success story is a superego ideal which taunts the incel. Worse, for incels it's a form of sexual despotism in which they are an oppressed caste. Their equivalent of the 'oppressive Tawaghit' of Islamic State propaganda. A fantasy image superimposed on layers of agonized self-loathing, anguished world- and women-hatred, sadism, masochism and death drive.

As the reference to Elliot Rodger made clear, Minassian was far from the first of his type. And many incels hope for more. During the rampage by former student Nikolas Cruz at a Florida high school in September 2017, incel communities were desperately rooting for the killer in the same ironic idiom: scorning the 'normies, stacies and chads' and praying the 'HERO' with the gun would also be 'ugly'. Years before, MRAs had cheered on the mass murderer Scott Dekraai when he shot his ex-wife and eight others during a custody battle over his son.

And yet, perhaps the most chilling aspect of Minassian's actions was the way he chose to announce his 'rebellion'. His post, written in the stylized, ironic jargon of trolling, implied a frightening degree of detachment. If one didn't know that the author was on the brink of mass murder, it would seem like a joke. It was as though the ironic folds had unravelled, revealing an ouroboros in which the 'literal' and 'ironic' existed on the same plane. He was a troll, in meatspace, and in the same move a vigilante murderer. His seriousness was couched in comic-book irony, much as Rodger's ghoulish videos and manifesto had been performatively laden with comic-book braggadocio.

Trolling irony was never what it appeared to be. Never detached, irony was just a container for ambivalence. The core of irony is almost always a passionate commitment which can't be expressed in any other way. To ironize about it, to make fun of it, is to allow it to be expressed while also reproaching it. In the case of the incels, irony tips over into passion, without losing the sense of self-reproach, or self-hatred. Trolling, as a tactic in a universal, web-mediated war, has acquired its misogynist wing. One every bit as futile, impossibilist and potentially dangerous as its Daesh counterpart.

CHAPTER FIVE

WE ARE ALL LIARS

Everywhere socialization is measured by the exposure to media messages. Whoever is underexposed to the media is desocialized or virtually asocial

Jean Baudrillard, *Simulacra and Simulation*

A human being takes in far more information than he or she can put out. 'Stupidity' is a process or strategy by which a human . . . commits him- or herself to taking in no more information than she or he can put out

Samuel Delany, *Stars in My Pocket Like Grains of Sand*

Not to lie about the future is impossible and one can lie about it at will

Naum Gabo, *The Realistic Manifesto*

I.

Edgar Maddison Welch carries two guns, one of them an automatic assault rifle bigger than his arm. It's an AR-15, a lethal weapon adored by the National Rifle Association, repeatedly used in several mass shootings. He has a third gun in his car, in case of trouble.

A young man with dirty fair hair and a scraggly beard, he is a small-time screenwriter and bit-part actor with minor credits in a string of slasher horror movies. He has come, dressed in light blue jeans and t-shirt, to 'self-investigate' rumours of an elite paedophile ring. Internet stories say that Hillary Clinton and top-level Democrats are trafficking child sex slaves out of the Comet Ping Pong restaurant in Washington DC: the infamous 'Pizzagate'.

Staff and diners at the pizzeria are faced with an agitated, gun-toting man who may be about to kill them. They flee, in hectic panic. He fires some shots into the floor and begins stalking the restaurant looking for the tunnels through which the children are allegedly being hustled. A restaurant employee who has gone to get some pizza dough from the freezer in the alley, comes back in to find Welch turning the rifle on him. He turns and runs, escaping with his life. After about twenty minutes, satisfying himself that there are no underage children on the premises, Welch surrenders peacefully to the police surrounding the restaurant.

All of this takes place within half an hour on a December afternoon in 2016, and it is more ridiculous and compelling than any script Welch is ever likely to write. He is not the first to go to the restaurant to investigate these claims. Since these allegations went viral, the owners have been bombarded with death threats and abuse, and vigilantes have turned up to look around the premises and live-stream their investigations. But Welch, clearly anticipating the sort of scenario in which he might have to be Vin Diesel, goes in armed and ready to kill. He ends up with a four-year jail sentence.

All of this derangement is apparently driven by a 'fake news' story, originating with far-right conspiracy websites and circulated on Facebook. There appear to be a surfeit of stories alleging Hillary Clinton's involvement in child sex trafficking. Lt Gen. Michael Flynn, then Trump's national security adviser, shared a similar tale, breathlessly tweeting about 'Money Laundering, Sex Crimes w Children, etc. . . MUST READ!'

It is not clear, could never be clear, whether the story is a deliberate troll or earnest lunacy. It may have been a dupe, or the true confession of someone who, as far-right conspiracy theorist Alex Jones once put it, smelled the body under the carpet. At this level, the difference between a fake story and a confession becomes moot. Nor is it possible to say whether, or why, people really believed it, or merely entertained it, or why either way they acted on it. Is it really a problem of 'fake news', or just another example of the paranoid vigilantism that has seen the rate of mass shootings in America soar, even as other violent crimes have plummeted?

In the same month that Edgar Maddison Welch undertook his one-man vigilante operation in Washington, the Pakistani defence minister was gulled into threatening Israel with nuclear strikes. He had read a story about Israel contemplating a nuclear attack on their country in the event that Pakistani troops entered Syria. Pakistan, he reminded Israel, was 'a nuclear state too'. The story was a fake, but it revealed something real nonetheless. The prospect of atomic genocide had been distilled for infotainment, only to expose a very real possibility already lurking in the global order.

In Giorgio De Maria's cult horror novel, *The Twenty Days of Turin*, high-minded city administrators are struggling to cope with the alienation of the dislocated migrants arriving in the city. A band of charming, fresh-faced youths, apparently idealistic and impossible to distrust, propose 'the Library'. In the Library, they don't want high-flown artifice; they want 'popular' literature: the confessional. In the Library, anyone can read anyone else's personal diaries, confessions, complaints, cries from the heart. One woman wants a young man to help her with constipation and is 'ready to give and give and give'. Another aches to satisfy 'some kind of poetic desire'. Old scrapbooks, notepads and diaries are recovered and enlivened by the invention of a new kind of audience.

Here is the Library as a kind of psychopharmacopoeia, an antidepressant, administering the suffering soul with writing. Appropriately, it is based in a wing of the sanatorium. For the blessing of an audience, some attention to their pains and yearning, citizens willingly give up their intimacy, their privacy, to the Library. Their confessions grow macabre, dark, malicious. Pages and pages of screeds are confected just to injure someone, or else disintegrate 'into the depths of bottomless madness'. They go from celebrity to trolling. And slowly it becomes clear that they have birthed a malevolent force, a 'collective psychosis' resulting in nightly mass murders.

The horror story of the Twittering Machine is told, cumulatively, in vignettes about 'fake news', in sustained augury about the 'post-truth' society being birthed, and in pithy denunciations of 'echo chambers' and 'content silos'. But what if we are in the position of De Maria's investigator, not knowing what we are faced with? There is a collective writing experiment, a descent into madness and violence. What force connects them is still, to us, an occult knowledge.

II.

Old media is not dying. The advertising-driven print and broadcast media will live, albeit smaller and much weaker than before. They are being inscribed within a new hierarchy of writing dominated by the digitus. And the characteristics of that new hierarchy are determined by the way that Silicon Valley venture capital has found its profit model.

The social industry is one powerful faction within a wider platform economy: what Nick Srnicek calls Platform Capitalism. This sector began to arise after the dot-com bubble burst, when a glut of spare financial capital was invested in tech upstarts experimenting with ways to make money. The 'platform' model, where the service is to connect businesses, customers and other businesses digitally, was a clear winner. As Srnicek documents, the logic of this platform connection is to make the processes of consumption and production more visible. Spotify, renting its musical product through a cloud-based streaming service, collects digital information from customers that enables far more precise marketing. General Electric, offering a cloud platform to allow industrial firms to connect production processes by sensor and chip all over the world, makes production systems legible in the form of electronic writing. This also permits a new form of rent-seeking. Instead of selling products, increasingly firms adopting the 'platform' structure just lease them as services. Rolls-Royce, rather than selling a jetliner engine, will now rent it out at an hourly rate.

The social industry giants have created a new form of advertising platform. The flow of marketing revenue is being massively redirected from newspapers to Facebook and Google. World advertising revenues for the newspapers fell by more than $15 billion from 2013 to 2017. In the US, newspaper readership fell to its lowest level since the 1940s. In the UK, print circulation is heading for a cliff fall. British press barons are discussing the formation of a cartel to negotiate advertising revenues, as a result of losing out to the internet. The same decline befalls the broadcasters, where social media ad spending is projected to be larger than the entire global television advertising market by 2020. The new giants are Facebook and Google – and their respective services, Instagram and YouTube. These companies took 90 per cent of all new digital-advertising revenue in 2017. Most of it came from smartphone users. Were it not for the smartphone becoming ubiquitous around 2011, things would be different.

Facebook beats a newspaper, hands down, precisely because it has nothing to do with journalism. Newspapers sell the attention of a cluster of demographics purchasing a fixed bundle of products. Their product is conditioned by factors extraneous to advertising, such as the ideological agenda of the owners, the professional ideology of journalists, and certain inherited cultural ideas of what a newspaper is and what 'news values' are.

Facebook doesn't care. It detaches the organization and distribution of content from that sort of editorial control. A piece of content originally procured for a Sunday newspaper, or a half-hour television news programme, is now an item in a flow of homogenized posts organized by algorithm. Facebook automatically selects for information what is impressive and seductive, rather than accurate or even meaningful. It degrades the ecology of information, while inflating it and adding a new volatility to it. And it radically accelerates the existing drive to infuse journalism with the imperatives of amusement and entertainment.

For the advertisers, this results in much better data. Attention is organised by far more exact demographics, indexed to clicks, searches, shares, messages, views, reacts, scrolls, pauses: the complete digital package. Google has an even more comprehensive set of tools. It is not just the search engine which allows Google to see what people are up to online. They have the Google Chrome browser, their Gmail service, their DNS server, YouTube, website analytics, Google Translate, Google Reader, Google Maps and Google Earth. They can analyse messages, contacts, travel routes and the shops visited by users. They have a deal with Twitter, giving them access to all tweets. Users hand over immense amounts of raw material to the platforms every time they access the app.

This new revenue system is transforming both the consumption and production of information, ripping it out of the control of Cold War-era broadcasters and print giants allied to the liberal state. Already in 2016, 62 per cent of Americans got some news on social media, and 44 per cent got their news regularly from Facebook. No other single company comes close. Those that are even remotely competitive are themselves advertising platforms. YouTube ranks second, with 10 per cent of American adults getting their news regularly from the video service, followed by Twitter with 9 per cent.

If the old news giants were advertising platforms in denial, Facebook is a media organization in denial. Neither Facebook nor Google invest in journalism. Indeed, they don't invest much in any new production at all. Their profits are so high and their costs so low that the vast majority of their wealth is invested in liquid financial stocks or hoarded offshore. In 2016, it was reported that Google offshored $43 billion.

Facebook uses the same tax-avoidance scheme. They are leaders of the pack among the top fifty American corporations hoarding $14 trillion offshore. Facebook, attempting to mollify old media monopolists losing out to Facebook without giving them a dime, has launched the 'Facebook Journalism Project'. The project proposes a new partnership with publishers, from *Bild* and *El País* to Fox News and the *Washington Post*, to help them use the medium to get new subscribers. This merely maximizes the ability of a small number of old media survivors to attract a diminishing pool of revenues. Google, in a similarly minuscule gesture, has set up a journalism fellowship.

Nonetheless, precisely because they have no responsibility to journalism, the social industry platforms are in a sense much purer media companies. When Mark Zuckerberg writes that 'news and media are not the primary things people do on Facebook', a claim he repeated to Congress in 2018, he is concealing something in plain sight. Facebook, Google, Twitter, YouTube, are nothing but media. They exist to generate information, as part of a cybernetic system of surveillance, control and extraction, without bias. Bias is about meaning, whereas social media platforms are fundamentally nihilistic.

This agnosticism about content purifies an existing trend in the old media. While newspapers owned by Axel Springer, or Rupert Murdoch, or the allies of ruling parties like *El País* in Spain, all had ideological axes to grind, they were also advertising platforms. And that business model was tendentiously already agnostic about content, as long as attention backed up by purchasing power was secured. In fact, this is true of all commodities produced under capitalism: investors are in principle (never entirely in practice) indifferent to content provided it increases the return on investment. Mark Zuckerberg's extreme agnosticism, to the extent that he openly declares that he has no problem with Holocaust denial appearing on Facebook if some users want that, is a pure distillation of this tendency. The fact that most of Facebook's editorial work is delegated to proprietary algorithms – automated agnosticism, digital nihilism – doesn't make it less of a media organization.

Facebook's old media competitors miss the mark by insisting, as the *Guardian* did in 2016, that Facebook covertly relies on old-fashioned 'news values'. The paper's story was based on leaked documents showing human intervention at various stages in its 'trending news' operation, 'injecting' some stories and 'blacklisting' some topics. As the documents suggested, Facebook's criterion for determining a top 'trending news' topic was its prominence in broadcast and print news outlets. But the point about any 'trending news' system is that it is, like 'trending topics', an echo chamber. It magnifies attention to a story simply because it already has attention. Facebook's editorial operation is a digital shrug at 'news values' which, exactly on that account, canalizes attention more efficiently.

The widespread recognition that the social industry giants are media organizations, the primary source of news for hundreds of millions of people, with enormous public agenda-shaping power, is leading to new pressures on both Facebook and Google. In Spain, in 2014, an intellectual property law was passed forcing Google to pay for links and excerpts of content displayed on its Google News feed. Google reacted as any good monopolist would, by shutting down its service in that country. This was a message for countries considering similar ideas, as the UK currently is, under pressure from its newspaper industry.

This is an extraordinary climatic shift. The old news industry, for decades, has told us that journalism is best served by private enterprise, free market competition and as little state intrusion as possible. Now they want the state to bail them out, but without as yet any serious conversation about what publicly funded, public interest journalism should look like, and to whom and how it should be accountable.

Rather than have this public conversation about what is happening with our degraded information ecologies, however, states are increasingly bringing the social industry giants to book over 'fake news'.

III.

Donald Trump's gleeful appropriation of the term 'fake news' ought to have been a red flag. It ought to have alerted us to the intrinsically authoritarian cadences of this language, and to the fact that it isn't saying exactly what we'd like to think it is.

In the United States, the term gained currency as part of an attempt to explain why the paragon of the Washington governing class, Hillary Clinton, lost to the far-right rank outsider Donald Trump. After all, Trump's candidacy was supposed to assure a Clinton win; leaked Democratic Party strategy documents showed that they sought to encourage the Republicans to veer as far right as possible, in the hope of building a broad centre to rival them. The *New York Times*, a paper very much of the Democratic Party establishment, conducted an in-depth investigation into these 'fake news' stories that it said had warped the outcome. Its showcase example was a tweet that went viral, claiming that anti-Trump protesters gathering in Austin were being professionally bussed in. The claim was illustrated by a photograph of ranks of buses and coaches that, it turned out, were for participants in an unrelated conference. This false claim was shared 16,000 times on Twitter and 350,000 times on Facebook, and the rumour was endorsed by Trump.

Other examples unearthed by the *Times* were far more morbid. Clinton was paying pollsters to skew results. Her campaign was planning a 'radiological attack' to stop voting. Her strategist John Podesta partook of occult rituals. Her opponents tended to die in suspicious circumstances. 'Fake news', so the argument went, had undermined the consensus necessary for effective government. As Martin Baron, executive editor of the *Washington Post*, complained: 'If you have a society where people can't agree on basic facts, how do you have a functioning democracy?'

The problem here is that this wasn't simply about disagreement as to the 'basic facts'. Disagreement about 'basic facts' is a condition of a functioning democracy. A fact is just a measurement, and there is always some legitimate disagreement over the relevance of the measurement, the tools used to make it, the authority of the people doing the measuring, and so on. There are no facts without values, so only in a police state can there be a factual consensus. The would-be arbiters of 'basic facts' once assured readers that Iraq possessed weapons of mass destruction, enabling the loss of hundreds of thousands of lives. No, the problem was deeper. These beliefs were, to differing degrees, suggestive of conspiracist paranoia. The kinds of people prepared to believe such stories were not only far from Clinton's core demographic; they were not even rooted in the sort of epistemological presuppositions that would be susceptible to a liberal press 'fact check'.

There is also little evidence that 'fake news' had much effect in 2016, and attempts to blame belief in 'fake news' stories risk shuffling cause and effect. For example, a study by researchers at Ohio State University looked at the correlation between belief in 'fake news' stories and defection from the Democratic ticket in 2016. It, quite ingeniously, controlled for alternative factors such as age, education, gender, race and ideological orientation. Remarkably, though, it omitted to control for the impact of Clinton's policies, statements or campaigning strategies. While establishing a weak correlation between belief in a fake news story and likelihood to defect, it was still unable to say whether this was a cause of defection or an effect of other factors causing defection. These other factors might include the effects of the credit crunch, the record of the Democratic Party in its rust-belt constituencies, and the disintegration of the political legitimacy of the party establishments.

There is a further difficulty posed by the way in which Clinton was damaged by true claims, which Trump was able to put to work. Among the leaked emails from Hillary Clinton's campaign, for example, was one discussing Clinton's speeches to Wall Street, wherein she is supposed to have said 'you need both a public and a private position'. In another, Democratic National Committee chair Donna Brazile said of the Democratic primary debates that she had received questions in advance from CNN. Another story, allegedly spread by Russian troll farms to depress black voter turnout, was that Clinton had once dubbed young black men 'superpredators'. This was also true. Trump's claim that she lied repeatedly and pathologically about her alleged heroics in Bosnia was also true.

If the term 'fake news' is widely used by the Right, including such conspiracy theorists as Alex Jones, this suggests it is semantically loaded. Indeed, Trump's appropriation of the term prompted a momentary fumbling for fine distinctions. The BBC suggested that 'unverified' was not the same as 'fake': fake news was untrue, whereas unverified news had not yet been proven to be true or false. The problem with such Jesuitical distinctions is that all 'fake news' is 'unverified' until someone proves it is 'fake'. When Trump used the term, he was using it to describe media organizations publishing a document concerning his alleged relationships with the Russian state that, they admitted, they couldn't verify. Moreover, this definition of 'fake news' would cover many stories critical of Trump. For example, the *Washington Post* alleged that Russian hackers had 'penetrated' the US electricity grid during the election, and that a range of left-of-Clinton websites were part of a Russian disinformation campaign. Both stories, aggressively promoted by the Post, were later humiliatingly edited, their central claims withdrawn.

Those bewailing 'fake news', overwhelmingly journalists from the legacy media, are also missing the real scoop. 'Fake news' is old news. After all, exactly when was the era of unalloyed truth-telling? It is child's play to list a century of official hoaxes, from Germany's 'corpse factory', to the Gulf of Tonkin incident, to Kuwaiti babies being ripped from incubators, to weapons of mass destruction capable of being unleashed within forty-five minutes. The availability of old media for state management is well documented, from the CIA's extensive operations in American newsrooms during 'Operation Mockingbird' to MI5's vetting of BBC journalists (and the BBC's covering up of this fact). Equally well documented is its involvement in what journalist Nick Davies called 'churnalism': the recycling of press releases as news. These include not just the usual run of celebrity fare or commercial propaganda, but also false stories from right-wing organizations like the anti-immigrant Migration Watch or the anti-Muslim Gatestone Institute.

To this extent, 'fake news' is a culmination and fusion of existing trends in the media: propaganda, churnalism and infotainment. The genre of faked celebrity deaths builds on a form of 'soft news' that emerged out of the fusion of entertainment and twenty-four-hour news. Alex Jones's far-right conspiracy website, Infowars, builds on talk radio's tradition of right-wing rage, conspiracy-as-infotainment and 'home shopping'. Much of what is classified as 'fake news' is just satire taken literally. For example, the satirical claim that the US would house a quarter of a million Syrian refugees at the Standing Rock Reservation was repeated in earnest by Sean Hannity of Fox News, and Donald Trump. In other cases, the old media concocts a false news story out of random detritus found on the internet. The *Toronto Sun*'s false story claiming that asylum seekers being temporarily housed at the Radisson Hotel Toronto East had 'slaughtered goats' in the bathrooms, was based entirely on unverified reviews left on the TripAdvisor website.

Nonetheless, 'fake news' has galvanized governments to act against Facebook, as part of the general attempt to invigilate liberal states against the populist menace. And Facebook's reticence has been noted as a black mark on its corporate character. In July 2018, for example, the head of Facebook's News Feed, John Hegeman, was asked by CNN to explain why Alex Jones's Infowars site was hosted. If Facebook was dedicated to eradicating fake news, why did it tolerate a site that disseminated nonsense rumours that the victims of the Sandy Hook massacre were 'crisis actors'? Hegeman insisted that Facebook was simply a place 'where different people can have a voice'. The baser truth is that Facebook profited from allowing advertisers to target people who liked the Infowars page. Facebook ultimately caved, only after Spotify and iTunes banned Infowars the following month. The result, illustrating how much value the platforms had added to the conspiracy site, was to cut its audience immediately in half.

In 2017, Facebook launched a 'war on fake news'. Having at first resisted attempts to hold it responsible for political events in 2016, the company struck a collaboration with the rumour-checking site Snopes, FactCheck.org, ABC News, and PolitiFact. Zuckerberg admitted that the problem was integral to the online attention economy: 'fake news sites are on the rise due to the profits which can be made from web advertising'. Subsequently, following Zuckerberg's appearance before Congress, the company released a mini-documentary pledging to join the 'fight against misinformation'. It would use AI and machine-learning tools to devalue 'fake news' so that it appeared in fewer feeds and thus had less effect. Predictably, the Trump-supporting Right claimed that Facebook's partners all had a record of 'left-wing' bias.

Twitter, which has been more resistant to this sort of policing operation, initially refused to join the 'war on fake news', sticking to its 'free speech' line. Twitter founder Jack Dorsey declared that Jones would continue to be welcome on the platform. If Jones 'spread unsubstantiated rumours', this was best dealt with by fact-checking journalists (acting at no cost to Twitter). The answer to bad speech was more good speech. This was either naive or sly. Hardly anyone is susceptible to 'fact-checking', particularly when it comes high-handedly and coercively from a self-appointed authority. Fact-checking is never as exciting as the 'facts' being checked, and it can have the perverse effect of driving certain stories up the ranks of the attention economy. Dorsey ultimately caved, too, but the social industry companies remain committed to minimizing the loss of content. By algorithmically orchestrating feeds with the aid of machine-learning, they hope to reduce the political pressure on them to ban users. In an effort to circumvent hate-speech restrictions, some alt-right activists flounced off to a right-wing wannabe Twitter, 'Gab', which gained almost half a million users within two years. But the majority of activists simply adapted their content and stayed put.

The Twittering Machine, in purifying existing tendencies towards informational nihilism in the media, has clarified that the truth value of information is not the same as its economic value. But 'fake news' is not, strictly, the issue. Insofar as outright fakery happens, it is easy to understand. People lie about their political opponents, or spread misinformation about celebrities, for obvious reasons. But the 'fake news' trope is like a conspiracy theory in that it asserts a huge epistemological gap between the knowledgeable elect, and a mass of deluded 'sheeple'. It is always assumed that someone, somewhere, knowingly concocted a lie that others are simply deceived by. But if a story is believed by tens or hundreds of thousands of people, it may have been believed by its original author.

And that's the hard question. Why did so many people want what Infowars was giving them? There are, of course, such things as conspiracies, political murders, occult rituals, terrorist false flags and sex slaves. These things are part of the world we live in. But growing numbers of people seem to want networks of conspiracy to do the work of shorthand political sociology, explaining how their lives got so bad, and how official politics became so remote and oppressive. They seem to want to believe that, rather than representing business as usual, today's centrist state managers are malign outsiders usurping a legitimate system. What accounts for this extraordinary hunger for paranoid tales of subversive evil?

IV.

We face a crisis of knowing. According to the explanation offered by theorists of a 'post-truth' society, this is a legacy of postmodernist dogma that also seeps into and informs today's insurgent right.

The argument about 'fake news' is thus further limned by a folk history of intellectual decline. According to this view, if false beliefs now gain acceptance, this is because the canons of Western reason have fallen into disuse.

This view arises in part because of the new political potency of the uneducated and unqualified. For the philosopher Steve Fuller, one of the red flags signalling the triumph of the post-truth situation was the defeat of Hillary Clinton, 'perhaps the most qualified person ever to run for the presidency', by the wildly unqualified Donald Trump. Michiko Kakutani, the esteemed journalist, likewise excoriates the Trump administration's appointment of 'unqualified judges and agency heads', as though the problem with the far right was their (often very real) incompetence. As though a competent far-right administration would not represent a far more assured doom. This reflects the spontaneous ideology of professionals, for whom education, qualifications and 'credentials' are the condition of good governance.

To treat political contests as elaborate job interviews implies a consensus: we already know what the job is, and only need to work out who can do it best. And if, rather than a struggle over competing interests and visions, an election is a meritocratic selection process, then Clinton's defeat can only be an injustice: popular sexism and unreason getting in the way of a logical career progression. From this perspective, democracy looks like lousy quality control. Indeed, the *New York Times* has reported survey evidence showing that it is political centrists who are most likely to overtly disapprove of democracy – especially in the United States. Unsurprisingly, both Brexit and the Trump victory have generated a flurry of 'scandalous' liberal think pieces asking whether democracy is such a good idea after all. As though the problem with the far right was too much democracy.

However, a claque of journalists and academics spearheaded by Michiko Kakutani argue that the crisis of knowing is a legacy of the 'postmodernist' assault on knowledge and the Enlightenment. The idea turns up everywhere. Philosopher Daniel Dennett complains that 'what the postmodernists did was truly evil'. The journalist Peter Pomerantsev, in a mini-documentary for BBC *Newsnight*, attributes the rise of politicians like Trump to postmodernism. The theory that postmodernism has promoted a pernicious subjectivism which relativizes truth to such an extreme degree that it provides cover to right-wing science-deniers, is ubiquitous.

'Postmodernism', however, turns out to be an elusive, slippery opponent. No one seems to be entirely sure what it is. For example, Kakutani cites without apparent irony a preening comment made by the American alt-rightist Mike Cernovich in an interview with the *New Yorker*. 'Look,' Cernovich explained, 'I read postmodernist theory in college. If everything is a narrative, then we need alternatives to the dominant narrative. I don't seem like a guy who reads Lacan, do I?' Cernovich may have read a little Lacan at college, but he is as likely to have understood him as Trump is to have ghostwritten *Finnegans Wake*. Lacan, a clinical psychoanalyst in the Freudian tradition, was as classically modernist as it was possible to be, and in no way aligned to the view that 'everything is a narrative'. In this context, 'postmodernist' appears to mean 'snooty French intellectual'. Yet Kakutani cites Cernovich's clueless aside as an example of 'the populist Right's appropriation of postmodernist arguments'.

The ostensible core of this appropriation is the denial of 'objective reality'. According to the thumbnail sketch of postmodernity offered by Kakutani and her co-thinkers, Foucault and Derrida can be blamed for this scandalous treason against reality. For British journalist Matthew D'Ancona, they were typical of the sorts of postmodern intellectuals who treated 'everything' as a 'social construct', thus engendering an extreme relativism. According to philosopher Lee McIntyre, Derrida interpreted 'everything' as a text. For Kakutani, the assault on reality independent of human perception has the insidious effect of demolishing 'rational, autonomous individuals', leading to the unwholesome claim that 'each of us is shaped, consciously or unconsciously, by a particular time and culture'. This argument would be appealing to those for whom Foucault and Derrida were unpleasant set texts at university. Among generic complaints about the oppressive abstruseness of their prose, it is reassuring to discover from third-hand distillations that it all boils down to the affirmation that 'everything is, like, a narrative or a social construct or something'.

Yet the argument disintegrates on examination. Neither Foucault nor Derrida had much to say about social construction, or the status of objective reality, or even postmodernity. The idea that people are shaped 'by a particular time and culture' is an Enlightenment, materialist hypothesis. Indeed, it is also just common sense. So is the motif of 'construction' which, Ian Hacking argues, can be traced to Immanuel Kant. To say that something is 'socially constructed' is to say that it wasn't handed down by a deity, but was built by humans: another Enlightenment idea. The way the term is often used today, to refer to how we partially 'construct' objects in the world by how we name them and talk about them, owes itself to the structuralist linguistics of Ferdinand de Saussure, who was about as postmodernist as a gramophone. The belief in 'objective reality' independent of human perception is not so much Enlightenment as pre-Enlightenment, traceable as much to Augustine of Hippo as to Kant. Scepticism about a reality independent of perception is really scepticism about the existence of unobservable entities, which is what in another context would be known as atheism. The atheist critique of religious belief often amounts to the claim that the theory is underdetermined by the data, so you may as well believe in a flying spaghetti monster. Beyond this, the fug about Enlightenment and 'postmodernism' is riddled with basic category errors, where these authors tend to juggle perfectly distinct concepts – language, objective reality and truth – as though they were equivalent.

Unfortunately, behind this scarecrow 'postmodernism' that is being waggled at us, there also lurks a fundamental misapprehension of the Right. The latter are disconcertingly instrumental in their approach to the facts. They are alert to the performative dimension of speech, the way in which statements make things happen. From Bolsonaro to Brexiteers, they show a keen appreciation of how information can be made to work. As Karl Rove put it, 'we create our own reality'. But, a few intellectual outliers notwithstanding, Trump and his supporters do not claim that truth doesn't exist, and that everything is narrative. They may disdain the truth claims of established experts, but they do not claim that there is no truth to be had. Far from it; the alt-right frequently claims to uphold reason, logic and facts against the 'snowflakes' of the Left, for whom feelings are said to be incorrigible. The meme, 'Not An Argument', popularized by the alt-right activist Stefan Molyneux, encodes a popular right-wing response to, for example, statements such as 'Trump is a racist'.

Moreover, like the 9/11 Truth movement, they are frequently distinguished by a touching faith in the existence of a discoverable and mind-blowing truth. From 'jet fuel doesn't melt steel beams' to 'Hillary traffics sex slaves', we are as far as can be from the terrain of epistemological relativism. Conspiracy theory covers the majority of the right-wing discourse called 'fake news'. And it is, if anything, a kind of epistemological absolutism, admitting of only one kind of truth: the clickbait kind of truth, the kind that says 'This One Weird Thing about the World Trade Center will Shock You'. It is also a kind of theodicy, an attempt to expose a 'hidden truth' that explains evil and suffering. But it is also an attempt to explain it away, to dispose of a complex problem by externalizing it: whether it is the Antichrist, Freemasons, the 'yellow peril', communists or Jews who are to blame, it is always an outsider sabotaging what would otherwise be a peaceful and just society. The telos of the clickbait economy is not postmodernism, but fascist kitsch.

Today, one of the dominant conspiracy theories of the Right is that left-wing intellectuals have been waging a slow, successful battle to overturn the canons of Western reason, logic and science: a process they describe as 'cultural Marxism'. This theory first gained notoriety when it appeared in the manifesto of neo-Nazi murderer Anders Behring Breivik. It has since gained ground in the alt-right, being repeated by the popular right-wing guru Jordan Peterson, best known for his theory that human gender relations are equivalent to the sexual habits of lobsters, as well as his curmudgeonly potpourri of self-help and Jungian mysticism. The sacked National Security Council officer Rich Higgins blamed 'cultural Marxism' for the opposition to Trump. It has also appeared in more mainstream quarters. The anti-Trump conservative Australian television news anchor, Chris Uhlmann, has decried the work of 'neo-Marxists' using 'critical theory as a vehicle for. . . the deconstruction of the West'.

This theory bears some alarming resemblances to the 'post-truth' accounts just assayed. The theorists of 'post-truth' share with their right-wing opponents a vocabulary, a counter-subversive zeal, a drive to externalize a complex problem, intellectual incuriosity and an authoritarian streak a mile wide. Their 'postmodernism' is a straw figure, the bogey-scapegoat of anglophone centrists losing an argument. Their 'Enlightenment' is, as Dan Hind once wrote of a similar frenzy of earnest rallying to reason, a kind of 'folk Enlightenment', a 'bowdlerised and historically disembodied Enlightenment' with eighteenth-century philosophers reduced to ciphers in contemporary battles. The native pomophobia of John Bullshitter was once leveraged as a kind of moral blackmail against the anti-war Left, who were blamed for an extreme cultural relativism that supposedly left the West defenceless. Now a similar rhetorical move aligns a disintegrating political consensus with, per Kakutani, 'the rule of raison'. With admirable economy, it thus creates a starkly simple polarity between the reasonable upholders of the status quo, and the beyond-reason hoi polloi. But, in appealing to an 'age of reason' that never existed, it seems to be far less interested in moral blackmail than in recovering what has been lost: the sure footing of the liberal state and its solid foundation in reason.

Conspiracy theories, though they have often come from threatened powers, today seem to be emerging from a more radical breakdown in meaning. They are the morbid symptoms, the excrescences, of a declining authority. When long-dominant ideologies break down, and when social interactions are increasingly governed by a confusing war of all against all, paranoia is a natural response. The rise of social industry platforms adds a new dimension to this. For they have created a machinery whose natural hero is the antisocial outsider, the hacker with no ties, the troll, the spammer. They have created a regime of competitive individualism in which perplexity and paranoia are a constant state of being. In that sense, the use of the platforms to create online communities galvanized by amateurish sleuthing, is an attempt to reclaim meaning.

This was already apparent in the early '9/11 Truth' communities. In surprise bestsellers by David Ray Griffin and Nafeez Mosaddeq Ahmed, as well as a plethora of tantalizing websites, the overwhelming thrust of the argument was that the official narrative makes no sense. These authors obsessively pored through the unfolding news narratives of events for contradictions, holes, oddities. Of course, there often are holes in the news, not to mention official redactions. And the '9/11 Truth' communities were often trying to exercise the kinds of critical reflection that there is generally little opportunity for. But they poked holes where there were none and interpreted those that did exist tendentiously. They were convinced that there was some hidden, forbidden knowledge somewhere, which only citizen journalists could uncover. This conviction that 'they' are hiding something from us was the shared ground of all the 'Truth' groups. Specific theories, such as that the Pentagon was hit by a missile strike, were secondary speculations.

Some of those used to being in power now feel embattled, and are beginning to collapse into the same logic. This is not unusual. As Emma Jane and Chris Fleming's analysis of conspiracy theories shows, the debunkers tend to share 'the epistemological orientations and rhetorical armoury' of those they critique. The performative contradictions become absurd, as when the behavioural economists Cass Sunstein and Adrian Vermeule recommended to the White House that it should take stringent measures against conspiracy theories – such as covert 'cognitive infiltration' of online communities, so as to plant doubts and undermine these groups from within.

Rather than emulate the paranoid style, the displaced centre needs to look deeper, because the collapse in sense that they are just now encountering goes back a long way.

V.

Expertise, as the ebullient Brexiteer Michael Gove reminded us, has made us sick. The crisis of knowing is, in part, a deep-rooted crisis of political authority: a credibility crunch following the credit crunch.

The decline of print giants linked to established parties and ideologies, and the rise of the social industry platforms, has accelerated the crisis. But it has done so largely by sharpening tendencies that were already in play in the old media. The complaints about 'fake news' indicate that the embattled political establishment has not yet mastered the new media. But the problem goes even deeper than that and, in a strange way, the myth of a 'post-truth' society is a bungled attempt to diagnose the rot.

In the sciences, there is an ongoing 'replication crisis' afflicting medicine, economics, psychology and evolutionary biology. The crisis consists of the fact that the results of many scientific studies are impossible to replicate in subsequent tests. In a survey of 1,500 scientists in the journal Nature, 70 per cent of the respondents failed to replicate the findings of another scientist's experiment. Half of them couldn't even replicate their own findings.

According to the historian of ideas Philip Mirowski, one of the main causes of the problem is that science is becoming commodified. As it becomes an outsourced research engine for corporations, quality control collapses. A 'parallel universe of think tanks and shadowy "experts"' emerges outside of academia, while inside, the state demands policy-oriented research but is increasingly indifferent to quality controls. Corporations – especially big tech – have little interest in research that doesn't pay off quickly with monetizable innovations and gizmos. Google has backed a proposal to incentivize scientists to think about the bottom line, wherein they place research ideas on something like a scientific stock market and the most promising ideas are snapped up by venture capitalists.

Among the worst examples of this degradation of scientific research by business might be the world's pharmaceutical industry and its effects on medicine. The industry is riddled with ostensibly scholarly papers ghostwritten by corporations, clinical trials carried out with unrepresentative samples and cherry-picked data: a 'murderous disaster' for patients, as Ben Goldacre aptly calls it. When a peer-reviewed survey of scientists published in 2009 found that 14 per cent admitted to personal knowledge of a fellow scientist falsifying results, medical researchers were the worst offenders.

This problem reverberates well beyond academia, because in the modern era the laboratory is the benchmark of legitimate knowledge. It is the historic model for authoritative truth claims, everyone implicitly trusting the boffin in the white coat. The industrial production of scientific deception would probably already be enough to make us sick of experts, even if we hadn't been through the global financial crisis with its damning implications for the economics profession, the majority of politicians and the global institutions supporting the economic system. If, for example, people were willing to believe that the MMR vaccine gave children autism, against the scientific consensus, or that Aids was a US government conspiracy, this suggests that the authority of science was already diminished. In some cases, this authority was weakened by real abuses, such as the Tuskegee experiment in the US, wherein syphilis-infected black men were misled, used as guinea pigs for medical experiments and never treated for their illness. This may be among the reasons why fact-checking and hectoring about 'the science' is so ineffectual.

For a while, 'big data' was offered as the answer to the problem of knowledge. Data was hailed as 'the new oil', and the raw material for a 'management revolution'. By turning company processes into readable electronic text, it would replace unscientific management techniques, hunches and intuitions with the brute force of facts. Google boss Eric Schmidt, exulting in the revolutionary potential of data, described it as 'so powerful that nation-states will fight over how much data matters'. In an excitable piece for *Wired*, former editor Chris Anderson enthused that such a scale of data collection would soon render theory and even the scientific method obsolete: 'with enough data, the numbers speak for themselves'.

The bonus of big data is omniscience: 'a full digital copy of our physical universe', as scientists Carlo Ratti and Dirk Helbing put it. We will be able to see all of existence as a stream of electronic writing. And for a while, it was even possible to believe this, if one set aside just how much of the physical universe is unknown and potentially unknowable. After all, the scale of data production is vast. The scale at which messages were exchanged was already quite enormous in the era of the analogue telephone. In 1948, 125 million telephone conversations were had in the US each day. But this was not captured and commodified information. The internet, as a writing machine, takes a note of everything.

Already by 2003, more data had been produced since the turn of the millennium than in the entirety of human history. By 2016, 90 per cent of the entire bulk of data in the world had been created in the previous two years, at a rate of 2.5 quintillion bytes of data a day. An increasing share of this data is on the internet, rather than on television or in print. By 2017, users had shared more than half a million photos on Snapchat, sent almost half a million tweets, made over half a million comments on Facebook and watched over four million YouTube videos every minute of every day. In the same year, Google was processing 3.5 billion searches per day.

With this much data, surely things would start to work without any applied theory. A prize example of this, for a long time, was Google Flu Trends. Beginning in the mid-2000s, Google began to develop the tool by comparing searches on its own search engine to the likelihood of outbreak. For a while, the results were eerily accurate. Google was able to predict the next outbreak up to ten days before the Centers for Disease Control and Prevention. Then, by 2013, it began to break down. Google's estimates overstated the spread of illnesses by almost a factor of two. And when that happened, the hyperbole of Google's promise became obvious.

The numbers never speak for themselves. Every data set requires treatment, processing and interpretation. The volume of data is not a sufficient criterion for judging how useful it is. And the treatment of it always implies a theory, whether or not it is acknowledged. Google, unwilling to concede that its own work implied a theory, simply developed a model for extrapolating from correlations established by the sheer bulk of data. They never tried to work out what the causal relationship was between search terms and the outbreak of flu, because that was a theoretical problem. Ironically, because they were only interested in what worked, their method stopped working.

Big data is no substitute for the scientific method. Far from having the magical cure, the pioneers of data extraction and analysis have contributed to today's degraded ecologies of information and research.

VI.

If our existing language could adequately account for the rapid degradation of information, we might know what a solution could look like. In shooting the messenger, however, 'post-truth' theorists are depriving themselves of some of the ways in which they could make sense of this situation.

Insofar as 'postmodernism' means anything, it refers to an attempt by a number of theorists to name something that seems to have changed. The 'postmodern' démarche, once faddishly declared across all fields of knowledge and culture, was more diagnostic label than manifesto. Some postmodern eristic came with emancipatory stylings, as though the collapse of totalizing claims and grand narratives would be innately liberating. For the ex-Marxists among the postmodernists, this was clearly an attempt at sublimating their historical defeat. Nonetheless, the identification of a postmodern era was an attempt to describe something that had happened to capitalism. That something – whether it went under the name of the post-industrial society, the knowledge economy or informational capitalism – was the growing importance of images and signs in everyday life.

The rise of information technologies and whole industries based around communications, signs and images, altered not only the economy but the structure of meaning. The growth of information economies fits well with the inherent and ever-increasing celerity of capitalism. Capitalism encounters time and space as obstacles in the way of making money. They would ideally like to realize their investment here and now. The development of information technologies enabling the instantaneous transmission of symbols and images around the world makes possible, as Marinetti's 'Futurist Manifesto' anticipated, the death of time and space. These technologies have been of most use in the financial sector. But now big data, by way of 'the cloud', claims to extend similar advantages to traditional manufacturing firms, by enabling them to choreograph production processes all over the world.

Ironically, the growth of information economies is catastrophic for meaning. No doubt, we have lived through a massive expansion in the amount of information that we are exposed to. In 1986, the average American was exposed to forty newspapers' worth of information each day. Two decades later, it was 174 newspapers. By 2008, the average American consumed about 36 gigabytes of information each day. And most of this information, insofar as it reaches us on social media, is designed to keep us typing and scrolling, producing more information. A headline tells us that a man was stabbed in front of his son on a train. A status argues that the poor and stupid should be sterilized. A viral video shows a politician dancing. A tweet claims that immigration makes us poorer. These snippets of information, appearing within microseconds of one another, have in common that they each set the wheels whirring, triggering mental and emotional work that often goes on throughout the day.

But we make a fundamental mistake if we assume that an increase in information corresponds to an increase in knowledge. When engineer Claude Shannon declared that information is entropy, he was saying something that would become starkly relevant in the age of social media. As an engineer, Shannon was interested in information as a storage problem. A coin toss could be said to contain two 'bits' of information, whereas a random card selection has fifty-two 'bits'. The more uncertainty, the more information. The same principle, applied to sentences, means that statements with less sense actually have more informational capacity. An increase in information could be proportionate to a reduction in meaning.

In the social industry, the incentive is to constantly produce more information: a perpetual motion machine, harnessed to passions of which the machine knows nothing. This production is not for the purpose of making meaning. It is for the purpose of producing effects on users that keep us hooked. It is for the purpose of making users the conduits of the machine's power, keeping its effects in circulation. Faked celebrity deaths, trolling, porn clickbait, advertisements, flurries of food and animal pictures, thirst traps, the endless ticker tape of messages, mean less than they perform. The increase of information corresponds to a decrease in meaning.

Moreover, this production is taking place in a simulacrum much like that described by the theorist of postmodernity Jean Baudrillard. A simulacrum is not a representation of reality. It is reality, albeit reality generated from digital writing and simulated models. It is simulation woven into our lives, with effects every bit as real as stock-market values, or the belief in God. It is reality as a cybernetic production. Like video game images, or virtual reality, the simulacrum is uncannily too perfect, too real: hyperreal, even. We are now far more incorporated into the system of images and signs, from gaming to feeds; but this simulacrum has its roots in capitalist culture's airbrushed advertising, seductive Hollywood dreams and slick gaming and infotainment industries.

With the coming of new virtual and augmented realities, the Twittering Machine may prove to have been a stage in the spread of the simulacrum – one with darkly dystopian potential. Jaron Lanier, effectively the inventor of virtual reality, argues that to make it work, you need to give the machine far more data about yourself than you do on the platforms. The result could be the most elaborate Skinner Box in history. What seems like a device for adventure and freedom could become 'the creepiest behaviour-modification device' invented thus far.

VII.

'Post-truth' politics is what we have long been living under in various forms: a technocracy, in a word. The rule of 'big data', now the most plentiful raw material in the history of the world, is not a departure from this: it is nothing but the rule of brute facts. It is the rule of technique, not truth, which has recently been found wanting. Or, as Wilde called it in 'The Decay of Lying', the 'monstrous worship of facts'.

But if the simulacrum is indeed the epitome of technocratic rule, disappearing meaning behind the coercive rule of information, it also represents a problem for power. The world of the simulacrum, a world increasingly drained of meaning, deprives power of its seemingly obvious legitimacy. The authoritative statements of politicians, attorney generals, senior journalists and academics come to seem arbitrary. The attempt to reinject meaning into the system by reviving Cold War ideologies and arousing public opinion against a scapegoat 'postmodernism' is doomed to fail, however. Since these efforts are themselves part of the simulacrum, they slip easily back into the cycle of meaningless information. The more sophisticated propagandists recognize this, and instead work with the grain of the collapse of meaning. For example, the BBC alleges that Russian disinformation campaigns no longer bother to promote a single narrative, but instead flood the internet with so many competing versions of a story that no one knows what to think. It would be prudent to assume that all parties now involved in disinformation are using similar techniques.

The problem is not that the internet is a web of lies. Of course it is. In 2016, a team of researchers published a study of online conduct which found that less than a third of users claimed to be honest about themselves on the internet. But the machine was invented to help us lie. From its first beginnings, even in the precocious French public-sector internet known as Minitel, the first thing users did was dissimulate their identities. Anonymity made it possible to wear new textual skins. In the early days of Silicon Valley idealism, anonymity and encryption was all the rage. The ability to lie about ourselves was thought to bring freedom, creative autonomy, escape from surveillance. Lying was the great equalizer. Silicon Valley, as it emerged in the 1980s and 1990s, was shaped by an aleatory fusion of hippy and New Right ideologies. Averse to public ownership and regulation, this 'Californian Ideology', as Richard Barbrook and Andy Cameron dubbed it, was libertarian, property-based and individualist. The internet was supposed to be a new agora, a free market of ideas.

This connection between lying and creative freedom is not as strange as it may appear. Milan Kundera, reflecting on Stalinist tyranny, argued that the injunction not to lie was one that could never be made to an equal because we have no right to demand answers from equals. Indeed, it is only when we acquire the capacity to lie that we really discover freedom of thought: since only then can we be sure that the authorities can't read our minds. It is only when we can lie about the future, the constructivists exhorted in the Realistic Manifesto, that we can begin to transcend the rule of brute facts. In this sense, there is a genuine utopian kernel to the Californian Ideology, even if its embodiment within social media is a utopia only for trolls and other sociopaths.

The problem is not the lies. It is information reduced to brute fact, to technologies with unprecedented and unforeseen powers of physical manipulation by means of information bombardment. We naively think of ourselves as either 'information rich' or 'information poor'. What if it doesn't work that way? What if information is like sugar, and a high-information diet is a benchmark of cultural poverty? What if information, beyond a certain point, is toxic?

One is struck, therefore, by the palpable timidity of commonplace diagnoses of 'fake news', opinion silos, filter bubbles and the 'post-truth' society. This, the 'sour grapes' theory of communications, is sensationalism. But all sensationalism is a form of understatement, all moral panic a form of trivialization, and this is glaringly so in the case of our 'fake news' panic. The problem is not the lies, but a crash in meaning. The problem is what the survivors, scrabbling in the rubble and detritus of the internet for answers, will believe.

The crisis of knowing has roots which run deep into the institutions from which authoritative knowledge was hitherto produced. The Twittering Machine didn't cause this crisis, but it is its current culmination. The Twittering Machine is a furnace of meaning.

CHAPTER SIX

WE ARE ALL DYING

Is it possible that in their voluntary communication and expression, in their blogging and social media practices, people are contributing to instead of contesting repressive forces?

Michael Hardt and Antonio Negri, *Declaration*

Silicon Valley calculates with, and not against, the Apocalypse. Its ever-implicit slogan is: 'Bring it on'

Geert Lovink, *Social Media Abyss*

Humanity rocks!

Elon Musk to Sam Harris, Twitter.com

I.

'I'm going to kill all Muslims,' he shouted, as almost a dozen worshippers and pedestrians lay injured and, in one case, dead. Almost as quickly, he retreated to a more grimly realistic declaration: 'I did my bit.'

Darren Osborne killed one Muslim, fifty-one-year-old Makram Ali. But he wanted to kill them all. He was psychologically fuelled for genocide.

He had rented a van and driven it to Finsbury Park Mosque, in a working-class north London community. He arrived at quarter past midnight, on 19 June 2017, driving up Seven Sisters Road without much of a plan other than to kill. The night before, he had bragged in a pub that he was a 'soldier', and that he was going to 'kill Muslims'. It is unclear what he would have done, had he not happened on a group of Muslims who had just performed night-time prayers and were attending to a man who had collapsed at a bus stop.

Like other 'lone wolf' attacks that had taken place over the previous two years, this one was chaotic, low-tech, disorganized. He simply drove up the road, ploughing the van into the crowd. When the van struck, he was driving at 16 mph. In the moment of his supposed triumph, he was heard saying, 'kill me'.

Finsbury Park Mosque is a hate symbol for the British far right. Indeed, on the day after the attack, British fascist Tommy Robinson called it a 'revenge attack', blaming the mosque for producing terrorists.

In fact, the mosque hadn't seen a jihadist cadre for almost fifteen years, when the leadership of the Islamist preacher Abu Hamza was ousted. Even if Osborne was the 'avenger' that he desperately wanted to be, no one at the mosque, or huddled at a bus stop outside it, could have given him anything to avenge. Nonetheless, Robinson's claim echoed Osborne's own incoherent self-justification, that the attack was revenge for an earlier massacre by jihadist militants on London Bridge.

It had taken only weeks for an unemployed man living in Wales to become an ideologically obsessed murderer. According to his relatives and estranged partner, Osborne had never before exhibited any racism. He had been troubled, alcoholic, violent, abusive, depressed – he had even attempted suicide, and made a failed attempt to get himself committed. In fact, according to a neighbour, he had always been a 'complete cunt', but never a racist. He was barely politically aware. He wouldn't even know who the Prime Minister was, according to his sister.

But then Osborne started consuming content made by fascist group Britain First, and far-right activist Tommy Robinson, chugging it like antidepressants. From alcoholism and drug dependency, he went straight to the 'red pill'.[4] Only then was all of this misery politically weaponized.

Osborne had, a few weeks before the attack, seen a BBC docudrama about a child-grooming scandal in the northern English town of Rochdale. Like most such scandals, it involved middle-aged men, some hitherto respected, taking advantage of underage girls. The girls were often particularly vulnerable because of their class, or because they were in care or in foster homes. In this case, the men were Muslim and the girls were white. And for Osborne, their being Muslim must explain their evil. Indeed, it was as if he had concluded that Islam explained all evil: a universal theodicy.

Nor was Osborne arriving at this conclusion in isolation. In Britain in 2018, Islam had long been a punching bag for politicians and the

4 The 'red pill' is a metaphor used by right-wing activists for the process of ideological conversion. Taken from the movie *The Matrix*, it ostensibly entails making people aware of harsh, painful realities. As in the movie, however, the real promise of the red pill is that it is both an escape from a depressing life and the beginning of an adventure.

press, the all-purpose bogey-scapegoat comparable only to those other anti-nationals, immigrants. The psychoanalyst Octave Mannoni once remarked on the surprising numbers of Europeans who, having never been to the colonies or seen a colonial subject, dreamed of them. The same could be said of many Britons who had encountered Islam only as a manifestation of their own unconscious. The propaganda of Twitter Nazis and YouTube fascists tuned into this dreamwork and turned the volume up by several orders of magnitude. Tellingly, on the day after the murder outside Finsbury Park Mosque, Tommy Robinson took advantage of an ITV platform to say that the Quran was an incitement to violence. For Robinson, having never demonstrated any expertise on the Quran, this too was dreamwork.

It is not difficult to imagine the compensatory, antidepressant effects of consuming such racist propaganda. It puts a name to an otherwise nameless misery and rage. It identifies a specific evil, points to a remedy and a community to which one might belong. It tells its audience – often white men younger than Osborne – that their seething sense of resentment is rational and justified. And it is exciting, and briefly empowering. The eagerness with which the 'red pill' is swallowed, and cult figures made of manipulative fascists like Tommy Robinson, is not in that sense hard to explain. Redpilling is, for many of its users, potent self-medication, better than any combination of cognitive behavioural therapy and prescription drugs.

To that extent, fascist propaganda works well on the Twittering Machine, which, among the many things it is, is a pharmacological device. Its economic model presupposes a surplus of misery which, Rumpelstiltskin-like, it spins into gold. As endless correct but point-missing liberal critiques maintain, the social industry does not deal in truth. Of course it doesn't; it deals in addictive substances, which it administers to the melancholic.

II.

What are the politics of the simulacrum? In cyberspace, the great 'consensual hallucination' as William Gibson called it, what we experience as social and political reality is increasingly a graphic representation of digital writing. Whoever masters the rapidly evolving idioms of this system of writing has a share in the production of virtual reality.

Fascists have proven to be avid early adopters of new technologies. They were among the first to use email in order to organize without being disrupted by the authorities. A 1993 march by German neo-Nazis in commemoration of Rudolf Hess eluded an official ban by using email communication. Throughout the early 1990s, far-right, Holocaust-denying groups used bulletin board systems and, later, the emerging ecology of 'alt' areas within Usenet.

This colonization of new technologies was not just an imperative for such groups, weakly rooted, their supporters scattered, unlikely to gain sympathetic coverage without subterfuge as to their politics. It was a far-sighted attempt to build a space for white-supremacist and Nazi ideologies within the new mediascape almost before anyone noticed. For example, Stormfront, a hub of far-right activity, was launched by neo-Nazi and former grand wizard of the Alabama Ku Klux Klan, Don Black. He learned his computing skills while in prison for attempting a coup in the Dominican Republic. What began in the early 1990s as a small bulletin board was relaunched as a website in 1996, then evolved into a web forum with roughly 300,000 users. Its ratings on Alexa, the website ranking service, were comparable to commercial media outlets. This is despite the fact that the forum is outmoded in its features and appearance, having changed little since 2001.

In the subsequent settling of the platforms, the far right has arguably been most successful with YouTube. Alt-right broadcasters have been 'monetizing' like microcelebrities, and 'influencing' like beauty bloggers. Fascists like Richard B. Spencer, Stefan Molyneux and Tommy Robinson are celebrities of the 'intellectual dark web', helped along by outriders such as the libertarian Joe Rogan and conservative Dave Rubin – and, often enough, broadcast media.

And they don't merely leverage the techniques of microcelebrity and 'influencing'. They benefit from specific features of the YouTube business model. Journalist Paul Lewis and academic Zeynep Tufekci have each gone down the rabbit hole of YouTube's 'up next' recommendations algorithm. The algorithm is there to keep users glued to the screen with content likely to be addictive. As with the other social industry platforms, the priority is time on device or, in the case of YouTube, 'watch time'. Each found that no matter the viewing history of the dummy accounts they used, the algorithms kept pointing them progressively towards more 'extreme' content: from Trump to neo-Nazis, from Hillary Clinton to 9/11 Truth.

But what is so addictive about 'extreme' content? Part of the answer is that much of what is characterized as extreme in this context is conspiracy infotainment: for example, in the run-up to the 2016 presidential election, the algorithms were promoting anti-Clinton conspiracy stories. When so many distrust the news, and find it frustrating and confusing, infotainment seems to be less 'hard work'. It offers what can feel like critical thinking in a recognizably digestible and pleasurable way. In the face of official agnotology – the practice of deliberately producing mass ignorance on major issues – it can feel empowering. But it may also be that the algorithms pick up on dark yearnings simmering below the supposedly consensual surface of politics.

So not only do far-right YouTubers network, collaborate and signal-boost one another's brands, driving their collective content up the viewing charts. Not only are they careful enough to avoid trigger words likely to be caught by an anti-hate speech algorithm. They can expect the platform to promote them precisely because of how riveting their content is supposed, by the algorithms, to be. Zeynep Tufekci argues that 'YouTube may be one of the most powerful radicalizing instruments of the 21st century'.

'In the old days', wrote Irish academic John Naughton, 'if you wanted to stage a coup, the first thing to do was to capture the TV station. Nowadays all you have to do is to "weaponize" YouTube.' A coup, of course, is a very twentieth-century technology. And one which, as yet, would be beyond the wherewithal of the networked far right. Nonetheless, it would be foolish to discount the aggregate impact of propaganda. Like advertising, it has to work on someone, otherwise the industry would die. YouTube's liberal critics have a point when they underline the reality-bending effects of this kind of simulacrum. As former Google engineer Guillaume Chaslot put it, YouTube 'looks like reality, but it is distorted to make you spend more time online'.

From Twitter revolutions to YouTube coups, technological determinism is attractive because of the way it simplifies problems. But if we succumb to the lure, we miss the real story. The obvious question is, why should neo-Nazi material, or conspiracist infotainment, be so riveting? When pundits complain of 'radicalization', the assumption appears to be that it is sufficient to be exposed to far-right material to be conveyed along an escalator belt towards 'extremism'. Yet, of course, most of the pundits who have viewed this material don't claim to have been 'radicalized' by it. And YouTube isn't deliberately promoting an agenda. Rather, the platforms, by their nature, are magnetically drawn to drama, whether political or personal. The user becomes, in China Miéville's term, a 'dramaphage'.

The content agnosticism of computational capitalism has political valences, but the algorithm's effects go well beyond political content. The artist James Bridle has written of the surprisingly outré and noir YouTube content for kids, which involves erotic or violent content: Peppa Pig eating her daddy or drinking bleach, for example. This material was created to meet a demand identified by the algorithms – in other words, it reflected data coming from users: searches, likes, clicks and watch time. In this respect, it was not unlike the algorithm-driven merchandise of previous years: t-shirts with such slogans as 'Keep Calm and Rape a Lot', 'Kiss Me I'm Abusive' and 'I Heart Boiling Girls'. And platform behaviour obeys what the ethnographer Jeffrey Juris calls a 'logic of aggregation'. It herds users together in temporary groupings based on this data. It establishes correlations over whole data populations between certain types of content and certain behaviours: stimulus and response. It works only because of the response. There has to be something in some viewers waiting to be switched on. The algorithms, by responding to actual behaviour, are picking up on user desires, which may not even be known to the user. They are digitalizing the unconscious.

The platforms thus listen intently to our desires, as we confess them, and give them a numerical value. In the mathematical language of informatics, collective wants can be manipulated, engineered and connected to a solution. And new technologies have only been as successful as they have been by positioning themselves as magical solutions. Not just to individual dilemmas, but to the bigger crises and dysfunctions of late capitalism. If mass media is a one-way information monopoly, turn to the feed, the blog, the podcast. If the news fails, turn to citizen journalism for 'unfiltered' news. If you're underemployed, bid for jobs on TaskRabbit. If you've got little money but own a car, use it to make some spare money on the side. If you're undervalued in life, bid for a share in microcelebrity. If politicians let you down, hold them to account on Twitter. If you suffer from a nameless hunger, keep scrolling. The business model of the platforms presupposes not just the average share of individual misery but a society reliably in crisis.

III.

Why does the far right thrive on YouTube? Why, by the same token, does Donald Trump win Twitter? Why is it that none of his clever online interlocutors, though often more knowledgeable than he is, ever lay a glove on him? What about the Twittering Machine is so congenial to Trump's performance art? Isn't trumping the enemy half the pleasure of being on the machine? We should begin to take seriously the possibility that something about the social industry is either incipiently fascistic, or particularly conducive to incipient fascism.

The 'networked individualism' of the internet is both social and a machine. It binds social interactions to protocol. Information, far from wanting to be free, as Californian folk wisdom has it, desires control. It wants hierarchy and infallible instruction: the smack of firm leadership. How the protocols are designed reflects social and cultural values, in a way that is obscure to users. And these values have a distinctly antisocial thrust. Alice Marwick, an academic and former Microsoft researcher, has shown that the culture of the Northern California tech scene where the platforms are based is deeply committed to competition, hierarchy and social status. The most admired, cult-like figures among the largely affluent white men who predominate in the scene, are successful businessmen.

In the 1990s, when the net was being built, the purview of Silicon Valley was essentially that of the Republican right-winger, Newt Gingrich. Gingrich lobbied hard for an internet run along 'free market' lines. The aim was that it would result in innovation driven by start-ups, tech geeks and bold venture-capitalist pioneers, and the techno-idealists lapped it up. So did the Clinton White House, an early evangelist for the globalization of the net. In practice, predictably, it resulted in an internet dominated by tech giants and Wall Street. When Marwick says that social media tools 'materialize' neo-liberal ideology, therefore, she's describing the way in which the tech teaches users to think of themselves as the kinds of 'entrepreneurs' that tech geeks and Silicon Valley businessmen idealize. The Twittering Machine, organized as a competitive like-hunt, status-hungry and celebrity-obsessed, ideally suited to marketing and commerce, is the technical version of a social machine that preceded it: a stock market of status. This is one of the things that cultural critic Jonathan Beller is getting at when he calls the machinery of computational capital 'formations of violence'. It is the abstract technical expression of unequal relationships produced by complex histories of political violence: racism and riots, class struggles and countercultures, mobsters and McCarthyism. This violence was coded into the machine; presupposed by it.

The machinery produces, industrially, a social life bent around the imperatives of states and markets. As a technology, it is almost custom-designed for a post-democratic age, for the rule of technocracy and cruelty. To that extent, it builds on existing patterns. The 'if. . . then' logic of algorithms is not in itself a new machinery. It is used all the time in policymaking, often without the aid of computing: if the passenger has been to x country, then a further search will be carried out; if the applicant has savings, then unemployment benefits will be docked. Many forms of algorithmic control are too complex, thus far, to be handled entirely by machine: border controls and immigration law, for example. However, what big data enables is an extension and depth of control-by-protocol that has never before been seen. It enables the corporate clients of the platforms to algorithmically size up their targets and customize each user's experience. It permits governments who use the data to scale their bureaucratic action down to the most minute level of analysis, thus improving their efficiency in everything from traffic control to aerial bombardment.

Post-democracy was well advanced in most of Europe and North America well before the digital platforms appeared. As the political scientist Colin Crouch defines it, a post-democratic society is one that retains the institutions of mass democracy, but where these have negligible effects on policymaking. It reduces elections to a spectacle of stage-managed debates and poll-driven simulations of 'voter demand'. Whereas mass democracy means that popular desires and interests have to be taken seriously, post-democracies are in the business of population management. Like cybernetic systems, post-democracies are far less interested in consent than in moderating the behaviour of elements within the system. Like the algorithmic protocols of the digital platforms, they hit below the intellect, working underneath the surface of persuasion, building realities into our everyday experience. It doesn't negotiate with our wants, it shapes what we are capable of wanting. And, as the Italian anarchist Errico Malatesta once put it, 'everything depends on what the people are capable of wanting.'

The underground persuasion of reality-shaping is what big tech does really well. It is quite different from what used to be called hegemony. Hegemony is a strategy of obtaining leadership of a broad civil society coalition to achieve political goals. It means building alliances with other groups by taking their interests and desires seriously, rather than just coercing them. It means offering moral leadership rather than simply material incentives. At their most successful, ruling groups are able to explain their own interests in terms of an 'historic mission' for the whole society. In the Cold War era, the struggle against communism was this sort of mission. While it surveilled and repressed communists, left-wing trade unionists and radical civil-rights activists, it also won broad popular consent.

What the platforms have done is far more subterranean. The Twittering Machine proposes nothing, declares nothing good or bad, but works on the infrastructures of everyday life. It might be called a sub-hegemonic practice.

IV.

This is clearly an emerging form of techno-political regime. And it is not the participatory online democracy, or agora, that has been vaunted. But nor is it yet clear what that regime will look like in ten or twenty years' time.

As John Naughton has written, comparing the internet with the printing press, faced with world-changing technologies we always tend to overstate the short-term consequences and underestimate the long-term consequences. How could, for example, the early book readers have known that the technologies they wielded would inspire the Reformation, let alone forming an indispensable basis for the modern industrial nation-state? The spontaneous assumption might instead have been that the Catholic Church would be empowered. The first mass market created by print was in standardized indulgences.

The values that have shaped the creation of the Twittering Machine don't necessarily determine its destiny. Skinner's fantasy of a utopia without conflict or human authority broke down. The early hope of cybernetics, to design a system of control by means of organizing communication, turned into its opposite. It helped create, as Justin Joque put it, 'a globally networked system so complex that no known model could ever describe it, let alone regulate it'. And by the same logic, the neo-liberal values that aligned Silicon Valley bosses with the Obama White House are not necessarily the same as the real ideological effects of the machine. We might say that if the machine has its conscious uses, it also has an unconscious. We feign omniscience at our peril. One of the pleasures of the 'backlash' style is to be a Cassandra, seeing it all so clearly, yet so impotently. 'I told you so' is a dubious consolation. What is more, hasty denunciations risk leaving us with the misapprehension of knowing what we've got ourselves into, while injecting an unhelpful nastiness, condescension and paranoia into the conversation. There has been a bonfire of digital vanities, bromides stacked upon platitudes, 'digital democracy', 'the networked citizen', 'Twitter revolutionaries' all going up in smoke. We, who stand in its glare, should be sceptical of provisional analyses being offered with too much certainty.

We should nonetheless take seriously the fascist potential of the social industry, or its potential to intensify and accelerate proto-fascist tendencies already at work. The forms of fascism that we see in the twenty-first century may not resemble those of the past. The fascist movements of the interwar period were rooted in imperialist ideologies, popular militarism, paramilitary organizations and a world system run by colonial empires and menaced by socialist revolution. These circumstances will not return. The colonies are dead, most armies are professional and there isn't an abundance of popular organization of any kind, let alone paramilitary organization. Nonetheless, liberal capitalism shows itself to be vulnerable, crisis-ridden and open to challenge by the racist, nationalist far right. And what, in such circumstances, are the cultural valences of the social industry that produces so much of our social life now? Which tendencies would it select for, and which would it mute?

There is something about the way in which we interact on the platforms which, whatever else it does, magnifies our mobbishness, our demand for conformity, our sadism, our crankish preoccupation with being right on all subjects. Ironically, this despotic rectitude is allied with exactly the kind of 'swarm' propensities that were once idealized as the basis for a new kind of grass-roots power. The 'swarm', which began as a metaphor for conscientious citizens holding power to account, might well become a metaphor for the twenty-first century version of fascist street gangs.

The mistake would be to see this as someone else's problem, a problem affecting only obvious villains like trolls, hackers and alt-right bullies. Take, instead, something as simple and everyday as the critique-by-quote tweet. Holding aloft a specimen of a really degenerate opinion, we mock it for having the quality of being an opinion, which is that it gets something wrong. Inviting others to join in, we treat disagreement, not as constitutive of any society, but as malevolence, idiocy or the cry of the loser. It is to be settled by group humiliation, sudden orchestrations of mob fury, the stiletto-stab of sadism. This is the context in which, Devorah Baum argues, it's suddenly as if being wrong is the most intolerable thing in the world and being right is almost like a human right. The troll, the witch-hunter, the celebrity, the snowflake who can't stand being disagreed with: this is all of us, every day. We are not all so, equally, but insofar as we are on the platforms, we are all involved.

We are denizens, not citizens, of a machine that keeps us addicted, amid endless boring scrolling, with sudden volatile rages, excitements, adrenaline rushes of hate – charmingly euphemized as 'variable rewards'. A machine that makes wannabe celebrities of all of us, enjoining us to worship those above us in the status ecology while in the same move harnessing our sadism and rage, and directing it with laser-like focus to the schmuck-of-the-day. A machine that reduces information to meaningless stimuli which it jet-sprays at us, much as Trump bombards us with exclamation marks and block capitals. A machine that habituates us to being the manipulable conduits of informational power. There is, in this, a fascist potential.

V.

It wasn't supposed to be like this. The new platform technologies were supposed to be liberal, modern, participatory. The second wave of cyber-utopianism had been much like the first, headlined at the zenith of global power by a Democratic administration in Washington evangelizing for tech, for the globalization of the 'free and open' net built in Silicon Valley, and for the 'new economy' as a modernizing upgrade.

If the Clinton administration sought to hardwire as the universal framework for online social interactions a very parochial and eccentric Californian culture of rich white men, the Obama administration wanted to bring tech into the White House. The digital giants were essential, both for Obama and Hillary Clinton's State Department, to the modernizing of the government and the economy, and to achieving US foreign policy objectives. The White House met Google representatives more than once a week during Obama's tenure, and he was the first president to host a Twitter 'town hall' meeting. Eric Schmidt of Google, Jack Dorsey of Twitter and Mark Zuckerberg of Facebook all supported Obama and had close ties to the White House.

Clinton, in a major 2010 speech, attacked the usual enemies like hackers and repressive regimes, in defence of an 'open' internet. She milked the last dismal vestiges of Californian hippy idealism: alluding to the hoary old sentiment that 'information wants to be free', as the hippy entrepreneur and Silicon Valley legend Stewart Brand didn't quite say. She also took to task, as enemies of openness, those countries who didn't trust the global regulatory oversight of ICANN, an industry-aligned Californian non-profit. Championing an open net was, in addition to being congruent with Washington's liberal self-image, both a projection of American power and a logical political alliance. Democrats had always been close to telecommunications capital. The wave of monopolization taking place in mass media, resulting in six corporations controlling approximately 90 per cent of the flow of information, had been helped along by Clinton's 1996 Telecommunications Act. What is more, unlike the old economy giants allied with the Bush administration, such as Halliburton, these new economy giants were clean-cut, had no coal under their fingernails. They seemingly traded a mysterious substance – communication, the cloud – of which everyone was in favour, and which was pristine and high-status.

However, it was also complicated. It was easy enough for the White House to gloat about free information if it inconvenienced Iran. It was easy for the State Department to lobby Twitter to hold off maintenance work during Iran's Green Movement, telling them that a 'Twitter revolution' was happening. But when WikiLeaks shared a virtual library of classified State Department documents, the results were embarrassing. It was hardly mind-blowing that US diplomats fawned over dictators like Egypt's Hosni Mubarak. But these revelations came as the regimes in Tunisia and Egypt were about to fall to popular revolutions. Similar movements would then appear in Bahrain, Algeria, Yemen, Libya, Syria and even Saudi Arabia.

And suddenly information didn't want to be free any more. Abruptly, the US had to conduct a series of foreign policy pivots. At first, it tried to defend the Egyptian dictatorship, with Vice President Joe Biden telling Tahrir Square protesters that Mubarak was no dictator but 'an ally of ours'. This proved unavailing; it tacked briefly in the wake of the demand for electoral democracy before swerving behind a new, blood-bath-inaugurated coup led by General Sisi. The US supported the Saudi invasion of Bahrain and aerial assault on Yemen, crushing both of those uprisings. It used limited military force to intervene in the Libyan uprising and to pilot a pro-US leadership to power, with ultimately disastrous results.

And amid its embarrassment and its perplexity, the administration sought to indict everyone associated with the WikiLeaks revelations. This, for the old Washington establishment, exemplified the bad, irresponsible side of the internet. It was the net as Assange or Pirate Party activists fantasized it could be: a stateless anarchy, without intellectual property rights. The fact that they made leaking 'sexy', as security experts put it, and that the enormously modish trolling group Anonymous had joined the war on secrecy, raised the stakes and demanded examples be set. Private Chelsea Manning, blamed for the leaks, was held in solitary confinement at a supermax prison and subject to what the UN special rapporteur on torture called cruel, inhuman and degrading treatment. The Justice Department demanded access to the Twitter accounts of WikiLeaks volunteers, dismissing privacy and free speech concerns as 'absurd'.

It appeared, for a moment, as though the White House had misunderstood the real potential of the social industry, skewered by its own hype about 'Twitter revolutions' and the advantages of tech. Indeed, there was and is a tension here, and it revolved around the politics of information management. The security state's ancient dream had been that it would monopolize the management of information. The cutting edge of encryption, storage and control should be in the gift of the National Security Agency. This twenty-first century Leviathan would have unique 'back door' access to any information system. That is not how the tech giants see it. For them, their monopoly over content and over the management of user information is part of a system of private property from which they profit. User information and data is itself valuable property, whose value diminishes if it is not secured.

Washington thus found itself in a number of direct battles with the tech giants. Twitter fought the Justice Department on its demands for the account information of WikiLeaks volunteers, in a case brought jointly with the American Civil Liberties Union, which it ultimately lost. Yahoo fought the National Security Agency in a secret Foreign Intelligence Surveillance Act court case over the latter's demand for user account details under its PRISM program. Google resorted to internal encryption to evade surveillance when it was revealed that both the NSA and GCHQ had wiretapped the firm's communications. Apple fought the FBI to a standstill over encryption on its phones. The FBI wanted to force Apple to unlock an iPhone belonging to Rizwan Farook, one of the shooters in the San Bernardino massacre in December 2015. Apple resisted in the courts, and ultimately the FBI backed off when it used third-party software to hack the phone, revealing nothing of pertinence. FBI director James Comey complained that Apple allowed 'people to hold themselves beyond the law'. This was revealing, suggesting that he expected there to be no area of life not potentially scrutable by the law. If the internet was nothing but an elaborate surveillance mechanism, the law should be the beneficiary. The American state had been a vigorous champion of tech, its property regime and its global commercial success. Yet their property claims were now disrupting the security state's fantasy of omniscience.

Washington nonetheless continued to champion the tech giants. Indeed, the government found that it was able to hijack the features of the social media platforms to extend its surveillance, building the biggest domestic spying programme in US history. It used Facebook to launch cyberwar programmes aimed at enemies, implanting malware and stealing files from personal hard drives. It was this attack on the security of the platform that led to an incensed Mark Zuckerberg calling the White House to complain about the lack of transparency in NSA programmes. He said that such secretive, counter-security measures not only put users at risk but would also incline them to 'believe the worst' – and, he implied, disconnect. The security state was threatening the informational property of the platforms. Despite such tensions, the platforms remained close to Washington. Theirs was not a battle over values, but a turf struggle over informational control. It was platforms like Google, Facebook and Twitter which, in the first place, had created this unprecedented surveillance, presenting ample legal and illegal ways for government agencies to exploit the resulting data.

The social industry monopolies have duly been evolving ways to cooperate with the security state, suggesting lines for a potential fusion. This calls into question the cyber-futurist notion of 'cloud' logic displacing sovereign power, breaking up sovereignty into the politics of data packets, dissipating it in networks criss-crossing borders and territories. Rather than networked flows of information bypassing centralized bureaucracies, the flows are bureaucratically regimented and organized in such a way as to augment the traditional power of governments and corporations, at least in the short term. It also suggests that the emancipatory hopes of the era of Occupy, Anonymous and Pirate Parties pinned to such claims were at best wildly premature. Networks, which were expected to outflank the old sovereigns, have also extended their power.

And yet, as the philosopher Gilbert Simondon pointed out, we learn most from a technology when it breaks down. It is breakdown that stimulates scientific research and new knowledge. And the platforms have induced a crisis in an older machinery of governance and control. The Washington establishment, in its globalizing zeal and technological modernization drive, didn't quite anticipate what it was embracing. Whether it is Facebook's notorious motto 'Move Fast and Break Things', or Google's practice of never asking for permission, this was a force that could and would disturb the old, embedded alliances of state and media. That meant it could and would disrupt Washington's power.

VI.

Did Twitter make the 'Twitter revolutions', or did they make Twitter? From the Iranian Green Movement in 2009 to the Gezi Park protests in Turkey in 2013, the social industry was reported on as if it was a primary driver of unrest. Twitter, Facebook and YouTube were not just the digital media of the story. They were the story, the technological vanguard of dramatic, world-changing events. They were associated, by connotation, with progress, youth, the new, the next big thing.

It would be impossible to quantify the commercial value of the 'Twitter revolutions' for the social industry. It is in the nature of the medium to massively complicate causality. The bare data shows that from the inception of the Green Movement to the end of the Gezi Park protests, Twitter's active user base had increased sevenfold from 30 million to over 220 million. Facebook's already much larger user base had increased from almost a quarter of a million to 1.2 billion users. How much this was due to these earth-shaking events and how much to other commercial strategies and 'network effects', is not clear. But the growth was conditioned, and probably very strongly conditioned, by the insertion of the platform brands into a captivating story of a global youth uprising.

The term 'Twitter revolutions' had, of course, always glossed over salient realities. Whether in Iran or Tunisia, the numbers of users connected to social media were a small and disproportionately middle-class share of the total population. In Tunisia, there were just two hundred active Twitter users. Most social industry users, still a minority of the population, were on Facebook. In Egypt, where the social industry had much deeper penetration, with 60 per cent of under-thirties using it, the April 6 Youth Movement was able to use Facebook as a communications hub. Other activists, however, found that mobile texting was far more important for organizing. Nonetheless, when the desperate Tunisian market seller, Mohamed Bouazizi, set himself on fire after being harassed by police, it became known only because the images were shared on Facebook and resonated with an existing mood of fury with the regime. When the Tahrir Square protesters flooded timelines with the riveting detail of their audacious actions, they not only increased the costs of repression for the regime and weakened the position of its overseas backers, but gave confidence to others to join in.

Whatever the political purposes to which users put them, however, the most successful users are those who understand the informational politics of the platform. The infamous Facebook experiment, published in 2014, on 'emotional contagion', built on the well-known fact that sentiment is catching. By manipulating users' moods, it found that this contagion can now be orchestrated on a massive scale by networks. The virality and celerity of the information economy piggybacks on this tendency, aggregating and herding sentiment, assembling makeshift alliances around a mood, building towards a euphoric climax and then dissipating. The experiment also showed that it is possible for the medium to fabricate and manipulate the mood of users, which of course Facebook already does on a molecular level through its management of feeds. But it doesn't necessarily need to mass-produce emotional hype: opportune sentiments will arise as a matter of course.

In 2011, what went viral was a model of protest. In Tahrir Square, a coalition of Islamists, liberals and Nasserists had built a city-within-a-city, a mini-metropolis managing lighting, accommodation, waste disposal, medicine, food, water, security checkpoints to guard against frequent government attacks, and inter-communal protection for Christians and Muslims at prayer. It would be tempting to say that, with opportunity came competence in the techniques of self-government, cooperation and mutuality. But the organizers of Tahrir Square were veterans of past struggles, from anti-war protests to the 2008 general strike. They had built coalitions and acquired their repertoires of protest and social media publicity over the course of almost a decade. What is more, the symbolically central revolt in Tahrir Square had to spread to other parts of the country, including to armed sectors of the population, in order for the dictatorship to be overthrown. In retrospect, even then it bypassed huge swathes of the population which later became the popular constituency for General Sisi's armed coup.

Nonetheless, Egypt's revolutionaries were giving other people ideas. They suggested a format of protest that could be taken up by anti-austerity and pro-democracy activists from New York to Nepal. It was not even just a protest. Tahrir Square was also an organizing hub at which other actions could be discussed and the diverse components of the movement tentatively federated. More importantly, it prefigured the self-rule that protesters wanted to achieve. It was, in embryo, an alternative way of organizing legitimate power. This gave rise to #Occupy, not so much a movement as a brand, a hashtagged franchise, a repertoire of symbols and tactics available to Indignados in Spain, labour activists in Nigeria, democracy protesters in Malaysia.

The digital swarms descended, from Puerta del Sol, Madrid to Oakland. The global core of this movement was Occupy Wall Street. There, heteroclite alliances of anarchists, Anonymous trolls, communists and libertarians shot a populist arrow across the bow at the One percent. They attempted new model communes, prefiguring a more democratic and egalitarian social order – although with little agreement as to what that might actually mean. Indeed, the absence of agreement was regarded as a virtue. They emphasized consensus over ideology, in the spirit of 1990s anti-capitalism and the Zapatista ethos: 'Many Yeses, One No'.

Organizationally, these protests looked very little like Tahrir Square. In some cases, the #Occupy brand and repertoire was worked into an existing social movement with its own tactics and traditions, as in Spain and Greece. But most of the time, #Occupy involved small groups of experienced activists setting up camp and relying on digital connections to attract otherwise scattered, disconnected participants. In New York, for example, the organizers of Occupy Wall Street were veterans of another recent alliance, New Yorkers Against Budget Cuts. In London, they were activists from the environmentalist movement Climate Camp. These were the handfuls of activists with the skills, resources and free time to organize. To their momentary advantage, they were tech-savvy and could exploit ubiquitous smartphone and platform use. And for a period of time in 2010 to 2011, it seemed as if all that was needed was to set up an event on Facebook, share it across the platforms, hashtag it, meme it and wait: build it, and they will come. Activists were flush with apparent success, surfing the crest of a viral wave.

#Occupy adopted the abstract schema of Tahrir Square's insurgency, without being able to emulate its substantial organized base, while tailoring it to fit with cyber-libertarian ideologies about the emancipatory possibilities of the 'network' and horizontal organization. They were emboldened in this approach by a flurry of academic and journalistic clichés celebrating the networked individual, the swarm and the reduced costs of collective organizing entailed by digital democracy. Such boosterism recognized real tendencies but underestimated the fragility of any organization so cheaply had.

The reduced costs of organizing also reduced the costs of quitting – as well as the costs of infiltration and disruption. Moreover, the proprietary algorithms were designed to advance individual networking, not collective organization. At most, because of their surging towards hype, they could generate a quick, expedient aggregation of individual sentiments. And, as Paolo Gerbaudo's analysis in his book *The Digital Party* recognizes, far from encouraging horizontal organization, digital networking tends to promote charismatic leaders and shallow forms of 'participation' and 'feedback' from within a largely passive layer of supporters. Insofar as these structures do translate into more sustained organization, as is arguably the case with Italy's populist Five Star Movement, they lend themselves less to democratic empowerment than to a business model. The digital euphoria generally passed and was replaced by demoralization. Occupy, emanating from a political mood that was suspicious of parties, was, organizationally, the meatspace equivalent of the shitstorm. It attracted giant bursts of feeling, energy and confidence, galvanized moments of unity and conviction and generated some impressive actions – most of which turned rapidly into passive despair.

The state didn't wither away; Occupy did. Beyond a few places where #Occupy was linked to already powerful social movements, the protests proved impossible to sustain, being more steam than piston, and not much steam at that. The enthusiasm for the network vanished like a trending topic. The 'movements of the squares' either dissipated into parties aimed at taking electoral power, as in Greece and Spain, or melted away and empowered authoritarian states, as in Turkey after the Gezi Park protests. The fate of the 'Arab Spring' would soon demonstrate just how exceedingly difficult it is to achieve lasting social and political change, even with much more sustained organization behind it.

And by 2014, a malevolent twist on the political mobilization of hip young digital natives was about to appear. Benefiting from civil war in Iraq, and outright carnage escalating to a state-orchestrated Götterdämmerung in Syria, it would add an obscene irony to every wholesome net-utopian cliché.

VII.

'Put down the chicken wings and come to jihad, bro.' This was the wry, savvy voice of an ISIS recruiter on Twitter. On Ask.fm, another recruiter answered questions about his favourite desert, his beard, life in the battle. Images circulated of jihadists cuddling kittens, eating Snickers, playing video games, beheading their enemies.

Five years after the Iranian Green Movement and three years after the 'Arab Spring' birthed such a brief reprise of cyber-utopianism, here was a 'Twitter revolution' that was actually in the middle of taking power. Here was a makeshift theocratic state, of all things, assembled with the logic of the swarm, occupying and keeping public space. Here was a right-wing, networked social movement, a reactionary guerrilla campaign, a band of mercenary adventurers, a brand, a hashtag, which had fully mastered the idiom of the platforms.

The Islamic State had emerged from a hard core of jihadist combatants affiliated to the 'Al-Qaeda' franchise during the occupation of Iraq and the ensuing civil war. At first dominated by 'foreign fighters', in the years since 2006 they had developed social roots in parts of Iraq's Sunni population. It had become a far-right social movement, armed and intent on challenging the territorial authority of the state bequeathed by the occupation. By 2012, as Syria descended into civil war, and jihadists, released from prison by Assad to sow chaos amid the opposition, opened a new front in the civil war, it gained its first territorial footprint, rebranding itself as the 'Islamic State in Iraq and Syria' (ISIS). By 2014, as the Iraqi government suppressed Sunni protests against their political exclusion with the use of death squads, ISIS was gaining political support even from hard-core secular Ba'athists. Indeed, many ISIS recruits were former Ba'athist soldiers. Moreover, the Iraqi army would not have disintegrated so rapidly in the face of ISIS assault were it not ushered in by a civilian uprising against the troops regarded as agents of a sectarian regime.

In the summer of 2014, as they began their invasion of Mosul, ISIS deployed a sophisticated social industry strategy. Far from trying to leverage surprise, they sought to inspire dread, broadcasting and live-tweeting their coming with the hashtag #AllEyesOnISIS. Through the Twitter-linked app, Dawn of Glad Tidings, they used supporters' smartphones to disseminate messages, carefully tailored to avoid triggering spam filters. The app was downloaded ten thousand times, permitting sophisticated Twitter-storming operations. As their forces marched towards Baghdad, the number one search result for 'Baghdad' on Twitter was an image of a jihadist contemplating an ISIS flag flying over the city. They successfully hijacked World Cup-related hashtags to spread links to their propaganda video. By February 2015, it was estimated that there were anything from 90,000 to 200,000 pro-ISIS tweets on Twitter every day. By mid-2015, Twitter had come under pressure from the US government to delete pro-ISIS accounts, and had to take down some 125,000 of them. They shared slick videos aimed at Western millennials, some most likely produced by the former German rapper turned jihadist, Denis Cuspert. Jihad was being marketed, very efficiently, as the epitome of masculine cool.

Sedimented into this barrage of self-publicity was a stream of snuff videos, as members braggingly broadcast images of the beheadings and war atrocities they had been party to. Although this initially alarmed the ISIS leadership, worried about its effects on Muslim support and the criticisms it was drawing from the Al-Qaeda leadership, it didn't slow down or reduce the flow of recruits. If anything, ISIS became known for the extravagance of its displays of violence and its pointed refusal to acknowledge limitations. It is even possible that these irruptions of obscenity demonstrated for some supporters the authentic commitment of these 'lions': their #nofilter reality, as opposed to the pervasive fakery of online celebrity.

In the first six months of the US-led bombing campaign to oust ISIS, the Pentagon reported 19,000 new recruits to the organization, most of them from outside the Middle East, 3,000 from Europe, North America and Australia, and a surprisingly large number of them religious novices – including at least one recruit whose entire training in the religion came from a copy of *Islam for Dummies*. International combat tourists filtered into training camps, ostensibly to avenge the humiliations of empire by enslaving Yazidi women and beheading infidels, perhaps just as attracted by the prospect of survivalist nirvana. The morbid fascination with the group, sanctioned by lurid news coverage of the ISIS 'way of life', was akin to the Nazi or satanic fixations of ostracized American teenagers contemplating a school shooting. It self-consciously incarnated the antithesis of everything liberal modernity stood for.

Twitter did not create the sumps of misery from which recruits could be found in small Welsh towns, among Swedish teenagers or from put-upon Muslim minorities in the suburbs of the Île-de-France. No more than it had created the injustices giving rise to Occupy. Far less did it create the sorts of feelings that would lead to surprisingly widespread passive support for the group. At the height of the group's notoriety, it was more popular in Europe than in the Middle East. Polling controversially suggested that 7 per cent of British citizens and 16 per cent of French citizens responded favourably to ISIS, a share much larger than the entire Muslim population in each society. Nor did Twitter create the patterns of state breakdown allowing ISIS to gain territorial footholds, or induce the Iraqi government to unleash death squads to quell a restive Sunni population, thus making them briefly receptive to ISIS rule. Nor did it build the torture chambers during the anti-occupation insurgency in Iraq, or the television shows modelled on twentieth-century show trials in which terrified and beaten 'guests' were interrogated for supposed terrorism offences, all of which had helped mint these hard-boiled jihadists.

Nonetheless, it is hard to see ISIS spreading terror among its opponents, and excitement among its members, so efficiently without the social industry. The tens of thousands of demoralized Iraqi government troops who fled Mosul without a fight were prompted in part by the belief that an overwhelming armed force was coming. In fact, the invasion forces consisted of just two thousand jihadists, compared to thirty thousand government troops. And it afforded ISIS a new means of ideological dissemination, quite different from the hierarchical, vanguard model of Al-Qaeda communications. ISIS instead made short propaganda clips modelled on Hollywood fare, and games like its own ripped version of *Grand Theft Auto* exploited the volatility of Twitter, Instagram and Facebook, deploying crowdsourcing, apps, bots and hashtag-hacking. It used the logic of the Twitterstorm to insinuate its short, digestible bites of propaganda into popular culture.

ISIS did not propose anything like the global, millenarian political philosophy of Al-Qaeda, but it disseminated a ready-to-hand narrative about emancipation from the 'oppressive Tawaghit' – the system of regimes bequeathed by the colonial partition of the Middle East. It leveraged the free labour of users of its app, in the congealed form of smartphone data, the better to orchestrate its tweetstorms. It asked users to participate in its propaganda by sharing hashtags, articles and videos. At one stage, ISIS accounts asked followers to video themselves waving the ISIS flag in a public place and share it on social media. It created a sense of identity and belonging. Its promise – as the chicken wings tweet showed – was that users would find greater meaning and value in life by migrating to the sunny Wilaya of Raqqah and building the Islamic State. It focused, to that end, on recruiting not just for military purposes, but potential citizens for what they claimed was a flourishing earthly utopia living as God intended.

ISIS was a franchise with a central hierarchical structure, not an autonomist collective. Its utopian fantasies were not cyber-utopian. It therefore exploited social media far more efficiently than the protest movements of 2011, without unconsciously mimicking or depending on the model of association found on the platforms. It harnessed the medium's viral and swarming properties, using digital connections to encourage unpredictable acts of terror beyond its territorial grasp, as in Beirut and the Bataclan. But it didn't rely on networks to outflank centralized power. Centralized power was already collapsing, and ISIS was building a new regime in its place, taxing a population of some seven or eight million subjects and controlling profitable oilfields. It was armed and disciplined, internally coercive and seeking ideological homogeneity. It tacitly recognized that the forms of association on the platform are not 'horizontal' but built around complex informational hierarchies that could be manipulated.

US counter-insurgency, confronting ISIS, was likewise opportunistic in its use of the medium. While the greatest emphasis was placed on coordinated aerial bombardment, racking up tens of thousands of bodies according to the US Military, the Obama administration began to talk cyberwar. This was already in vogue in the administration. It had used cyber-sabotage against North Korea's nuclear weapons programme. It cooperated with Israeli intelligence in writing code for the Stuxnet worm – a viral attack that shut down Iran's nuclear power facilities in Natanz. In 2015, State Department counterterrorism official Alberto Fernandez argued that the US, in a break from the 'marketplace of ideas' rhetoric, needed its own 'troll army' to combat ISIS. Later the same year, the US Air Force bombed a 'command and control' building discovered by combing ISIS's social media streams and associated metadata. By 2016, they were vaunting their ability to use 'cyberbombs' to hack and disrupt ISIS computer networks. ISIS, for its part, allegedly responded by using the social industry to accumulate background information on a hundred US Military personnel and posting a 'hit list' for supporters to target. But in an example of the *mise en abyme* of online trolling, wherein one never knows for sure who the enemy is or what game they're playing, the Associated Press later suggested that the threat was actually the work of Russian trolls. The logic of the online network thus superimposed itself on the more conventional logic of asymmetrical war.

ISIS's territorial control was ended by factors extrinsic to its use of the social industry. Its brutality undercut its social basis and eroded the cooperation of notables in Iraqi, Syrian and Libyan territories that it held. Its early successes had come easily, in a lightning streak, conferring on it an image of divine omnipotence. The first serious military setbacks blew away that aura and recruitment slowed down dramatically. And, of course, its fantastical project of building a theocratic state while conducting an asymmetrical war with the powers that had already devastated Iraq, was in its own terms a huge overreach. It created more deadly enemies than its tens of thousands of recruits could fight. It's difficult to believe their project was ever anything other than a grandiose delusion.

Yet the technological basis of ISIS' international recruitment still left them with an added weakness. Most of their recruits, as the UN reported in 2017 after ISIS lost Raqqah, were either irreligious or knew nothing about the fundamentals of Islam. Still less did they grasp the elaborate political ideologies emanating from Islamist thinkers like Syed Qutb, the Egyptian theologian and Muslim Brotherhood member who so strongly influenced this strain of jihadism. They were largely young men, socially marginalized, economically and educationally disadvantaged, travelling to Syria or Iraq without really understanding what they were getting into. Many of them, the study suggested, were criminalized men seeking redemption. Another study by George Washington University found a recruit from Texas who moved to the Islamic State looking for a role as an English teacher. The ideological thinness of the attraction to ISIS among those reached by Twitterstorm and hashtag-hacking is likely to be part of the reason for the rapid outflow of recruits as the war turned harsher.

The Islamic State has fallen, with fighters controlling just 4 per cent of the territory they once did, but the organization known as ISIS remains. It is, among other things, a form of twenty-first-century fascism. Its use of the platforms shows us something about how new fascisms will work, in terms of their culture, communications and ideology. It is, to use Jonathan Beller's phrase, a form of 'fractal fascism'. If the spectacle is a social relationship mediated by images, what Guy Debord called the concentrated spectacle of Führer celebrity worship has given way in the social industry to the diffuse spectacle of commodity images. In the social industry, it's one, two, three, many Führers.

From ISIS to the alt-right, new fascisms are emerging around microcelebrities, mini-patriarchs and the flow of homogenized messages. If classical fascism directed narcissistic libido investments into the image of the leader, as the embodiment of the people and its historical destiny, neo-fascism harvests the algorithmic accumulation of sentiment in the form of identification-by-Twitterstorm. If the image of the fascist mass was once best captured by the bird's-eye view of aerial photography, it is now available in a much higher-resolution bird's eye view as metrics. And if classical fascism built its organization through recruitment from social organizations, such as veterans' clubs, germinal neo-fascism recruits from the loose associational practices of the platforms. The networked social movement has acquired jackboots.

VIII.

Is Donald Trump the future, or a transitional tremor? A great deal of alarm about the social industry has been concerned with its effects on electoral systems: the dark arts of the algorithm propelling 'populists' (or, according to taste, 'authoritarians') to power.

The world's first 'Twitter president' is indeed a natural social industry star. And as a Twitter celebrity, he was constructing his political profile from his first real tweet in 2011, when he signalled his participation in an online campaign claiming that Obama was not born in the US and was not eligible to be president. He has proven to be excellent at riding the waves of aggregated sentiment, far more effective than his opponents. As a presidential campaigner, Trump used digital media to orchestrate mass media interest. The campaign's tactic, according to one of his former digital strategists, was to keep saying 'off the cuff' apparently crazy things, that would compel the media to give him coverage. He succeeded, gaining 15 per cent more coverage than Clinton, despite the media being largely hostile to him.

Twitter also enabled him to shape the campaign as an exciting duel with his enemies. An analysis of Trump's tweets during the election found that they effectively substituted for campaign position statements. Most of his tweets attacked the Washington establishment, blaming it for uncontrolled migration, terror and job losses, rather than advocating a policy position. He limited public access to his governing agenda. Clinton's online campaign struggled, by contrast, to build hashtagged enthusiasm with #ImWithHer and such memes as the #pantsuit, soliciting the enthusiasm of upwardly mobile career women struggling against sexism. Some of her tactics downright failed, including a listicle identifying her with 'your abuela', where 'abuela' is the Spanish word for 'grandmother'. Latin voters, far from being impressed, began to post criticisms of her support for militarized border controls with the hashtag #NotMyAbuela quickly going viral.

As President, encircled by a hostile media and Congress, subject to investigation and hamstrung by intelligence leaks, Trump used Twitter as a refuge of uncompromised sovereignty. There, he could announce policy, denounce his enemies, praise his own record and attack the legacy media (with the exception of the sunny, far-right morning show, *Fox and Friends*) as #fakenews and #fraudnews. It is clear that Trump has been able to use the platforms to consolidate a political base in a way that would not have been possible if the old set of relations between mass media and the liberal state remained intact.

Nonetheless, as with such figures as Narendra Modi of India, Rodrigo Duterte of the Philippines and Jair Bolsonaro of Brazil, Trump has benefited mainly from the political weaknesses of his opponents. While Modi, Duterte, Bolsonaro and Trump have all used the social industry and messaging services effectively to bypass legacy media, they have each benefited from the (perceived and actual) corruption and stalemate of the political establishment.

In office, Trump has thus far mainly demonstrated the weakness of the nationalist right. On trade, despite repudiating the potentially lucrative Trans-Pacific Partnership, he has been unable to propose a serious alternative to the institutions of liberal globalization. On foreign policy, despite his public deference to Putin, he has largely acceded to the lines of action demanded by the Pentagon in Syria and North Korea, albeit that he has freed them to pursue that agenda in a more radical way than they were able to under Obama's micromanagement. On his promised massive structural investment, he got nowhere. On his trade war with China, he has raised tariffs, but the total levels still remain historically low. Much of what he has achieved required the connivance of Congressional Republicans, such as the standard Republican tax cut for the rich, or the promotion of a hard-right Federalist Society judge to the Supreme Court. Unsurprisingly, by the summer of 2017, Trump's ousted ally Steve Bannon lamented that the presidency the far right 'fought for, and won, is over'.

The difficulty faced by the far right is that political success has outrun social and political organization. Historically, the far right has succeeded by building roots in thick networks of civic associations, from fraternal organizations in the US South to veteran and military clubs in Germany. It has, in this context, developed a 'grass-roots' paramilitary presence to control the streets. Such civic organization is far more patchy and thin today. The technological harvesting of sentiment can briefly aggregate electorally sufficient crowds, given a crisis of the establishment. But it is a poor substitute for the kind of organized and armed power that could actualize the YouTube coup that Naughton describes. And if this was the sole basis for fascism in the future, it is more than likely that the traditional governing centre would reassert its dominance. The latter's entitled cry of protest in the face of failure – per Wilde, the rage of Caliban not seeing his own face in a glass – would, and will, give way to a hard-headed and resourceful campaign to stabilize the relationship of the medium to political power.

The fascist potential of the social industry doesn't necessarily lie in its short-term electoral consequences, ominous and damaging as these may be. Rather, far more lethally, it may be indicated by the phenomenon fashionably known as 'stochastic terror'. This concept, anonymously minted in 2011, refers to the way that communications can be used to incite random violence and terror. The violence, though statistically predictable within a given population, is individually unpredictable. The Twittering Machine is designed for just this kind of stochastic influencing. The use of algorithms to customize user experience depends on the idea that, statistically, x content will generate y number of z behaviours over a given population. Though someone must choose, in some way, to act on the stimulus, the machinery bypasses the question of individual responsibility by administering a data set.

Currently, part of the strategy of the rump ISIS group is to use social media campaigns to work on and put to motion existing reservoirs of sentiment, existing capacities for murder. Just as it once encouraged supporters to wave the ISIS flag, it now asks them to extend its physical reach and project violence into otherwise unreachable states. Most of the attacks are in Iraq and Afghanistan, where the jihadists have their own forces. But from stabbings in Marseille, Westminster and Edmonton (Canada), and vehicle attacks in New York, Nice, Barcelona, Ohio, Stockholm and London, to shootings in Toronto, Paris and Orlando, ISIS has claimed a global body count. It has used its hashtagged franchise model to motivate disparate, random attacks by lending them an appearance of global coherence, direction and belonging.

The networked far right, from its 'gendertrolling' MRA wing to its overt white supremacists, has generated its own share of 'lone wolf' desperadoes: far more, in the United States, than the jihadists. In the decade from 2008 to 2017, according to the Anti-Defamation League, 71 per cent of fatalities from individual terror attacks were caused by the far-right. The tactical repertoire ranges from disorganized and low-tech, such as the neo-Nazi James Fields' vehicular assault on anti-fascist protesters in Charlottesville resulting in the death of Heather Heyer, to more planned armed assaults, such as the mass shootings at the Quebec City Mosque and the Tree of Life Synagogue. Media commentary has begun to argue that the internet is partly to blame. For example, the Quebec shooter Alexandre Bissonnette avidly consumed racist content from right-wing activist Ben Shapiro and neo-fascist Richard Spencer. Robert Bowers, who shot up the Tree of Life Synagogue during a Shabbat service, was an active user of the alt-right Twitter epigone, Gab. The so-called 'MAGA bomber', who tried to bomb George Soros, Hillary Clinton and Barack Obama, had recently threatened a Twitter user with death: Twitter's moderator had declined to take action, explaining that the tweet didn't violate Twitter's community standards.

Blaming social media activity for the actions of these murderers in any direct and individualized way would simply beg the convoluted question of cause and effect. To what extent, for example, was Alexandre Bissonnette a fan of Ben Shapiro's content because he was already on the road to becoming a racist killer? How much did whatever he saw on Gab enable Robert Bowers' belief that the Hebrew Immigrant Aid Society, by helping settle refugees, was bringing 'invaders' that 'kill our people'? In what way, if at all, did it tip him over the edge, leading him to declare: 'I can't sit by and watch my people get slaughtered. Screw your optics, I'm going in'? There could, by definition, be no answer to this. The effects of content in the social industry, as with advertising, are collectivizing: they are designed to work across a population.

We are, to some extent, working in the dark. At present, there is no single dominant far-right brand or franchise capable of aggregating and shaping these attacks as part of a global narrative. There is no armed right-wing hub of attraction able to draw a swarm of like-minded warriors: no fascist answer to Occupy. Fascism, in most cases, dares not speak its name. Fascist terror is 'stochastic' because fascism is still fractal: the armed shitstorm, a material possibility of the medium every bit as much as the meatspace troll, has yet to materialize. But these are early days for the networked fascism of the twenty-first century.

CONCLUSION

WE ARE ALL SCRIPTURIENT

Writing is pre-eminently the technology of cyborgs

Donna Haraway

If anyone knew with what impatience and vexatiousness I pen down my Conceptions, they might be very well assured that I am not only free from, but incapable of the common disease of this Scripturient age

Henry More,
'An Explanation of the Grand Mystery of Godliness'

I.

The chronophage is a monster that eats time. Squatting, insectoid, on top of the Corpus Clock in Cambridge, it mechanically turns the wheel, and snaps its jaws to consume each second. On the hour, a chain drops into a small wooden coffin in the back of the clock.

An industry that monetizes 'time on device' is a chronophage of a different order, with the tick of the clock replaced by the click of keys or the tap of thumbs on screen. A social machine that organizes and measures our scarce attention, assigning a numerical value to every scroll, pause, keystroke and click. A near-death experience, measuring out its approach by the second.

It makes time itself a commodity, albeit a very unevenly distributed one. Every time we average life expectancies, we bracket the worlds of plunder and prey, the centuries of colonial and class history concentrated in the huge differences of life chances across the planet. What *is* universal is that time is scarce. There are only so many hours in a day, so many days in a year and so many years in a life. The fictional 'average' human being on the planet has seventy years, or approximately six hundred thousand hours. Four hundred thousand of those will be spent awake.

If a life is defined by what we attend to, then from this aerial view, screen time, watch time, and time on device are ways of quantifying the life consumed as raw material by the social industry and its sister industries in amusement, entertainment and news. The spread of smartphone ownership has expedited the colonization of more and more of life by these attention-seeking industries. They work themselves into the interstices of the bulks of time we spend at work, eating, going to the toilet, socializing or in transit, and gradually enlarge their share.

The time taken by the Twittering Machine expands every year, both individually and in aggregate. The average global internet user now spends 135 minutes per day on the social industry platforms. If spread uniformly over a life, this would amount to fifty thousand hours. Statista conservatively estimates that between 2010 and 2020, social industry users will have trebled from approximately one billion to three billion. This is in the context of an even larger share of life spent interacting with screens, much of it in computerized workplaces. For example, Americans spend eleven hours every day interacting with screens: most of their waking reality is a simulacrum. Such figures, of course, merely gesture with a hefty pinch of salt towards a scale, a quantity of decisions taken.

Addiction occurs through choices, but somehow it also happens behind our backs. No one consciously sets out to devote themselves to the machine, to become its addict. Its veto power over all other possible attentions takes place, cumulatively, through every apparently free choice made as a user. We drop into the dead zone, the 'ticker trance' of feed addiction, by increment. The way the chronophagic machine fights for our attention recalls what Eastern Christianity used to call the demon of *acedia*. This was a predecessor of the modern concept of melancholia, and it was used in monasteries (those ancient writing machines) to describe an affliction of the devoted. In the original Greek, 'akedia' meant 'lack of care'. In the Latinized Christian use propagated by Evagrius of Pontus, it described a lack of care about one's life; a listless, restless spiritual lethargy. The condition left one yearning for distraction and continual novelty, exploiting one's petty hates and hungers. It dissolved one's capacity for attending, for living as if living mattered, into a series of itches demanding to be scratched. Ultimately, it was dehumanizing, corrosive of meaning: it was spiritual death.

This way of describing our predicament runs the risk, innate to Christian demonology, of paranoia. It is less 'they're all out to get me' than 'evil is something that happens to me, rather than something I am involved in'. As with conspiracy theory, it externalizes evil. After all, the platforms are not only *not* demons; they are ostentatious about it. 'Don't be Evil', as the Google slogan has it. They don't, by themselves, generate the acedia, the generalized depression and weariness that they monetize. No more than the pharmaceutical industry does. They offer us a solution, an addiction which magnifies and potentiates acedia. But, as with all addictions, we succumb to it with our choices and our rationalizations. We are, after all, only staying in touch, only seeing what's happening, only looking for the news, friends, entertainment: the mood-altering substance which is euphemized as 'variable rewards' is something that affects other people.

Given the time this addiction demands of us, we are entitled to ask what else we might be doing, what else we could be addicted to. A near-death experience often forces us to take a more executive view, to see our micro-decisions in the context of an absolute scarcity of life. It imposes a rigour which is counter to acedia. If we had, for example, just one year to live, and really intended to live, how much of that time would we spend doing what we now do on the Twittering Machine? If we are suddenly 'scripturient', if we feel compelled to write to one another, could we find a better platform for doing so? And if cyber-utopianism has collapsed, what would a utopia of writing really be like?

II.

It would be hard to overstate the scale of the change we're going through. Writing is fundamentally conservative. It is a conventional system of markings that, to be comprehensible, has to be preserved. As the historian of writing Barry Powell argues, this conservatism is supported by political power. The use of writing stabilizes language, suppresses local variation, gives the impression of homogeneity. Even revolutionaries, as Mao discovered, struggle to transform writing systems.

That makes it, curiously, harder to see the cultural and political impact that each specific technology of writing has. Writing is a technology whose materiality – whether it is with papyrus and reed, pen and paper, movable type or computer – is never neutral as to its possible uses. But the more it stays the same, the less there is to contrast it with. Alphabetic writing has dominated in most parts of the world for 2,500 years. Printed writing has dominated for six hundred years. Partly because of their longevity, there has been no direct way to see their deep cultural effects in everyday life: to see how the material properties of our writing systems favour some kinds of expression and prejudice others. Making these visible has been the work of archaeologists and historians.

The digital revolution over recent decades has suddenly offered a freshet of contrasts. The ease of associative linking with hypertext underlines just how deeply embedded linear writing – and therefore linear thinking – has been in print culture. The internet spontaneously achieves the kind of montaging and remediation of content that in the print era was the preserve of cultural margins: scrapbooking, for example, or modernist poetry. The availability of real-time written communication has revived the use of logographic and pictographic elements in writing, the emoticon for example, to efficiently convey aspects of spoken conversation such as register and expression. This abruptly highlights how contrived the dominance of exclusively alphabetic writing has been, and the degree of formality and protocol in expression that it has required of us.

The emerging economy of digital writing, with drastically reduced costs of reproduction, upends economies of scale by which writing has been organized into note, letter, article, essay, novel, encyclopedia. A couple of ordinary sentences can be of enormous economic value, as demonstrated by Snapchat's loss of $1.3 billion stock value after a single tweet by Kylie Jenner. It shows us how much our inherited standards of punctuation, rubrication and letterform are a legacy of the early modern reinvention of the book as, in Marshall McLuhan's words, the 'first uniformly repeatable commodity, the first assembly line, and the first mass-production'. It also upsets centred hierarchies of writing, where all texts ultimately refer to and are legitimized by a single, sacred text such as a bible or constitution. On a distributed network of writing, there is no single centre.

Above all, the digital revolution blurs the social distinction between reader and writer. Part of the allure of the Twittering Machine has been the way it extends the privilege of writing. The history of literacy is also a history of repression and exclusion. Of fictional women, burning 'like beacons' in the literature of men, as Virginia Woolf put it in her essay 'A Room of One's Own', while real women were 'locked up, beaten and flung about the room'. Of slaves forbidden to write, secretly acquiring the means to send private letters, or learning to read only to burn incandescently at their captivity. 'The more I read,' Frederick Douglass wrote in 1845, 'the more I was led to abhor and detest my enslavers'.

In Charlotte Perkins Gilman's feminist short story from 1892, 'The Yellow Wallpaper', men are desperate to control writing. Writing, the protagonist is told, is her symptom. It rots her brain. All these morbid fantasies. It is not motherly. It is not wifely. It gives rise to her hysterical illness. In fact, as becomes clear in the story, writing is both her symptom and her only hope of a cure. It is the return of the repressed. 'The subject cries out,' Lacan exclaimed, 'from every pore of his being what he cannot talk about.' Her writing sweats with an overplus of meaning. There's something the writer can't say; it pours out of her anyway.

Since the men in her life, terrified of her sexuality and its potential violence, can't hear her, Gilman's protagonist must write. She compulsively writes and writes, and suffers boredom, withdrawal and restless visions when prevented from writing. Writing and its absence exercise a despotic power over her life, no less than the patriarchs do.

We are, abruptly, writing more than we ever have before. Our 'scripturient' disease, the writing symptom, shows, in part, how much was waiting to be expressed before the digital upheaval incited a new revolution in mass literacy. Handwriting was once the privilege of a few, before the first explosion of mass literacy in the late nineteenth century. Where it was taught, penmanship was indexed to social class, gender and occupation: merchants, lawyers, women and upper-class men were taught distinct letterform styles. The very appearance and configuration of the shapes and spacing of letters allowed a reader to quickly understand its social significance. Even in the printed word, there emerged an association of letterform with social class: think, today, of the different fonts deployed by 'popular' newspapers and those of the broadsheets. Writing has always been laden with hierarchies of significance and signification.

What distinguishes the new mass literacy from its nineteenth-century predecessor is the spread of writing, in the homogenized fonts of the computer, the smartphone, the Twittering Machine. The characteristic experience of literacy prior to the Internet was reading; now it is writing. Amid a collapse in trust in the old media, whose commercial strategies and political affiliations have drawn it further and further away from the priorities of its audiences, the people formerly known as the audience have become the producers. We still read, but differently. We read less for edification than to be productive: scanning and scavenging material from a flow of messages and notifications. And as we do so we are, behind our backs as it were, writing in digital script. The practices of the computerized workplace overflow into those of the Twittering Machine.

Our dilemmas are therefore not those of the nineteenth century, when the spread of writing often had the inflection of social rebellion, as women, slaves and workers wrote against the wishes and purview of their masters and superiors. While there remain regimes, institutions and individuals who wish to shut us up, power more often works by making us speak, coaxing our confessions, our testimonies, our cries from the heart, out of us. Today Gilman's narrator, instead of encountering the assured authority of doctors and husbands, would be besieged by swarms of wishful online patriarchs, gendertrolls, far less assured but no less terrified of what she might say. But she would also encounter the even more anonymous, semi-occulted means by which her writing is extracted: the Twittering Machine.

The old story in which the vital truth is repressed, and cries out to be told, isn't for the most part the story of the Twittering Machine. If we have nothing to write, or we don't know what to write, the machine will goad us. There will always be something to react to. The content agnosticism of the machine means that we can sometimes use it to break unjust silences, from #MeToo to Black Lives Matter. But the format in which even this writing takes place is coercive, harnessed to ceaseless production. In a way, the hyper-productivity of the machine might have the effect of producing a new kind of silence. The cathartic effect of writing, reacting to stimulus, can be a way of filling the void with endless monetizable chatter. A new form of stifling that leaves no space to say what matters. As Colette Soler put it, 'The gag has not been lifted: it has only changed its terms.'

If we want 'free expression' today, it is no longer enough to demand the abolition of political constraints. We have to free expression from the ceaseless production of redundancy, and ourselves from the compulsion to labour. We have to withdraw our labour and reclaim the pleasures of writing as leisure time.

III.

Things could have been different. Before the cyber-utopianism of the California tech scene, there was the cyber-utopianism of Paris's Left Bank. Before the internet, French hipsters were experimenting with online anonymity, an experience they called 'fading'. Before the Twittering Machine, there was a public-sector platform, open to all, which was at the cutting edge of communications technology, the envy of Silicon Valley.

They called it Minitel. The Médium Interactif par Numérisation d'Information Téléphonique: France's internet *avant la lettre*. Except that Minitel was not exactly like the internet. The terminal was a small, sleek wood-brown box with a keyboard that flipped out to reveal a screen. It was a videotex service, a service that allowed users to access pages of text and images in a computer-like format. It used slightly different technological principles from the internet, resulting in a more limited system. For example, Arpanet used a distributed network, rather than a centralized information system. It implemented a form of packet-switching, wherein a message is broken into bits of data, distributed over optimal routes and reassembled at destination, and which is still used today in the foundational protocols of the internet.

These systems were chosen, in part, for their military virtue. An alluring myth of the internet's origins has it that it was essentially invented by Paul Baran, of the RAND Corporation, as a way for communications to survive nuclear war. The Arpanet system was actually designed separately, without Baran's direct involvement. Nonetheless, it used remarkably similar ideas, and Baran was one of the major inventors of the distributed network and the packet-switching method. The underlying idea for a 'distributed network' of writing, published in a 1964 article, was that in the event of a nuclear strike, the communications system would best survive if it wasn't centralized. This necessitated plenty of redundancy in the network. As Sandy Baldwin puts it: 'you design a distributed network full of waste to guarantee that it can communicate beyond the apocalypse.' Even if every last human life was obliterated, there would still be bots messaging one another, Microsoft's 'TayTweets' riffing on new languages with Facebook's 'Bob' and 'Alice'.

The French government paid close attention. It had just withdrawn from NATO a few years before Arpanet was launched in 1969, and it was trying to build a competitive economy. It was desperate to outdo Britain and Germany by modernizing the French economy first. The Gaullist state was ploughing money into advanced technological research, to update its telecommunications system. In 1973, engineers at the Institut de Recherche en Informatique et en Automatique had developed a network to rival Arpanet: CYCLADES. It was based on similar practices of decentralized networking. And it deployed its own version of packet-switching, using the 'datagram' invented by Louis Pouzin, which had been a major influence on the Arpanet design. The first CYCLADES terminal with television and keyboard calling was made public in 1974. This combination of telephone and computer was the earliest echo of what would later be called, with official gusto, 'telematics'.

The public sector threw its weight behind the development of this system. Gérard Théry, the French director general of telecommunications, drew up plans to develop a 'telephone for all' system as the infrastructural basis for 'computing for all'. In 1978, a government report anticipated the 'computerization of society' and called for state investment to expedite the future. CYCLADES was ultimately defeated, however, by the internal politics of the public sector. France's telecommunications department, Postes, télégraphes et téléphones (PTT), had been developing its own system, Transpac. Transpac used, instead of packet-switching, a circuit-switched network. Circuit-switching is a much older system initially designed in 1878 for handling phone calls, using dedicated point-to-point connections for the duration of the call. At the insistence of the PTT, CYCLADES was defunded and the Transpac system was the basis for the emerging videotex service, Minitel.

Minitel was pioneered in 1981, in a small experiment in Velizy, connecting 2,500 homes with an experimental range of services. Central to this, and the major incentive for households to adopt the device, was that it offered a computerized file of the telephone directory so that calls to anyone could be made quickly and easily. By 1983, the service was successful enough to be extended throughout the whole of France. And the terminal was free, distributed by local authorities. France Télécom astutely surmised that the public couldn't be expected to buy something without knowing in advance what services would be available. Users were billed, not by subscription fee, but on a play now, pay later basis. The number of terminals in use soared to 531,000 by 1984. By the mid-1990s, just as the internet was being launched, there were over six and a half million terminals.

The advantage of Minitel was that it was an open platform, guaranteed by the public sector. Anyone could offer any service or promote any idea. All one had to do was register and pay a fee. Initial press hostility diminished as the newspapers saw an opportunity to sell their product in a new medium. The services available included online shopping, chatting, booking tickets, interactive gaming, checking bank accounts – even the rudiments of what we today call 'smart homes', such as remote control of thermostats and home appliances.

New online visual arts flourished. So did a certain cosmopolitan cyber-utopianism. 'I am dreaming', wrote artist Ben Vautier, 'of a Minitel with which we should send a message in French and it would be received in Bantu at Tombouctou and in Basque in Bayonne.' On the Left and within social movements, the technology generated breathless radical enthusiasm. There was good reason for this, as social organizations proved able, from the start, to turn the technology to their advantage.

In late 1986, for example, social movement organizations created a new Minitel service: 36-15 Alter. This combined twenty-five associations representing psychiatric patients, anti-racist students, farmers and other heterogeneous groups. They all paid the fee together, and collectively managed the informational commons. Alongside the 'free radio' movement, it showed that the old one-way communications system was breaking down. The old mass media had wielded the power of hypnotic mass suggestion, with audiences reduced to passive recipients of mediated messages. Philosopher Félix Guattari, a participant in 36-15 Alter, looked forward to the vanishing of 'the element of suggestion', and the emergence of a 'post-media era'. The 'machines of information, communication, intelligence, art and culture' could be collectively and individually reappropriated.

In the same year as the launch of 36-15 Alter, student protesters used the message system of Libération, a left-wing daily which supplied Minitel content, to organize mass protests against education minister Alain Devaquet's reforms to the university system. The government's plan was to impose more selection in universities and charge fees. Within days of the mass protests, during which the student protester Malik Oussekine was killed in police custody, the law was withdrawn and Devaquet resigned. In 1988, nurses used the network to coordinate their strike action against health cuts, staff shortages and low wages. During the strike, they forged a new union, La Coordination Nationale Infirmière, and used Minitel as, in the words of sociologist Danièle Kergoat, 'a tool for transforming social reality'. On Minitel, they could collectively discuss their situation, share notebooks of grievances, maintain shared status updates. Guattari enthused that the nurses 'knew how to use Minitel for transversal communication' to cut across old lines of division. They were able 'to dialogue' between different practices in different fields. They could fuse 'individual points of view with the collective movement' and allow 'minority positions' to be taken into account.

Minitel was not, however, a leftist utopia. In fact, it was far more akin to the agora that enthusiasts of the internet would later celebrate. Among other things, it was a state-maintained free market. Because it was open, one could just as easily use it to sell sex as incite revolution. In fact, the burgeoning online sex industry became one of its major hives of activity. The telecom entrepreneur Xavier Niel made his fortune running cybersex services on Minitel. This was, as a former Minitel sex worker described, an industry that demanded industrial work rates. He was compelled, for example, to work with four terminals, using four different (usually female) identities at the same time, 'processing' clients as quickly as possible. What wasn't commercialized was the infrastructure itself. There was no way to make money from taps and clicks, and therefore no technological incentive for addiction, celebrification, trolling and the regular moments of explosion around aggregated sentiment that characterize the Twittering Machine.

It was also limited by its narrowly national basis. There was a chance that French technique could have globalized. For a brief moment, Minitel had the ear of the California tech scene, its cultural leaders, ravers, tech geeks and anyone else who might be interested. In the early 1990s, before the internet was launched, France Télécom approached the influential West Coast guru John Coate, who had popularized the online bulletin board system The WELL. Coate was successful in gaining the attention of the tech scene, whose vanguard was impressed by Minitel. A system was duly pioneered, called '101 Online'. The problem is that, rather than providing the sort of open platform, the 'electronic "meeting place"', that Minitel provided in France, it ended up being a version of the proprietary services already available for the wealthy few from CompuServe and AOL.

Minitel failed for other reasons, too. Its technical basis was not kept up to date, and it relied too much on a national telecommunications infrastructure using circuit-switching. Minitel was outmoded and unable to compete with the World Wide Web. Its antiquated video transmission services couldn't beat the power of hypertext. In addition, France Télécom stopped supplying terminals free of charge, so user growth began to fall for the first time. The European Commission, seeing the global potential of the internet, recommended that the EU adopt the Californian 'free market' model as the basis for its dissemination. France Télécom began to link the Minitel network to the global internet, but with personal computing these terminals were no longer necessary and too restrictive. The dissemination of computing technology and, soon, mobile phones outstripped Minitel's accomplishments.

Yet, despite all of its limitations, the continuing affection for Minitel meant that it didn't immediately disappear. Millions of users continued to work with this antiquated model of 'télématique', and the platform wasn't finally shut down until 2012.

IV.

Silicon Valley mythology holds that Minitel failed because it was too dirigiste, too state-directed. As Julien Mailland points out, however, both Minitel and the internet were the products of different quantities of state investment, private capital and thriving cultures of amateur enthusiasts and experts improving the technology and proselytizing for it.

Both Minitel and the internet show that there is no 'free market' without substantial public-sector intervention and backing. The internet's history also shows us that when we rely on the private sector and its hallowed bromide of 'innovation', quite often that will result in technical innovations that are designed for manipulation, surveillance and exploitation.

The tax-evading, offshore wealth-hoarding, data-monopolizing, privacy-invading silicon giants benefit from the internet's 'free market' mythology, but the brief flourishing of Minitel shows us that other ways, other worlds, other platforms, are possible. The question is, given that there's no way to reverse history, how can we actualize these possibilities? What sort of power do we have? As users, it turns out, very little. We are not voters on the platforms; we are not even customers. We are the unpaid producers of raw material. We could, if we were organized, withdraw our labour power, commit social media suicide: but then what other platforms do we have access to with anything like the same reach?

The fate of minimalist Facebook alternatives like Ello demonstrates the dilemma of users. Ello was launched in 2014, with almost half a million dollars of venture capital funding. Its unique sell was that it would not turn users into commodities: 'You Are Not a Product', it offered. The majority of users ruefully rejoined, 'Oh Yes We Are'.

Over a million people signed up – hardly negligible, but it barely made a dent in the Facebook leviathan. Any competitor to Facebook would have to offer something special to counter the 'user effects' which favour monopoly, let alone its addictive propensities. And the truth is that Ello, because it is not addictive, has very little eye candy and is not based on creating a hive of users goaded into frenzied activity, is rather boring. It's hard to imagine, during a conversation or train ride, repeatedly pulling out one's smartphone and irritably navigating to the Ello app to check the notifications. And that, in a nutshell, is the problem.

There are democratic potentials in the internet. Even if it is in essence a commercialized system of surveillance and controls, there have always been ways of writing against the grain. Radical movements, from Bernie Sanders' campaign in the United States to the Jeremy Corbyn-led Labour Party, have used professional social media campaigns to outflank and subvert the old media monopolies. Even in the People's Republic of China, the spread of online communications technologies has created new enclaves outside of the state's and companies' control. While the regime harnesses computerization and big data to state surveillance and the disciplinary system of 'social credit', workers use popular social industry platforms such as QQ and Sina Weibo – Chinese equivalents of Facebook and Twitter – to organize walkouts, discuss strategies and collate demands.

There may also be ways to fight the social industry, incrementally, for control of the social media platforms. In the United Kingdom, the Labour opposition is experimenting with ideas of a public service platform run by the BBC, one of the few brands with perhaps more global clout than Facebook. To some extent user-governed, and stripped of the data-hoarding, privacy-invading propensities of the existing social industry platforms, this has been proposed as part of a wider agenda of democratizing mass media. A successful public-sector competitor to Facebook and Google would be a significant problem for these giants, and for the advertisers that rely on them, given that the UK provides 40 million of Facebook's most affluent active users. However, whatever advantages it could have, it may also face the same problem as existing commercial competitors: a collective, culturally reinforced addiction, and the self-reinforcing tunnel of attention and satisfactions that it has generated.

And this is where the story is not just about corporations and technologies. The Twittering Machine may be a horror story, but it is one that involves all of us as users. We are part of the machine, and we find our satisfactions in it, however destructive they may be. And this horror story is only possible in a society that is busily producing horrors. We are only up for addiction to mood-altering devices because our emotions seem to need managing, if not bludgeoning by relentless stimulus. We are only happy to drop into the dead-zone trance because of whatever is disappointing in the world of the living. Twitter toxicity is only endurable because it seems less worse than the alternatives. 'No addiction', as Francis Spufford has written, 'is ever explained by examining the drug. The drug didn't cause the need. A tour of a brewery won't explain why somebody became an alcoholic.'

To break an addiction, the neuroscientist Marc Lewis has argued, is a unique act of reinvention. It requires a creative leap. The addict gives up meth not by going cold turkey or taking a pharmaceutical substitute, but by breaking the compulsory force of habit. It is not a matter of a single 'crossroads' decision, like a vote or a purchase in which everything immediately resolves into clarity. It is a process of becoming different. For the individual addict, that might mean undergoing intensive psychotherapy, learning a new art or skill, or religious conversion. The beauty of neuroplasticity, says Lewis, is that while brain tissue is lost during addiction, as the attention tunnel prunes and shears unused synapses, once the addiction is over, the lost matter is not only replaced but actually increases. Recovering addicts don't simply get back what they have lost: they tend to develop entirely new and more sophisticated capacities. New ways of being in the world.

The question is what, collectively, would such a reinvention look like? How could we acquire new and better habits, better ways of writing to one another? If we've written our way into this situation, how can we write our way out of it?

V.

What could a utopia of writing look like? There is, and could be, no answer to that. If anyone knew what utopia looked like, it would have ceased to be utopia: we would be living in it.

Utopia is, literally, a non-place, meaning that utopias at their best are not prescriptions but imaginative placeholders for human desires. At its worst, cyber-utopianism has been a neo-liberal sublimation of 1960s communalism, reflecting the journey from the hippy Stewart Brand and the *Whole Earth Catalog* to *Wired* magazine. The whole earth, according to this dispensation, is a 'global, massively interconnected system of technology vibrating around us', as executive editor of *Wired*, Kevin Kelly, put it. This conception, which he calls 'the technium', saw Kelly, Brand and their confederates serenaded by venture capital and lauded at Davos. But for Kelly, it had a more mystical significance. The technium was 'actually a divine phenomenon that is a reflection of God', he told *Christianity Today* in doxological tones. More circumspect in his book, he ventured that 'if there is a God, the arc of the technium is aimed right at him'. This literally assigned a holy significance to the global triumph of Silicon Valley.

At its best, however, cyber-utopianism has revelled in untold possibility. From Manuel Castells' celebration of online 'creative autonomy' to Clay Shirky's egalitarian 'communities of practice', cyber-utopianism has welcomed, not so much a desired end state as the expansion of new horizons. The openness and indeterminacy of the network seemingly permitted what John Stuart Mill would have called 'experiments of living'. This is the utopian side of liberalism. The virtue of a platform model, from this point of view, is that it would enable everyone to write as uniquely as they must and as weirdly as they will.

The destruction of an ill-founded cyber-utopianism, insufficiently attentive to the political economy of platform capitalism and its pathologies, has given rise to a counter-utopian backlash. It manifests in the proliferation of articles with headlines like, 'I quit social media and it changed my life'. TED talks such as Cal Newport's 'Why you should quit social media'. Books like Jaron Lanier's *Ten Arguments For Deleting Your Social Media Accounts Right Now*. Alongside these are the innumerable head-shaking think pieces about how to combat 'fake news' and stop Russian trolls from destroying democracy. Increasingly, the rich absent themselves, professionalizing and delegating their social media accounts. Platform bosses, of course, never get high on their own supply: social media abstinence is not an affliction of the poor, but the cultural distinction of the affluent.

'A world without utopias', as the historian Enzo Traverso writes, 'inevitably looks back'. Without them, our thwarted longings sour and turn reactionary. And the backlash style, despite having the advantage that it disputes the inevitability of our assimilation into the Borg, is reactionary. It is compromised by a subtending fantasy that it could somehow be sufficient to exhort others to quit. Which is further underpinned by a fantasy that the frequent flights into mob irrationality, paranoia, nihilism and sadism characteristic of the social industry could be solved simply by 'going back'. As though these phenomena had no deeper and farther-reaching roots.

This is the sort of position that is incorrectly derided as neo-Luddite. By now it is well known that the Luddites have been historically misrepresented, their struggle against exploitation and destitution having been unjustly caricatured as technophobia. They were not against machines, but skilled in their use. Their utopia, such as it was, was not a pre-industrial Arcadia, but an incipiently socialist one in which the machines were dominated by workers, rather than workers being dominated by the machine. They smashed the tools to disrupt an emerging social machine that treated them as expendable units of a production process.

The Luddites were also excellent trolls. They were, like the movement that was massacred at Peterloo a few years later, a prototypical class insurrection: but they carried it off with tremendous elan. The very name 'Luddite' deliberately evoked a fictitious leader, Ned Ludd, a product of legend and fantasy, fear of whom had British authorities and spies searching high and low for sign of him. His supporters decided that Mr Ludd lived in Sherwood Forest, home of the equally legendary Robin

Hood, and signed their letters, 'Ned Ludd's Office, Sherwood Forest'. They cross-dressed and marched as 'General Ludd's wives'.

Luddism in the twenty-first century is an entirely defensible position; indeed, a desirable one. But what would it look like? It could hardly begin by smashing the machine. It is far too distributed, globally. And at any rate, many of the things we call tools are abstractions: we can't 'smash' the like button. And our immediate problem with the Twittering Machine is not that it drives us into unemployment, but that it works us without remuneration the better to sell us as a product. It gives us tasks in the form of a casino-style game: it is in the vanguard of the gamification of capitalism. And if all that happened was that, in a giant digital suicide, we killed off the social industry, the media, amusement and entertainment complexes would fuse with venture capital to do it all again only more efficiently. We need more than this. We need an escapology, certainly, a theory of how to get out before it's too late. We also need to free up our time and energy and shape them to better purpose. We need something to long for, the better to devise grander escapologies. We need the 'intercalary gush' of Catholic poet Charles Péguy, a moment of rupture in our daily habits through which to escape not only the Twittering Machine but the unnecessary burden of misery that it successfully monetizes.

Cyberspace is dreamspace, a place for exploration and reverie. Reverie is a dream, and a dream is a wish fulfilment; a momentary pleasure wherein a desire is partially satisfied. This is something to be cautiously optimistic about. If desire, as opposed to need or an instinctual programme, is distinctly human, then so is the ability to satisfy it indirectly, through fantasy. Indeed, since most desires can't be satisfied in any other way, reverie seems to be essential to a pleasurable life. The theft of the capacity for reverie by the social industry, the way it has used gaming-industry techniques to lead us into a guided trance, down pathways lit up with virtual rewards, is therefore no trivial matter. We might ask whether there are other technologies for reverie in modern life, what the neo-Luddite approach might be to that.

We feel a compulsion to participate, to react, to keep up to speed, to be in the know. There is something to be said for refusing to be in the know. Robert Frost's poem from 1916, 'Choose Something Like a Star', speaks of an entity that both shows itself and hides itself. It appears in remote, dark obscurity and will only say 'I burn'. Even as it reveals itself to us, Frost suggests, something of its being remains mysterious, elusive. It asks of us, not understanding, but 'a certain height'. He says, when 'the mob is swayed to carry praise or blame too far', then, 'we may choose something like a star' to stay our minds. And with that, we can escape – from the hot flows of information, the flux, the bombardment, of impressions, of exposure to messages, more now than ever before, a data apocalypse, from which nothing intelligible can ultimately be wrested – to a fixed point of unknowing.

What would happen if we applied Delany's strategy of 'stupidity': that is, of only taking in as much information as we could put out? What if we were not in the know? What if our reveries were not productive? What if, in deliberate abdication of our smartphones, we strolled in the park with nothing but a notepad and a nice pen? What if we sat in a church and closed our eyes? What if we lay back on a lily pad, with nothing to do? Would someone call the police?

REFERENCES AND BIBLIOGRAPHICAL NOTES

FOREWORD

p. 15: **All technology, as the historian Melvin Kranzberg put it . . .** Melvin Kranzberg, 'Technology and History: "Kranzberg's Laws"', *Technology and Culture*, Vol. 27, No. 3 (Jul., 1986), pp. 544–560.

CHAPTER ONE

p. 21: **The Museum of Modern Art explains:** Paul Klee, Twittering Machine (Die Zwitscher-Maschine) 1922, MoMA: https://www.moma.org/collection/works/37347.

p. 22: **Thomas More wondered . . .** Quoted in Karl Marx, Capital, Volume I: *A Critique of Political Economy*, Dover Publications, Inc: Mineola, NY:, 2011, p. 761.

p. 22: **At first, says historian Warren Chappell . . .** Warren Chappell & Robert Bringhurst, *A Short History of the Printed World*, Hartley & Marks: Point Roberts, WA, 1999, pp. 9–10.

p. 22: **Without print capitalism . . .** Benedict Anderson, *Imagined Communities: Reflections on the Origin and Spread of Nationalism*, Verso: London and New York, 2006.

p. 23: **It is a form of shorthand propaganda . . .** Marcus Gilroy-Ware astutely draws on Todd Gitlin's concept of 'instant propaganda' to describe the work that such phrases do. Marcus Gilroy-Ware, *Filling the Void: Emotion, Capitalism and Social Media*, Repeater Books: London, 2017, Kindle loc. 288.

p. 23: **As William Davies has argued . . .** William Davies, 'Neoliberalism and the revenge of the "social"', *openDemocracy*, 16 July 2013.

p. 24: **Our lives have become . . .** Shoshana Zuboff, 'Big Other: surveillance capitalism and the prospects of an information civilisation', *Journal of Information Technology*, 2015, No 30, pp. 75–89.

p. 24: **. . . redolent of the 'Skinner Box' . . .** B. F. Skinner, *The Behavior of Organisms: An Experimental Analysis*, B. F. Skinner Foundation: Cambridge, MA, 1991.

p. 25: **. . . according to former editor-in-chief . . .** Chris Anderson, 'The End of Theory: The Data Deluge Makes The Scientific Method Obsolete', *Wired*, 23 June 2008.

p. 26: **We no longer have to believe, as neo-liberal economist . . .** F. A. Hayek, *The American Economic Review*, Vol. 35, No. 4. (Sep., 1945), pp. 519–530.

p. 26: **Estimates of social platform usage vary wildly but . . .** Hayley Tsukayama, 'Teens spend nearly nine hours every day consuming media', *Washington Post*, 9 November 2015.

p. 26: **And the number of us checking our phones . . .** Deloitte, 'Global mobile consumer trends', 2nd edition, 2017 <www2.deloitte.com>.

p. 26: **. . . violent, eroticized, animated fantasies aimed at children . . .** James Bridle, 'Something is wrong on the internet', *Medium.com*, 6 November 2017.

p. 26: **This is the 'modern calculating machine' . . .** Jacques Lacan, 'Seminar on "The Purloined Letter"', in *Écrits: The First Complete Edition in English*, W. W. Norton & Company: New York, 2006, p. 45. On the cybernetic origins of Lacan's thinking here, see Lydia H. Liu, *The Freudian Robot: Digital Media and the Future of the Unconscious*, University of Chicago Press: Chicago, MI, 2011, Chapter Four.

p. 27: **He blames the 'short-term, dopamine-driven feedback loops' of social media . . .** Julie Carrie Wong, 'Former Facebook executive: social media is ripping society apart', *Guardian*, 12 December 2017; Alex Hern, '"Never get high on your own supply" – why social media bosses don't use social media', *Guardian*, 23 January 2018.

p. 28: **Sean Parker, the Virginia-born billionaire hacker . . .** Thuy Ong, 'Sean Parker on Facebook: "God only knows what it's doing to our children's brains"', *The Verge*, 9 November 2017; Olivia Solon, 'Ex-Facebook president Sean Parker: site made to exploit human "vulnerability"', *Guardian*, 9 November 2017.

p. 28: **It was another former Twitter adviser and Facebook executive . . .** Antonio García-Martínez, 'I'm an ex-Facebook exec: don't believe what they tell you about ads', *Guardian*, 2 May 2017.

p. 28: **As the Silicon Valley guru Jaron Lanier puts it . . .** Jaron Lanier, *You Are Not a Gadget: A Manifesto*, Alfred A. Knopf: New York, 2010, p. 11.

p. 29: **We would enjoy 'creative autonomy' . . .** Manuel Castells, *Communication Power*, Oxford University Press: Oxford, 2009.

p. 29: **Multitudes would suddenly swarm . . .** Michael Hardt & Antonio Negri, *Multitude: War and Democracy in the Age of Empire*, Penguin Books: New York, 2004.

p. 31: **A 2015 study . . .** Eric P. S. Baumer, Shion Guha, Emily Quan, David Mimno, and Geri Gay, 'Missing Photos, Suffering Withdrawal, or Finding Freedom? How Experiences of Social Media Non-Use Influence the Likelihood of Reversion', *Social Media and Society*, 2015.

p. 31: **For those who are curating a self . . .** Mike Elgan, 'Social media addiction is a bigger problem than you think', *CIO*, 14 December 2015.

p. 31: **. . . the 'gamification of capitalism'.** Byung-Chul Han, *Psychopolitics: Neoliberalism and New Technologies of Power*, Verso: London and New York, 2017.

p. 31: **Even Skinner's rats were not Skinner's rats . . .** Bruce K Alexander, 'Addiction: The View from Rat Park', 2010 www.brucekalexander.com.

p. 31: **Marcus Gilroy-Ware's study of social media . . .** Marcus Gilroy-Ware, *Filling the Void: Emotion, Capitalism and Social Media*, Repeater Books: London, 2017.

p. 32: **. . . our online avatar resembles a 'virtual tooth' . . .** Hans Bellmer, *Little Anatomy of the Physical Unconscious, or The Anatomy of the Image, Dominion*: Waterbury Centre, VT, 2004, p. 5.

p. 32: **The global rise in depression . . .** Laura Entis, 'Depression is Now the World's Most Widespread Illness', *Fortune*, 30 March 2017.

p. 32: **Steven Rudderham had been targeted . . .** Steve White, 'Steven Rudderham: Dad falsely accused of being paedophile on Facebook found hanged', *Mirror*, 24 May 2013; Keith Kendrick, 'Dad "Driven to Suicide" by Facebook Trolls Over False Paedophile Claims', *Huffington Post*, 14 August 2014.

p. 33: **. . . Chad Lesko of Toledo, Ohio . . .** Camille Dodero, 'Viral Facebook Post Alleges Man Is a Wanted Rapist, But He's Not', *Gawker*, 24 May 2013.

p. 33: **Garnet Ford of Vancouver, and Triz Jefferies of Philadelphia . . .** Doug Ward, 'Man wrongly accused through social media of Surrey homicide', *Vancouver Sun*, 12 October 2011; Jessica Hopper, 'Wrong Man Shown in Wanted Photo for Philadelphia "Kensington Strangler"', ABC News, 21 December 2010; Stephanie Farr, 'Wrong Man Shown in Wanted Photo for Philadelphia "Kensington Strangler"', *Philadelphia Inquirer*, 21 December 2010.

p. 34: **In 2006, a thirteen-year-old boy named Mitchell Henderson . . .** Mattathias Schwartz, 'The Trolls Among Us', *New York Times*, 3 August 2008; Whitney Phillips,

'This Is Why We Can't Have Nice Things: Mapping the Relationship between Online Trolling and Mainstream Culture', *MIT* Press: Cambridge, MA, 2015, pp. 28–30.

p. 35: **. . . an eleven-year-old boy from Tennessee, Keaton Jones . . .** 'How is a bullied child like "Milkshake Duck"?', *BBC Trending*, 17 December 2017; Joanna Williams, 'Poor bullied Keaton Jones has become a Milkshake Duck, the latest viral victim of fake celebrity compassion', *Daily Telegraph*, 12 December 2017.

p. 36: **Ashawnty Davis, who, her parents say . . .** Doug Criss & Laura Diaz-Zuniga, 'Parents say 10-year-old daughter killed herself because of bullying', CNN, 2 December 2017.

p. 37: **. . . domesticate them with the 'rule of law' . . .** See Martha Nussbaum, *Anger and Forgiveness: Resentment, Generosity, and Justice*, Oxford University Press: New York, 2016.

p. 37: **. . . the workings of the liberal state.** See Corey Robin, *Fear: The History of a Political Idea*, Oxford University Press: New York, 2006.

p. 37: **The spectacle . . .** Guy Debord, *Society of the Spectacle*, Rebel Press: London, 2014.

p. 38: **The debacle . . .** Nick Cohen, '"Twitter joke" case only went ahead at insistence of DPP', *Observer*, 28 July 2012; Owen Bowcott, 'Twitter joke trial became confrontation with judicial establishment', *Guardian*, 27 July 2012.

p. 38: **Less well known . . .** 'Azhar Ahmed sentenced over Facebook soldier deaths slur', BBC News, 9 October 2012.

p. 38: **This is what happened . . .** Taylor McGraa, 'Exclusive: Bahar Mustafa Speaks to VICE After the Police Drop "#KillAllWhiteMen' Charges", *Vice*, 3 November 2015; Charlie Brinkhurst-Cuff, 'I'm glad the CPS saw Bahar Mustafa's #killallwhitemen tweet in context', *Guardian*, 5 November 2015.

p. 39: **Trolls programmatically search . . .** On 'exploitability', see Whitney Phillips, *This is Why We Can't Have Nice Things: Mapping the Relationship between Online Trolling and Mainstream Culture*, MIT Press: Cambridge, MA: 2015.

p. 39: **The late writer, Mark Fisher . . .** Mark Fisher, 'Exiting the Vampire Castle', *Open Democracy*, 24 November 2013.

p. 40: **'Language is mysterious' . . .** Karen Armstrong, *The Bible: A Biography*, Atlantic Books: London, 2007, p. 1.

p. 40: **So that a future reader can breathe . . .** Seamus Heaney, 'A Kite for Aibhin', *Human Chain*, Faber & Faber: London, 2010.

p. 40: **The religious historian . . .** David Frankfurter, 'The Magic of Writing and the Writing of Magic: The Power of the Word in Egyptian and Greek Traditions', *Helios*, Vol. 21, No. 2, 1994.

p. 40: **The Polish-American grammatologist . . .** I. J. Gelb, *A Study of Writing*, University of Chicago Press: Chicago & London, 1952.

p. 42: **According to the software developer . . .** Joel Spolsky, 'The Law of Leaky Abstractions', *Joel on Software*, 11 December 2002.

p. 44: **But it is also to loop . . .** Louis R Ormont, 'Cultivating the Observing Ego in the Group Setting', *International Journal of Group Psychotherapy*, Vol. 45, No. 4, 1995.

p. 44: **Jonathan Beller, the film theorist, has argued . . .** Jonathan Beller, *The Cinematic Mode of Production: Attention Economy and the Society of the Spectacle*, Dartmouth College Press: Hanover, NH, 2006.

CHAPTER TWO

p. 47: **. . . 'bright dings of pseudo-pleasure' . . .** Paul Lewis, '"Our minds can be hijacked": the tech insiders who fear a smartphone dystopia', *Guardian*, 6 October 2017.

p. 47: **Leah Pearlman was a user . . .** Victor Luckerson, 'The Rise of the Like Economy', *The Ringer*, 15 February 2017; Julian Morgans, 'The Inventor of the "Like" Button Wants You to Stop Worrying About Likes', *Vice*, 6 July 2017.

p. 47: **Apple's design strategist . . .** Mark Sullivan, 'Jony Ive says "constant use" of iPhone is "misuse"', *Fast Company*, 6 October 2017.

p. 48: **Yet, according to David Kirkpatrick's history . . .** David Kirkpatrick, *The Facebook Effect: The Inside Story of the Company That Is Connecting the World*, Simon & Schuster: New York, 2011, p. 118.

p. 48: **One of the site's earliest users . . .** Julia Carrie Wong, 'I was one of Facebook's first users. I shouldn't have trusted Mark Zuckerberg', *Guardian*, 17 April 2018.

p. 48: **He told a friend . . .** Josh Halliday, 'Facebook: Mark Zuckerberg college messages reveal steely ambition', *Guardian*, 18 May 2012.

p. 48: **But one of Twitter's early founders . . .** Nick Bilton, *Hatching Twitter: A True Story of Money, Power, Friendship, and Betrayal*, Penguin: New York, 2013, p. 152.

p. 49: **As he told the university newspaper . . .** Alan J. Tabak, 'Hundreds Register for New Facebook Website', *The Harvard Crimson*, 9 February 2004; see also Tom Huddleston Jr., 'Here's how 19-year-old Mark Zuckerberg described "The Facebook" in his first TV interview', CNBC, 17 April 2018.

p. 49: **By 2005 . . .** David Kirkpatrick, *The Facebook Effect: The Inside Story of the Company That is Connecting the World*, Simon & Schuster: New York, 2011, p. 319.

p. 49: **Harvard sociology professor Nicholas Christakis . . .** Stephanie Rosenbloom, 'On Facebook, Scholars Link Up With Data', *New York Times*, 17 December 2007.

p. 49: **As William Davies points out . . .** William Davies, *The Happiness Industry*, Verso: London and New York, 2015, pp. 241–243 and 253.

p. 50: **This was an example . . .** Declan McCullagh, 'Knifing the Baby', *Wired*, 5 November 1998; Bruce Sterling, *The Epic Struggle of the Internet of Things*, Strelka Press: Moscow, 2014, Kindle Loc. 200.

p. 51: **Drug use . . .** Bruce Alexander & Anton Schweighofer, 'Defining "addiction"', *Canadian Psychology* Vol. 29, No. 2:151–162 April 1988.

p. 51: **The model for research . . .** Kimberly S Young, *Caught in the Net: How to Recognise the Signs of Internet Addiction – and a Winning Strategy for Recovery*, John Wiley & Sons: New York, 1998; see also the website for Young's Center for Internet Addiction <www.netaddiction.com>.

p. 52: **Facebook's founding president . . .** Olivia Solon, 'Ex-Facebook president Sean Parker: site made to exploit human "vulnerability"', *Guardian*, 9 November 2017.

p. 52: **The anthropologist Natasha Dow Schüll . . .** Mattha Busby, 'Social media copies gambling methods "to create psychological cravings"', *Guardian*, 8 May 2018; see also Natasha Dow Schüll, *Addiction by Design: Machine Gambling in Las Vegas*, Princeton University Press: Princeton, NJ, 2014.

p. 52: **Nora Volkow . . .** Abigail Zuger, 'A General in the Drug War', *New York Times*, 13 June 2011.

p. 53: **Adam Alter . . .** Adam Alter, *Irresistible: The Rise of Addictive Technology and the Business of Keeping Us Hooked*, Penguin: New York, 2017.

p. 53: **. . . a 2013 study . . .** Joanna Stern, 'Cellphone Users Check Phones 150x/Day and Other Internet Fun Facts', ABC News, 29 May 2013.

p. 53: **One recent survey . . .** '1 in 10 of us check our smartphones during sex – seriously', *Daily Telegraph*, 13 May 2016.

p. 53: **In his book . . .** Marc Lewis, *The Biology of Desire: Why Addiction is Not a Disease*, Scribe: London, 2015.

p. 54: **Thomas De Quincey's . . .** Thomas De Quincey, *Confessions of an English Opium-Eater and Other Writings*, Oxford University Press: Oxford, 2013.

p. 54: **When the Catholic mystic . . .** Francis Thomson, 'The Poppy', *Selected Poems of Francis Thomson*, Amazon Edition.

p. 55: **Technology has never . . .** The psychoanalyst Sherry Turkle is insightful on this. See *Alone Together: Why We Expect More From Technology and Less From Each Other*, Basic Books: New York, 2011.

p. 55: **This is how the telecommunications firm . . .** This commercial, known as 'Anthem', is widely quoted. For a useful analysis, see Lisa Nakamura, '"Where Do You Want To Go Today?": Cybernetic tourism, the Internet, and transnationality,' in Nicolas Mirzoeff, *The Visual Culture Reader*, Routledge: London and New York, 2002.

p. 55: **Facebook's first video advertisement . . .** Sadly the ad is no longer available. It is described in detail by Tim Nudd, 'Ad of the Day: Facebook', *Adweek*, 4 October 2012.

p. 55: **But as the cyberpunk writer . . .** Bruce Sterling, quoted in Virginia Heffernan, *Magic and Loss: The Internet as Art*, Simon & Schuster: New York, 2017, p. 25.

p. 56: **What Bruce Alexander calls . . .** Bruce Alexander, *The Globalization of Addiction: A Study in Poverty of the Spirit*, Oxford University Press: Oxford, 2011.

p. 56: **. . . 'uniform distancelessness' . . .** Christopher Bollas, *Meaning and Melancholia: Life in the Age of Bewilderment*, Routledge: London and New York, 2018, p. 49.

p. 56: **We prefer the machine . . .** Sherry Turkle's research finds a surprisingly large constituency of people who would prefer a robot as a romantic or sexual partner, because they wouldn't come with the oddities that human partners bring. *Alone Together: Why We Expect More From Technology and Less From Each Other*, Basic Books: New York, 2011.

p. 56: **First, a sharp decline . . . The decline in violence is linked to a general decline in all sorts of crime since the mid-1990s.** For an overview of some of the evidence, see A. Tseloni, J. Mailley, G. Farrell, & N. Tilley, 'Exploring the international decline in crime rates', European Journal of Criminology, 7(5), 2010, pp. 375–394; and Jan van Dijk, A. Tseloni and G. Farrell, *The International Crime Drop: New Directions in Research*, Palgrave Macmillan, 2012. Despite efforts to link the crime drop to improved property security or changes in policing tactics, it is so sustained and general as to elude that type of explanation. It is indicative of a deeper social threshold having been reached.

p. 56: **. . . a decline, almost a crash, in rates of alcohol and nicotine consumption . . .** See, for example, 'Under-25s turning their backs on alcohol, study suggests', BBC News, 10 October 2018; Linda Ng Fat, Nicola Shelton and Noriko Cable, 'Investigating the growing trend of non-drinking among young people; analysis of repeated cross-sectional surveys in England 2005–2015', *BMC Public Health*, 18 (1), 2018; Sara Miller Llana, 'Culture shift: What's behind a decline in drinking worldwide', *Christian Science Monitor*, 3 October 2018; Denis Campbell, 'Number of smokers in England drops to all-time low', *Guardian*, 20 September 2016; 'Adult smoking habits in the UK: 2017', Office for National Statistics, 3 July 2018; 'Why young people are now less likely to smoke', BBC News, 7 March 2017; Frank Newport, 'Young People Adopt Vaping as Their Smoking Rate Plummets', Gallup, 26 July 2018.

p. 56: **Analysis of American . . .** Jean Twenge, *iGen - Why Today's Super-Connected Kids Are Growing Up Less Rebellious, More Tolerant, Less Happy – And Completely Unprepared For Adulthood*, Atria Books: New York, 2017.

p. 57: **It is no accident . . .** Darian Leader, *Hands: What We Do With Them – And Why*, Penguin Random House: London, 2016, Kindle Loc. 686.

p. 57: **. . . 'post-scarcity' . . .** for one version of this fashionable theory, see Jeremy Rifkin, 'The Rise of Anti-Capitalism', *New York Times*, 15 March 2014.

p. 57: **The literary critic Raymond Williams . . .** Raymond Williams, *Television: Technology and Cultural Form*, Routledge: London and New York, 2003, pp. 19–21.

p. 57: **The psychoanalyst Colette Soler . . .** Colette Soler, *Lacan: The Unconscious Revisited*, Karnac Books: London, 2014, Kindle Loc. 3239.

p. 58: **In an arresting image . . .** Marcus Gilroy-Ware, *Filling the Void: Emotion, Capitalism and Social Media*, Repeater Books: London, 2017, Kindle Loc. 610.

p. 58: **. . . rules which English philosopher Thomas Hobbes, in a pregnant metaphor, compared to the 'laws of gaming'.** Thomas Hobbes, *Leviathan*, Oxford University Press: Oxford and New York, 1998, p. 230.

p. 59: **B. F. Skinner was not . . .** Daniel W. Bjork, 'B. F. Skinner and the American Tradition: The Scientist as Social Inventor', in Daniel W. Bjork, Laurence D. Smith and William R. Woodward, eds., *B. F. Skinner and Behaviorism in American Culture*, Lehigh University Press: London, 1996; Daniel N. Wiener, *B. F. Skinner: Benign Anarchist*, Allyn & Bacon: Boston, MA, 1996.

p. 59: **The behavioural scientists . . .** Kaya Tolon, 'Future Studies: A New Social Science Rooted in Cold War Strategic Thinking', in Mark Solovey and Hamilton Cravens, *Cold War Social Science: Knowledge Production, Liberal Democracy, and Human Nature*, Palgrave Macmillan: New York, 2012; see also Robert L. Solso, *Mind and Brain Sciences in the 21st Century*, MIT Press: Cambridge, MA, 1999.

p. 59: **The programme was surprisingly successful . . .** On 'Project Pigeon', see C.V. Glines, 'Top Secret WWII Bat and Bird Bomber Program', *Aviation History*, May 2005; and James H. Capshew, 'Engineering Behaviour: Project Pigeon, World War II, and the Conditioning of B. F. Skinner', in Laurence D. Smith and William R. Woodward, eds., *B. F. Skinner and Behaviorism in American Culture*, Lehigh University Press: London, 1996.

p. 59: **In *Science and Human Behavior* . . .** B. F. Skinner, *Science and Human Behavior*, The Free Press: New York, 2012.

p. 60: **As long as he had the means . . .** Here is the rub. As William Davies argues, the plausibility of such agnosticism is only plausible as long as the agnostic 'is privy to huge surveillance capacities'. William Davies, *The Happiness Industry*, Verso: London and New York, 2015, p. 254.

p. 60: **This was first fully outlined . . .** B. F. Skinner, *Walden Two*, Hackett Publishing Company Inc.: Indianapolis, IN, 2005.

p. 61: **They have to give up and mourn . . .** For arguments along these lines, see Marshall Wise Alcorn Jr., *Resistance to Learning: Overcoming the Desire Not to Know in Classroom Teaching*, Palgrave Macmillan, 2013; K Daniel Cho, *Psychopedagogy: Freud, Lacan, and the Psychoanalytic Theory of Education*, Palgrave Macmillan, 2009; Stephen Appel, ed., *Psychoanalysis and Pedagogy*, Bergin & Garvey: Westport, CT, 1999.

p. 61: **Perhaps it is no coincidence . . .** Byung-Chul Han, *Saving Beauty*, Polity Press: Cambridge, 2018.

p. 61: **A small number of real-world . . .** Richard Feallock and L. Keith Miller, 'The

Design and Evaluation of a Worksharing System for Experimental Group Living', *Journal of Applied Behavior Analysis*, Vol. 9, No. 3, 1976, pp. 277–288; Kathleen Kinkade, *A Walden Two Experiment: The first five years of Twin Oaks Community*, William Morrow, 1973; Hilke Kuhlmann, *Living Walden Two: B. F. Skinner's Behaviorist Utopia and Experimental Communities*, University of Illinois Press: Champaign, IL, 2010.

p. 62: **This belief was . . .** Henry L. Roediger, 'What Happened to Behaviorism', Association for Psychological Science, 1 March 2004; Richard F. Thompson, 'Behaviorism and Neuroscience', *Psychological Review*, Vol. 101, No. 2, April 1994, pp. 259–65. The significance of the behaviourist infiltration of neuroscience and psychology can hardly be overstated. The prestige of neuroscience in particular, thanks to great advances made in the 1990s, became phenomenal. There were some interesting efforts at producing a new synthesis, for example by fusing neuroscience and psychoanalysis. Eric R. Kandel, Psychiatry, *Psychoanalysis, and the New Biology of Mind*, American Psychiatric Publishing, Inc.: Arlington, VA, 2005. But the more general pattern was a misleading and ideologically charged reductionism, in which social stereotypes were given ostensible scientific validity. See Cordelia Fine, *Delusions of Gender: The Real Science Behind Sex Differences*, Icon Books, London: 2005. Moreover, it tended to corroborate the strategies of authority, by reducing human behaviour to brain behaviour, thus making it more eminently governable. See Suparna Choudhury and Jan Slaby, eds., *Critical Neuroscience: A Handbook of the Social and Cultural Contexts of Neuroscience*, Wiley-Blackwell, Oxford: 2016; and Nikolas Rose, *Neuro: The New Brain Sciences and the Management of the Mind*, Princeton University Press: Princeton, NJ, 2013.

p. 62: **Nir Eyal . . .** Nir Eyal, *Hooked: How to Build Habit-Forming Products*, Penguin: New York, 2004.

p. 62: **Strikingly . . .** Laura Entis, 'How the "Hook Model" Can Turn Customers Into Addicts', *Fortune*, 11 June 2017.

p. 62: **We are digital 'serfs' . . .** Jaron Lanier, *You Are Not A Gadget: A Manifesto*, Alfred A. Knopf: New York, 2010, p. 117; Bruce Sterling, *The Epic Struggle of the Internet of Things*, Strelka Press: Moscow, 2014, Kindle Loc. 32.

p. 63: **Every time we fill . . .** Moshe Z. Marvit, 'How Crowdworkers Became the Ghosts in the Digital Machine', *The Nation*, 5 February 2014.

p. 63: **From the point of view of freedom, says Shoshana Zuboff . . .** Shoshana Zuboff, 'Big Other: surveillance capitalism and the prospects of an information civilisation', Journal of Information Technology, 2015, No. 30, pp. 75–89; Shoshana Zuboff, *The Age of Surveillance Capitalism: The Fight for a Human Future at the New Frontier of Power*, Profile Books, 2019.

p. 63: **Ludwig Börne . . .** Quoted in Walter Benjamin, *The Arcades Project*, Harvard University Press: Cambridge, MA: 1999, p. 514.

p. 63: **Tristan Harris . . .** Tristan Harris, 'The Slot Machine in Your Pocket', *Der Spiegel*, 27 July 2016.

p. 64: **Adam Alter adds . . .** 'Users were gambling every time they shared a photo, web link, or status update.' Adam Alter, *Irresistible: The Rise of Addictive Technology and the Business of Keeping Us Hooked*, Penguin: New York, 2017, p. 118; Schüll quoted in Mattha Busby, 'Social media copies gambling methods "to create psychological cravings"', *Guardian*, 8 May 2018.

p. 64: **When we're on the machine . . .** Natasha Dow Schüll, *Addiction by Design:*

Machine Gambling in Las Vegas, Princeton University Press: Princeton, NJ, 2014, pp. 18–32.

p. 64: **Some gambling-machine addicts . . .** Natasha Dow Schüll, *Addiction by Design: Machine Gambling in Las Vegas*, Princeton University Press: Princeton, NJ, 2014, p. 33.

p. 64: **As one former gambling addict . . .** Quoted in Jim Orford, *An Unsafe Bet?: The Dangerous Rise of Gambling and the Debate We Should Be Having*, Wiley-Blackwell: London, 2010, p. 58.

p. 64: **Schüll calls it the 'machine zone' . . .** Natasha Dow Schüll, *Addiction by Design: Machine Gambling in Las Vegas*, Princeton University Press: Princeton, NJ, 2014, p. 34.

p. 65: **Marc Lewis describes . . .** Marc Lewis, *Memoirs of An Addicted Brain: A Neuroscientist Examines His Former Life on Drugs*, Public Affairs: New York, 2011, p. 295.

p. 65: **For gamblers . . .** 'Such intoxication depends on the peculiar capacity of the game to provoke presence of mind through the fact that, in rapid succession, it brings to the force constellations which work . . . to summon up in every instance a thoroughly new type of reaction from the gambler. The fact is mirrored in the tendency of gamblers to place their bets, whenever possible, at the very last moment – the moment, moreover, when only enough room remains for a purely reflexive move.' Walter Benjamin, *The Arcades Project*, Harvard University Press: Cambridge, MA, 1999, pp. 512–513.

p. 65: **The ensuing trance-like state . . .** David Berry, *Critical Theory and the Digital*, Bloomsbury: New York, 2014, p. 80.

p. 65: **Whereas gambling was controlled . . .** Jim Orford, *An Unsafe Bet?: The Dangerous Rise of Gambling and the Debate We Should Be Having*, Wiley-Blackwell: London, 2010, pp. 3–44.

p. 66: **As the late literary scholar . . .** Bettina L. Knapp, *Gambling, Game and Psyche*, SUNY Press: Abany, NY, 2000. Similar references to gambling as a divine, or divinatory, practice pepper James George Frazer's classic, *The Golden Bough*, Heritage Illustrated Publishing: New York, 2014.

p. 67: **Repetition is then . . .** See, for examples of this very pervasive argument, G F Koob, 'Negative reinforcement in drug addiction: the darkness within', *Current Opinion in Neurobiology*, 23(4), August 2013, pp. 559–63; Marc J Lewis, 'Alcohol: mechanisms of addiction and reinforcement', *Advances in Alcohol and Substance Abuse*, 9(1–2), 1990, pp. 47–66.

p. 67: **A study of 'internet addiction' . . .** Phil Reed, Michela Romano, Federica Re, Alessandra Roaro, Lisa A. Osborne, Caterina Viganò & Roberto Truzoli, 'Differential physiological changes following internet exposure in higher and lower problematic internet users', *PLOS ONE*, 25 May 2017.

p. 67: **According to the neuroscientist . . .** Robert Sapolsky, 'Dopamine Jackpot! Sapolsky on the Science of Pleasure', 2 March 2011, lecture available on <www.youtube.com>.

p.67: **Dopamine, as the anthropologist Helen Fisher puts it . . .** Helen Fisher, *Anatomy of Love: A Natural History of Mating, Marriage, and Why We Stray*, W. W. Norton & Company: New York and London, 2016, p. 95.

p. 67: **The psychologist Stanton Peele . . .** Stanton Peele and Archie Brodsky, *Love and Addiction*, Broadrow Publications, New York, 2014.

p. 68: **Addicts who quit . . .** Marc Lewis, *The Biology of Desire: Why Addiction is Not a Disease*, Scribe: London, 2015, p. 59.

p. 68: **And it suggests . . .** Jeffrey A Schaler, *Addiction is a Choice*, Open Court: Chicago & Lasalle, 2009, pp. xiii–xiv.

p. 69: **It breaks up our day . . .** Adam Greenfield, *Radical Technologies*, Verso: London and New York, 2017, p. 36.

p. 69: **What we refer to . . .** For an excellent dissection of 'cloud' ideology, see Tung-hui Hu, *A Prehistory of the Cloud*, MIT Press: Cambridge, MA, 2015.

p. 69: **. . . 'everyware' . . .** Greenfield wrote of this trend long before the ubiquitous ownership of smartphones and similar devices. Adam Greenfield, *Everyware: The Dawning Age of Ubiquitous Computing*, New Riders: Berkeley, CA, 2006.

p. 70: **. . . Google's 'smart city' . . .** Ava Kaufman, 'Google's "Smart City Of Surveillance" Faces New Resistance In Toronto', *The Intercept*, 13 November 2018; Nancy Scola, 'Google Is Building a City of the Future in Toronto. Would Anyone Want to Live There?', Politico, July/August 2018.

p. 70: **It closely resembles . . .** Gilles Deleuze, 'Postscript on the Societies of Control', *October*, Vol. 59 (Winter, 1992), pp. 3–7.

p. 70: **As Donna Haraway once wrote . . .** 'Why should our bodies end at the skin, or include at best other beings encapsulated by skin?' Donna Haraway, *A Cyborg Manifesto: Science, Technology and Socialist-Feminism in the Late Twentieth Century*, University of Minnesota Press: Minneapolis, MN, 2016, p. 61.

p. 71: **So what happens if bits of us . . .** Brian Rotman, *Becoming Beside Ourselves: The Alphabet, Ghosts, and Distributed Human Being*, Duke University Press: Raleigh, NC, 2008.

p. 71: **. . . Lydia Liu argues . . .** Lydia H. Liu, *The Freudian Robot: Digital Media and the Future of the Unconscious*, University of Chicago Press: Chicago, MI, 2011, Kindle Loc. 227.

p. 71: **The drug addicts . . .** Bruce Alexander, *The Globalization of Addiction: A Study in Poverty of the Spirit*, Oxford University Press: Oxford: 2011, Kindle Loc. 281.

p. 71: **If their bet poses a question about destiny . . .** Rik Loose, *The Subject of Addiction: Psychoanalysis and the Administration of Enjoyment*, Karnac Books: London, 2002, p. 157.

p. 72: **Patrick Garratt wrote . . .** Patrick Garratt, 'My Life as a Twitter Addict, and Why it's More Difficult to Quit Than Drugs', *Huffington Post*, 29 April 2012.

p. 72: **Social media addiction has been linked . . .** Jaron Lanier breezily sums up this research in chapter seven of *Ten Arguments for Deleting Your Social Media Accounts Right Now*, Penguin Random House: London, 2018. On the link with teen suicides, see 'Social media may play a role in the rise in teen suicides, study suggests', CBS News, 14 November 2017; and J. M. Twenge, T. E. Joiner, M. L. Rogers & G. N. Martin, 'Increases in Depressive Symptoms, Suicide-Related Outcomes, and Suicide Rates Among U.S. Adolescents After 2010 and Links to Increased New Media Screen Time', *Clinical Psychological Science*, 6(1), 2018, pp. 3–17. For Facebook's reaction, see Sam Levin, 'Facebook admits it poses mental health risk – but says using site more can help', *Guardian*, 15 December 2017.

p. 72: **The dominant view . . .** Allen Carr, *The Easy Way to Stop Gambling: Take Control of Your Life*, Arcturus, 2013. Alas, the Allen Carr estate has yet to enlighten us as to the 'Easy Way' to stop social media addiction.

p. 73: **. . . Mary Beard . . .** Mary Beard, 'Of course one can't condone . . . ', Twitter.com, 16 February 2018. For a critique of Beard's stance, see Sita Balani, 'Virtue and Violence', Verso.com, 23 March 2018.

p. 74: **She ended the day . . .** Roisin O'Connor, 'Mary Beard posts tearful picture of herself after defence of Oxfam aid workers provokes backlash', *Independent*, 18 February 2018.

p. 75: . . . **'carrot and shtick'** . . . Jaron Lanier, *Ten Arguments for Deleting Your Social Media Accounts Right Now*, Penguin Random House: London, 2018, p. 9.

p. 75: . . . **Paracelsus** . . . See chapter twelve of Hugh Crone, *Paracelsus: The Man Who Defied Medicine*, The Albarello Press: Melbourne, 2004.

p. 75: **As Rik Loose** . . . Rik Loose, *The Subject of Addiction: Psychoanalysis and the Administration of Enjoyment*, Karnac Books: London, 2002, p. 117.

p. 76: **For the duration of our visit** . . . Virginia Heffernan describes this beautifully in chapter one of *Magic and Loss: The Internet as Art*, Simon & Schuster: New York, 2017.

p. 76: **As the sociologist Benjamin Bratton** . . . Benjamin H. Bratton, *The Stack: On Software and Sovereignty*, Massachusetts Institute of Technology: Cambridge, MA, 2015, p. 47.

p. 76: **To locate it** . . . Sigmund Freud, 'Beyond the Pleasure Principle', in *Complete Psychological Works Of Sigmund Freud*, Vol. 18, Vintage Classics: London, 2001.

CHAPTER THREE

p. 79: **She told them: just wait, you'll see, you'll understand** Lilia Blaise and Benoît Morenne, 'Suicide on Periscope Prompts French Officials to Open Inquiry', *New York Times*, 11 May 2016; 'Suicide sur Periscope: Océane "avait fait part de ses intentions suicidaires"', L'Express, 13 May 2016; Jérémie Pham-Lê and Claire Hache, 'Suicide d'Océane sur Periscope: "Elle m'avait dit que son ex avait abusé d'elle"', L'Express, 12 May 2016. Rana Dasgupta, 'Notes on a Sucide', *Granta* 140: State of Mind, August 2017.

p. 79: **Obviously it's going to slam into a wall** . . . Lucy Williamson, 'French Periscope death stirs social media safety fears', BBC News, 13 May 2016.

p. 80: **Freud, in 'Mourning and Melancholia', argues that** . . . Or, as Jacqueline Rose put it: 'All suicides kill other people'. Sigmund Freud, 'Mourning and Melancholia', in *On Murder, Mourning and Melancholia*, Penguin: London, 2005.

p. 80: **In the act of suicide, Lacan said** . . . Jacques Lacan, *Formations of the Unconscious: Book 5, The Seminar of Jacques Lacan*, Polity Press: Cambridge, 2017, p. 228.

p. 80: **Rana Dasgupta, in a powerful essay about** . . . Dasgupta, 'Notes on a Suicide', *Granta* 140.

p. 80: **By now, thanks in part to Kenneth Anger's classic account of Hollywood. . .** Kenneth Anger, *Hollywood Babylon: The Legendary Underground Classic of Hollywood's Darkest and Best Kept Secrets*, Bantam Doubleday Dell Publishing Group, 1983.

p. 80: **Research finds that suicide among celebrities** . . . Dianna T. Kenny and Anthony Asher, 'Life expectancy and cause of death in popular musicians', *Medical Problems of Performing Artists*, 3(1), March 2016, pp. 37–44; David Lester, 'Suicide in Eminent Persons', Perceptual and Motor Skills, 87(1), 1998, pp. 90–90. Kenny's findings are particular to popular musicians, but suggest a rate of suicide anywhere between three and seven times that of the general population. Lester's study of 'eminent persons' finds a suicide rate of 3 per cent, well above that for the general population, when the global mortality rate for suicide is 16 per hundred thousand.

p. 81: **as media critic Jay Rosen calls us** . . . Jay Rosen, 'The People Formerly Known as the Audience', *PressThink* (www.pressthink.org), 27 June 2006.

p. 81: **Writing before the advent of social media, Jonathan Crary** . . . Jonathan Crary, *Suspensions of Perception: Attention, Spectacle, and Modern Culture*, MIT Press: Cambridge, MA, 2001.

p. 81: **Autoplay means that audiovisual parts of your feed** . . . Georges Abi-Heila,

'Attention hacking is the epidemic of our generation', *UX Collective* (www.uxdesign.cc), 1 March 2018.

p. 81: **The ideological power of our interactions with . . .** Alfie Bown, *The Playstation Dreamworld (Theory Redux)*, Polity Press: Cambridge, 2017.

p. 81: **Neuroscientists tell us that, physically, the brain cannot focus . . .** John Medina, *Brain Rules: 12 Principles for Surviving and Thriving at Work*, Home, and School, Pear Press: Seattle, WA, 2014; Eyal Ophir, Clifford Nass and Anthony D. Wagner, 'Cognitive Control in Media Multitaskers', Proceedings of the National Academy of Sciences, Vol. 106, No. 37, 2009, pp. 15583–15587.

p. 82: **It can take over half an hour to recover . . .** Rachel Emma Silverman, 'Workplace Distractions: Here's Why You Won't Finish This Article', *Wall Street Journal*, 11 December 2012; Bob Sullivan and Hugh Thompson, 'Brain, Interrupted', *New York Times*, 5 May 2013; There is some research that suggests interruptions make people work faster, but at the cost of increased stress. Gloria Mark, Daniel Gudith and Ulrich Klocke, 'The Cost of Interrupted Work: More Speed and Stress', Proceedings of the SIGCHI Conference on Human Factors in Computing Systems, Florence, Italy, 5–10 April 2008, pp. 107–10.

p. 82: **The psychoanalyst Adam Phillips speaks of . . .** See Adam Phillips, 'On Vacancies of Attention', Provoking Attention conference, Brown University, May 2017 (www.youtube.com); and 'Forms of Inattention', in *On Balance*, Penguin: London and New York, 2010.

p. 82: **. . . according to historian Daniel Boorstin,** Daniel J. Boorstin, *The Image: A Guide to Pseudo-events in America*, Vintage Books: New York, 1992, p. 136.

p. 82: **Celebrity, detached from any context beyond itself . . .** Leo Braudy, *The Frenzy of Renown: Fame and its History*, Vintage Books, New York: 1986, p. 554.

p. 83: **For example, the *Guardian* reports that to become a 'micro-influencer' . . .** Leah McLaren, 'What would you do if your teenager became an overnight Instagram sensation?', *Guardian*, 22 July 2018; Emma Lunn, 'Putting you in the picture: yes, you can earn a living on Instagram', *Guardian*, 5 May 2017; Richard Godwin, 'The rise of the nano-influencer: how brands are turning to common people', *Guardian*, 14 November 2018.

p. 83: **The vast majority of people don't have . . .** The average number of followers/friends for Facebook, Twitter and Instagram is, respectively: 155, 707, 150. Sarah Knapton, 'Facebook users have 155 friends – but would trust just four in a crisis', *Daily Telegraph*, 20 January 2016; 'The Average Twitter User Now has 707 Followers', *KickFactory* (www.kickfactory.com), 23 June 2016; 'What Your Follower/Following Ratio Say About Your Instagram Account', WorkMacro (www.workmacro.com), 12 March 2018.

p. 83: **For example, Michelle Dobyne of Oklahoma . . .** Mark Molloy, 'Woman gives incredible interview after escaping house fire', *Daily Telegraph*, 12 January 2016; Dave Schilling, 'Viral video news memes bring fame – but still feel almost racist', *Guardian*, 14 January 2016; Zeba Blay, 'Why do we laugh at viral stars like Michelle Dobyne and Antoine Dodson?', *Huffington Post*, 16 January 2016. For a thorough discussion of this case, see Crystal Abidin, Internet Celebrity: Understanding Fame Online, Emerald Publishing: Bingley, 2018, pp. 38–41.

p. 83: **The anthropologist Hortense Powdermaker . . .** Hortense Powdermaker, Hollywood, the Dream Factory: An Anthropologist Looks at the Movie-Makers, Little Brown & Company: Boston, 2013, pp. 40–41, 93–8.

p. 84: **In 2015, the Instagram model Essena O'Neill . . .** Elle Hunt, 'Essena O'Neill quits Instagram claiming social media "is not real life"', *Guardian*, 3 November 2015; Madison Malone Kircher, 'Where Are You, Essena O'Neill?', New York, 4 November 2016.

p. 84: **Donna Freitas' research into young social media users . .** Donna Freitas, *The Happiness Effect: How Social Media is Driving a Generation to Appear Perfect at Any Cost*, Oxford University Press: New York, 2017, pp. 61–4.

p. 85: **If celebrities often spiral into public displays of self-degradation . . .** Chris Rojek, *Celebrity*, Reaktion Books: London, 2001, p. 11.

p. 85: **What hooks us is also what kills us . . .** Nadeem Badshah, 'Hospital admissions for teenage girls who self-harm nearly double', *Guardian*, 6 August 2018; Denis Campbell, 'Stress and social media fuel mental health crisis among girls', *Guardian*, 23 September 2017; J. M. Twenge, T. E. Joiner, M. L. Rogers and G. N. Martin, 'Increases in Depressive Symptoms, Suicide-Related Outcomes, and Suicide Rates Among U.S. Adolescents After 2010 and Links to Increased New Media Screen Time', *Clinical Psychological Science*, 6(1), 2018, pp. 3–17; 'Media Use, Face-to-Face Communication, Media Multitasking, and Social Well-Being Among 8- to 12-Year-Old Girls', *Developmental Psychology*, 48(2), March 2012, pp. 327–36; L. E. Sherman, A. A. Payton, L. M. Hernandez, P. M. Greenfield and M. Dapretto, 'The Power of the Like in Adolescence: Effects of Peer Influence on Neural and Behavioral Responses to Social Media', *Psychological Science*, 27(7), 2016, pp. 1027–1035. Benjamin Fong argues that these effects are good reason for progressives to quit. Benjamin Y. Fong, 'Log Off', Jacobin, 29 November 2018. For a sceptical review of such analyses, see Tom Chivers, 'The truth about the suspected link between social media and self-harm', *New Scientist*, 6 August 2018. As regards the tendency to compare ourselves with those above us in the social hierarchy, see Oliver James, *Britain On the Couch: How keeping up with the Joneses has depressed us since 1950*, Vermilion: Reading, 2010.

p. 85: **As Alain Ehrenberg put it . . .** Alain Ehrenberg, *The Weariness of the Self: Diagnosing the History of Depression in the Contemporary Age*, McGill-Queen's University Press: Montreal and Kingston, 2010, p. 4.

p. 85: **And revenues for social industry firms began to take off . . .** 'Twitter's revenue from 1st quarter 2011 to 3rd quarter 2018 (in million U.S. dollars)', *Statista*, 2019 (www.statista.com); Facebook's 'initial public offering' of shares was made in May 2012, reaching a peak market value of $104 billion. See Warren Olney, 'Facebook IPO: A Touchstone Cultural Moment for America?', To the Point, KCRW.com, 17 May 2012.

p. 86: **A Stasi for the Angry Birds generation' . . .** *Stewart Lee's Comedy Vehicle*, BBC Two, Series 3, Episode One, available on www.youtube.com, 24 February 2014.

p. 86: **Through years of 'invading people's privacy' . . .** Dan Sabbagh, 'Paul McMullan lays bare newspaper dark arts at Leveson inquiry', *Guardian*, 29 November 2011.

p. 87: **Morgan was an associate of Rees . . .** See Tom Watson and Martin Hickman, *Dial M for Murdoch: News Corporation and the Corruption of Britain*, Allen Lane: London, 2012; Nick Davies, *Hack Attack: How the truth caught up with Rupert Murdoch*, Vintage, London, 2015; and Alastair Morgan and Peter Jukes, *Who Killed Daniel Morgan?: Britain's Most Investigated Murder*, Blink Publishing: London, 2017; Cahal Milno, Jonathan Brown and Matt Blake, 'Beyond the law, private eyes who do the dirty work for journalists', *Independent*, 13 July 2011.

p. 87: **The reporter, having been read Lewis's suicide note at the inquest . . .** On both Stronge and Lewis, see Peter Burden, *News of the World?: Fake Sheikhs and Royal Trappings*, Eye Books Ltd: London, 2009.

p. 88: **The rising profile of 'celebrity worship syndrome'. . .** Randy A. Sansone and Lori A. Sansone, '"I'm Your Number One Fan" – A Clinical Look at Celebrity Worship', *Innovations in Clinical Neuroscience*, 11(1-2), January/February 2014, pp. 39–43.

p. 88: **Newspapers, working to the woke dollar . . .** Examples of which include: Maya Salam, 'Why "Radical Body" Live' is Thriving on Instagram', *New York Times*, 9 June 2017; Jess Commons, '15 incredible body positive people to follow on Instagram', *Evening Standard*, 11 May 2017.

p. 89: **The traditional celebrities who adapt best to the medium . . .** Alice Marwick and danah boyd, 'To See and Be Seen: Celebrity Practice on Twitter', *Convergence: The International Journal of Research into New Media Technologies*, 17(2), 2011, pp. 139–58; Alice Marwick, Status *Update: Celebrity, Publicity, and Branding in the Social Media Age*, Yale University Press: New Haven and London, 2013.

p. 89: **By 2015, social advertising . . .** Chris Horton, 'Is Social Advertising Subverting Social Media Marketing?', *Business 2 Community* (www.business2community.com), 2 May 2015.

p. 90: **It had proven wildly profitable . . .** Madeleine Berg, 'Logan Paul May Have Been Dropped By YouTube, But He'll Still Make Millions', *Forbes*, 11 January 2018; Gavin Fernando, 'How Logan Paul went from one of the world's most famous YouTube stars to universally hated', News.com.au, 3 November 2018.

p. 91: **Fellow YouTuber Japanese-American internet . . .** Reina Scully, 'I have a lot of intense feelings', Twitter.com, 1 January 2018.

p. 91: **Paul, being a savvy entrepreneur . . .** James Vincent, 'YouTuber Logan Paul apologizes for filming suicide victim, says "I didn't do it for views"', *The Verge*, 2 January 2018.

p. 91: **Katelyn Nicole Davis, a twelve-year-old from Georgia . . .** Shehab Khan, 'Man dies after setting himself on fire during Facebook Live stream', *Independent*, 15 May 2017; Travis M. Andrews, 'Turkish man, 22, fatally shoots himself on Facebook Live', *Washington Post*, 13 October 2016; Carol Marbin Miller and Audra D. S. Birch, 'Before suicide by hanging, girl pleaded in vain for mom's acceptance', *Miami Herald*, 15 March 2017; Kristine Phillips, 'A 12-year-old girl live-streamed her suicide. It took two weeks for Facebook to take the video down', *Washington Post*, 27 January 2017.

p. 92: **Desperate faces, on the brink of desperate acts . . .** Béla Bálazs, *Theory of the Film: Character and Growth of a New Art*, Denis Dobson Ltd: London, 1952, pp. 62–3.

p. 92: **What if Conrad's 'demon of perverse inspiration' . . .** Joseph Conrad, *The Secret Agent, in Joseph Conrad: The Dover Reader*, Dover Publications, Inc.: Mineola, NY, 2014, p. 439.

p. 92: **In 2017, for example, a young woman from Ohio . . .** Rob Crilly, 'Teenager accused of live-streaming rape got "caught up in the likes"', *Daily Telegraph*, 18 April 2016; Tyler Kingkade, 'Why Would Anyone Film A Rape And Not Try To Stop It?', *Huffington Post*, 21 April 2016.

p. 92: **According to the prosecutor, Lonina told police . . .** Jill Bauer and Ronna Gradus, *Hot Girls Wanted: Turned On, 'Don't Stop Filming'*, Season One, Episode Six, Netflix, 2017.

p. 93: **Josef Fritzel, Ted Bundy, Timothy McVeigh and Jeffrey Dahmer . . .**The erotic interest in Lonina was preceded by the fascination with Amanda Knox, who had stood trial for the murder of Meredith Kercher. In the UK, Channel 5's flagship daytime programme, *The Wright Stuff*, hosted a debate entitled, 'Foxy Knoxy: Would Ya?'

p. 93: **Daniel Boorstin called celebrity the condition of being well known . . .** Daniel J. Boorstin, *The Image: A Guide to Pseudo-events in America*, Vintage Books: New York, 1992, p. 136.

p. 93: **There is something spellbinding about . . .** 'Human attention tends to fall on objects whose forms it recognizes, under the spellbinding influence of the direction taken by the attention of others'. Yves Citton, *The Ecology of Attention*, Polity Press: Cambridge, 2017, p. 64.

p. 94:**. . . easily reproduced pieces of information, or memes . . .** Adam Clarke Estes, 'A Guide to Facebook's Announcements', *The Atlantic*, 22 September 2011.

p. 94: **The easy solution is to tell a clichéd story about what's happening . . .** Philip Elmer-Dewitt, 'On A Screen Near You', *Time*, 24 June 2001.

p. 94: **From MySpace to Snapchat, the platforms . . .** Brad Stone, 'New Scrutiny for Facebook Over Predators', *New York Times*, 30 July 2007; Bobbie Johnson, 'Wired hacker outs MySpace predators', *Guardian*, 17 October 2006; Marion A. Walker, 'MySpace removes over 90,000 sex offenders', Associated Press, 23 February 2009.

p. 94: **Complaints about narcissism are almost always . . .** Kristin Dombek, *The Selfishness of Others: An Essay on the Fear of Narcissism*, Farrar, Straus & Giroux: New York, 2016.

p. 94: **The morally charged language of the backlash . . .** Elisha Maldonado, '"Am I ugly?" YouTube trend is disturbing', *New York Post*, 27 October 2013.

p. 94: **Young people have taken 'the desire for self-admiration too far'. . .** You can like yourself just fine,' Twenge and Campbell advise youngsters in the tough-love style of Dr Phil, 'without loving yourself to excess'. Jean M. Twenge and W. Keith Campbell, *The Narcissism Epidemic: Living in the Age of Entitlement*, The Free Press: New York, 2009, p. 69.

p. 94: **A swelling library of head-shaking academic papers . . .** In addition to Twenge and Campbell, the following are examples of a common obsession: Laura E. Buffardi and W. Keith Campbell, 'Narcissism and Social Networking Web Sites', *Personality and Social Psychology Bulletin*, 34(10), 2008, pp. 1303–1314; Christopher J. Carpenter, 'Narcissism on Facebook: Self-promotional and anti-social behavior', *Personality and Individual Differences*, Vol. 52, No. 4, March 2012, pp. 482–6; Andrew L. Mendelson and Zizi Papacharissi, 'Look At Us: Collective Narcissism in College Student Facebook Photo Galleries', in Zizi Papacharissi, ed., *A Networked Self: Identity, Community and Culture on Social Network Sites*, Routledge: London and New York, 2010; Soraya Mehdizadeh, 'Self-Presentation 2.0: Narcissism and Self-Esteem on Facebook', *Cyberpsychology, Behavior, and Social Networking*, Vol. 13, No. 4, 2010; Adam O'Sullivan and Zaheer Hussain, 'An Exploratory Study of Facebook Intensity and its Links to Narcissism, Stress, and Self-esteem', *Journal of Addictive Behaviors, Therapy & Rehabilitation*, 06 (01), 2017; Agata Blachnioa, Aneta Przepiorkaa and Patrycja Rudnicka, 'Narcissism and self-esteem as predictors of dimensions of Facebook use', *Personality and Individual Differences*, Vol. 90, February 2016, pp. 296–301.

p. 94: **It fuses narcissism . . .** See Christopher Lasch on the 'narcissism of the mirror'. *The Culture of Narcissism: American Life in an Age of Diminishing Expectations*, W. W. Norton & Company: New York, 1991.

p. 94: **And we all fake it . . .** If, as Oliver Wendell Holmes said, the camera is 'a mirror with a memory', we are producing false memories on an industrial scale.

p. 95: **They reject the comforting idea . . .** Twenge and Campbell, *The Narcissism Epidemic*, pp. 65 and 71.

p. 95: **Zoe Williams worries . . .** Zoe Williams, 'Me! Me! Me! Are we living through a narcissism epidemic?', *Guardian*, 2 March 2016.

p. 95: **Jeffrey Arnett at Clark University . . .** The very trendy Implicit Association Tests, which they use to demonstrate 'unconscious' awesomeness on the part of their test subjects, have been savaged by a glut of peer-reviewed scholarship. It isn't clear that these gimmicks measure anything, let alone the unconscious. Christian Jarrett, 'Millennials are Narcissistic? The evidence is not so simple', BBC News, 17 November 2017; Jeffrey Jensen Arnett, 'The Evidence for Generation We and Against Generation Me', *Emerging Adulthood*, 1(1), 2013, pp. 5–10; E. Wetzel, A. Brown, P. L. Hill, J. M. Chung, R. W. Robins and B. W. Roberts, 'The Narcissism Epidemic Is Dead; Long Live the Narcissism Epidemic', *Psychological Science*, 28(12), 2017, pp. 1833–1847; Samantha Stronge, Petar Milojev and Chris G. Sibley, 'Are People Becoming More Entitled Over Time? Not in New Zealand', *Personality and Social Psychology Bulletin*, 44(2), 2018, pp. 200–13.

p. 95: **This is demonstrated in . . .** In 2017, amid considerable controversy, the American Psychiatric Association lifted the professional ban on members speculating on the mental health of public officials. Alessandra Potenza, 'Commenting on Trump's mental health is fine, psychiatry group says', *The Verge*, 25 July 2017. A bestselling book written by thirty-seven psychiatrists diagnosed Trump with pathological narcissism. Bandy X. Lee et al., *The Dangerous Case of Donald Trump: 37 Psychiatrists and Mental Health Experts Assess a President*, St Martin's Press: New York, 2017; the lead author of the DSM's definition of narcissistic personality disorder wrote to the *New York Times* to scold his colleagues, noting that there was no way they had sufficient information to make such a claim. Allen Frances, 'An Eminent Psychiatrist Demurs on Trump's Mental State', *New York Times*, 14 February 2017.

p. 96: **Twenge's work with 'Generation Z' . . .** Jean Twenge, *iGen: Why Today's Super-Connected Kids Are Growing Up Less Rebellious, More Tolerant, Less Happy – And Completely Unprepared for Adulthood*, Atria Books: New York, 2017.

p. 96: **But it does so using a technology that . . .** Adam Greenfield, *Radical Technologies*, Verso: London and New York, 2017, p. 45.

p. 97: **Through these, photographer Brooke Wendt suggests . . .** Brooke Wendt, *The Allure of the Selfie: Instagram and the New Self-Portrait*, Institute of Network Cultures: Amsterdam, 2014, p. 16.

p. 97: **From Toulouse-Lautrec's Self-Portrait Before a Mirror . . .** For a beautiful history of visibility and self-portraits, see Nicholas Mirzoeff, *How to See The World: An Introduction to Images, from Self-Portraits to Selfies, Maps to Movies, and More*, Basic Books: New York, 2016.

p. 97: **When Christopher Lasch diagnosed an emerging culture . . .** Lasch, *Culture of Narcissism*.

p. 98: **In our selfies we look . . .** Wendt, *The Allure of the Selfie*, p. 20.

p. 98: **It orchestrates a paradoxically distracted . . .** See Josh Cohen, *The Private Life: Why We Remain in the Dark*, Granta: London, 2013, p. 34.

p. 99: **'As if I wrote the Internet,' . . .** Sandy Baldwin, *The Internet Unconscious: On the Subject of Electronic Literature*, Bloomsbury: New York, 2015, p. 5.

p. 100: **The cultural critic Marie Moran cites . . .** Marie Moran, *Identity and Capitalism*, Sage Publications: London, 2014.
p. 101: **As soon as the infant is captivated . . .** Sigmund Freud, 'On Narcissism: An Introduction', in *Complete Psychological Works of Sigmund Freud*, Vol. 14, Vintage Classics: New York, 2001.
p. 102: **As the psychoanalyst Alessandra Lemma argues . . .** Alessandra Lemma, *The Digital Age on the Couch: Psychoanalytic Practice and New Media*, Routledge: London and New York, 2017, pp. 136–7.
p. 103: **The artist Sean Dockray's 'Facebook Suicide Bomb Manifesto' . . .** Sean Dockray, 'The Facebook Suicide Bomb Manifesto', *Wired*, 31 May 2010.
p. 103: **Facebook's own options for permanent deletion . . .** On the fate of these websites and Facebook's painstaking measures to prevent disconnections, see Tero Karppi, Disconnect: Facebook's Affective Bonds, University of Minnesota Press: Minnesota, MN, 2018; and also Tero Karppi, 'Disconnect.Me: User Engagement and Facebook', University of Turku: Turku, 2014.
p. 103: **Ironically, Snapchat's fall . . .** 'Kylie Jenner "sooo over" Snapchat – and shares tumble', BBC News, 23 February 2018; Mark Sweeney, 'Peak social media? Facebook, Twitter and Snapchat fail to make new friends', *Guardian*, 10 August 2018; Rupert Neate, 'Over $119bn wiped off Facebook's market cap after growth shock', *Guardian*, 26 July 2018.
p. 103: **Yet, 40 per cent of the world's entire population . . .** Brett Williams, 'There are now over 3 billion social media users in the world – about 40 percent of the global population', *Mashable*, 7 August 2017.
p. 104: **What would happen if . . .** Matthew Crawford, *The World Beyond Your Head: How to Flourish in an Age of Distraction*, Penguin Random House: New York, 2015, p. 13.
p. 104: **What if, as the psychoanalyst Josh Cohen proposes . . .** Cohen, *The Private Life*, Kindle loc. 127.

CHAPTER FOUR

p. 107: **In February 2011, schoolgirl Natasha MacBryde . . .** 'Natasha MacBryde: Rail death teen threatened online', BBC News, 21 July 2011; Andy Dolan, 'Coroner slams "vile" school bullies who taunted suicide girl, 15, in death', *Daily Mail*, 22 July 2011; 'Public schoolgirl fell under train after being taunted by bullies', Daily Telegraph, 15 February 2011.
p. 107: **Spotting an opportunity, a twenty-five-year-old 'RIP troll' from Reading . . .** Steven Morris, 'Internet troll jailed after mocking deaths of teenagers', *Guardian*, 13 September 2011; Paul Cassell, '"I begged for help for my sick troll son"', *Reading Post*, 7 June 2013; Rebecca Camber and Simon Neville, 'Sick internet "troll" who posted vile messages and videos taunting the death of teenagers is jailed for 18 WEEKS', *Daily Mail*, 14 December 2011; 'Sean Duffy case highlights murky world of trolling', BBC News, 13 September 2011.
p. 108: **The defence claimed that . . .** Robert Zepeda and Emily Shapiro, 'Matthew Shepard: The legacy of a gay college student 20 years after his brutal murder', ABC News, 26 October 2018.
p. 108: **Nor was Duffy's an isolated case . . .** Whitney Phillips, *This Is Why We Can't Have Nice Things: Mapping the Relationship between Online Trolling and Mainstream Culture*, MIT Press: Cambridge, MA, 2015, pp. 28–30; Kenny Rose Bradford, 'Drowned Teenager's Family Targeted By Vile Web Trolls', *Huffington Post*, 14 August

2013; Gregory Pratt, 'Cruel online posts known as RIP trolling add to Tinley Park family's grief', *Chicago Tribune*, 12 August 2013.

p. 109: **'We are a mass of vulnerabilities' . . .** Jon Ronson, *So You've Been Publicly Shamed*, Pan Macmillan: London, 2015, p. 273.

p. 109: **Whitney Phillips, author of *This Is Why We Can't Have Nice Things* . . .** Phillips, *This Is Why We Can't Have Nice Things*, pp. 27, 35, 115 and 121.

p. 109: **Their detached humour was epitomized by . . .** Phillips, *This Is Why We Can't Have Nice Things*, p. 117.

p. 110: **Most trolls are not RIP trolls . . .** Karla Mantilla, *Gendertrolling: How Misogyny Went Viral*, Praeger: Santa Barbara, CA, 2015.

p. 110: **Everyone has an inner troll . . .** Justin Cheng, Michael Bernstein, Cristian Danescu-Niculescu-Mizil and Jure Leskovec, 'Anyone Can Become a Troll: Causes of Trolling Behavior in Online Discussions', ACM Conference on Computer Supported Cooperative Work, Feb–Mar; 2017, pp. 1217–1230.

p. 110: **From the first trolls on the Arpanet 'TALK' system . . .** On the origins of trolling in the early pre-World Wide Web Arpanet system, see Jamie Bartlett, *The Dark Net: Inside the Digital Underworld*, William Heinemann: London, 2014, pp. 25–68.

p. 111: **This includes a skit by YouTuber Sam Pepper . . .** Olivia Blair, 'Sam Pepper heavily criticised for "vile" fake murder prank video', *Independent*, 30 November 2015; 'Parents reveal reason behind shocking prank videos', ABC News, 28 April 2017; Sam Levin, 'Couple who screamed at their kids in YouTube "prank" sentenced to probation', *Guardian*, 12 September 2017.

p. 111: **'Every joke', Freud wrote . . .** Sigmund Freud, *The Complete Psychological Works Of Sigmund Freud, Volume VIII: Jokes and their Relation to the Unconscious*, Vintage: London, 2001, p 151.

p. 111: **For Henri Bergson, comedy 'dreams . . . '** Henri Bergson, *Laughter: An Essay on the Meaning of Comic*, Cosimo Classics: New York, 2005, p. 1.

p. 111: **As Adam Kotsko has written . . .** Adam Kotsko, *Why We Love Sociopaths: A Guide to Late Capitalist Television*, Zero Books: Winchester, 2012.

p. 112: **Trolling, to borrow a phrase from Phillips . . .** Phillips, *This is Why We Can't Have Nice Things*, p. 53.

p. 112: **André Breton, who invented the term 'black humour' . . .** André Breton, 'Second Manifesto of Surrealism' in *Manifestoes of Surrealism*, University of Michigan Press: Ann Arbor, MI, 1969, p. 125.

p. 112: **An early guide to flaming . . .** Quoted in Bartlett, *The Dark Net*, p. 40.

p. 112: **Founder Christopher Poole ensured that . . .** David Kushner, '4chan's Overlord Christopher Poole Reveals Why He Walked Away', *Rolling Stone*, 13 March 2015.

p. 114: **Interviewed by the *New York Times* in 2008 . . .** Robert Munro, 'Craigslist troll nailed with a $75,000 judgment', *Inquirer*, 11 May 2009; Mattathias Schwartz, 'The Trolls Among Us', *New York Times*, 3 August 2008.

p. 114: **Public displays of grief are regarded as . . .** Quoted in Phillips, *This Is Why We Can't Have Nice Things*, p. 84.

p. 115: **Their mirth resembles what Hobbes called . . .** Thomas Hobbes, *Leviathan*, Routledge: London and New York, 2016, p. 34.

p. 115: **In August 2012, the Australian television host Charlotte Dawson tweeted . . .** 'Charlotte Dawson: How the cyber trolls beat me', News.com.au, 3 September 2012; Sophie Goddard, 'Charlotte Dawson commits suicide following extreme trolling',

Cosmopolitan, 24 February 2014; Nicky Park, 'Charlotte Dawson in trouble on Twitter', *New Zealand Herald*, 10 May 2012; Anna Leask, 'Charlotte Dawson's closest friends reveal her demons', *The Chronicle*, 15 March 2014.

p. 115: **From Project Chanology, wherein 4chan users targeted the Church of Scientology . . .** Patrick Barkham, 'Hackers declare war on Scientologists amid claims of heavy-handed Cruise control', *Guardian*, 4 February 2008.

p. 116: **Gabriella Coleman, basing her analysis on Lewis Hyde's classic analysis . . .** Benjamin Radford, *Bad Clowns*, University of New Mexico Press: Albuquerque, NM, 2016; Gabriella Coleman, *Hacker, Hoaxer, Whistleblower, Spy: The Many Faces of Anonymous*, Verso: London and New York, 2014.

p. 117: **When *Stranger Things* actor Millie Bobby Brown quit Twitter . . .** Alex Abad-Santos, 'The "Millie Bobby Brown is homophobic" meme is absurd, but that doesn't mean it's harmless', *Vox* (www.vox.com), 15 June 2018; Roisin O'Connor, 'Millie Bobby Brown quits Twitter after being turned into an "anti-gay" meme', the *Independent*, 14 June 2018.

p. 118: **Anti-spammer vigilantes often targeted . . .** Lisa Nakamura, '"I Will Do Everything That Am Asked": Scambaiting, Digital Show-Space, and the Racial Violence of Social Media', *Journal of Visual Culture*, 13(3), 2014, pp. 257–74; see also Lisa Nakamura, Cybertypes: Race, Ethnicity, and *Identity on the Internet*, Routledge: London and New York, 2002; and Lisa Nakamura, Digitizing Race: *Visual Cultures of the Internet*, University of Minnesota Press: Minneapolis, MN, 2007.

p. 119: **The machine is perfectly congruent with . . .** Raymond Williams, *Toward 2000*, Penguin: London, 1985.

p. 119: **They also lend themselves to a kind of hypervigilance . . .** Eve Kosofsky Sedgewick, 'Paranoid Reading and Reparative Reading, Or, You're So Paranoid, You Probably Think This Essay Is About You', in *Touching Feeling: Affect, Pedagogy, Performativity*, Duke University Press: Raleigh, NC, 2003.

p. 119: **When the irony-Nazi and celebrity troll Andrew Auernheimer, or 'weev', bombastically declared that . . .** Mattathias Schwartz, 'The Trolls Among Us', *New York Times*, 3 August 2008.

p. 120: **Trolls, in the subcultural sense . . .** On the demographic background of subcultural trolls, see Phillips, *This is Why We Can't Have Nice Things*, p. 2.

p. 120: **Their vaunted detachment performs . . .** Klaus Theweleit, *Male Fantasies, Volume 1: Women, Floods, Bodies, History*, University of Minnesota Press: Minnesota, MN, 1987.

p. 120: **As Jamie Bartlett describes . . .** Bartlett, *The Dark Net*, pp. 27–33.

p. 120: **Pew Research found . . .** Maeve Duggan, 'Part 1: Experiencing Online Harassment', *Pew Research Center*, 22 October 2014; Soraya Chemaly, 'Why women get attacked by trolls: A new study unpacks the digital gender safety gap', *Salon* (www.salon.com), 23 October 2014; *Danielle Keats Citron, Hate Crimes in Cyberspace*, Harvard University Press: Cambridge, MA, 2014, p. 14.

p. 121: **Jon Ronson mentions . . .** Ronson, *So You've Been Publicly Shamed*, p. 243.

p. 121: **In 2006, a thirty-one-year-old Neapolitan woman . . .** Stephanie Kirchgaessner, 'Tiziana Cantone: seeking justice for woman who killed herself over sex tape', *Guardian*, 13 October 2016; 'Tiziana Cantone: Suicide following years of humiliation online stuns Italy', BBC News, 16 September 2016; Rossalyn Warren, 'A Mother Wants the Internet to Forget Italy's Most Viral Sex Tape', *The Atlantic*, 16 May 2018.

p. 122: **Not only that, but the way in which social media mobs form . . .** '"Poor people don't plan long-term. We'll just get our hearts broken"', *Observer*, 21 September 2014; Michelle Goldberg, 'Linda Tirado Is Not a Hoax', *The Nation*, 11 December 2013; 'Duncan Storrar: The instant hero torn down in days', BBC News, 13 May 2016; Ruth Smith, 'Lucy Meadows was a transgender teacher who took her own life. Her story must be remembered', *Independent*, 19 November 2017.

p. 122: **The monstering of Justine Sacco . . .** Ronson, *So You've Been Publicly Shamed*, pp. 95–111.

p. 123: **'We suck at dealing with abuse and trolls on the platform,' . . .** Natasha Tiku and Casey Newton, 'Twitter CEO: "We suck at dealing with abuse"', *The Verge*, 4 February 2015.

p. 124: **The 'marketplace of ideas' . . .** Austin Carr and Harry McCracken, '"Did We Create This Monster?" How Twitter Turned Toxic', *Fast Company*, May 2018.

p. 124: **Rather than lose profitable content . . .** Carr and McCracken, '"Did We Create This Monster?"'; Will Oremus, 'Twitter's New Order', *Slate* Magazine (www.slate.com), 5 March 2017; Julia Carrie Wong, 'Twitter announces global change to algorithm in effort to tackle harassment', *Guardian*, 15 May 2018.

p. 124: **As Facebook's former chief technical officer, Ben Taylor, explained . . .** Casey Newton, 'Here's how Twitter's new algorithmic timeline is going to work', *The Verge*, 6 February 2016.

p. 124: **When Reddit was used to circulate leaked celebrity nude images . . .** Yishan Wong, 'Every Man Is Responsible For His Own Soul', Reddit blog, 6 September 2014; Adi Robertson, 'Was Reddit always about free speech? Yes, and no', *The Verge*, 15 July 2015.

p. 125: **For most of us, it is completely ineffectual . . .** Sarah Jeong, The Internet of Garbage, *Forbes*: New Jersey, NJ, 2015, pp. 69–90.

p. 125: **Nor did 'free speech' prevent Facebook from . . .** Levi Sumagaysay, 'Facebook hangs "Black Lives Matter" sign at its headquarters', SiliconBeat (www.siliconbeat.com), 9 July 2016; Sam Levin, 'Facebook temporarily blocks Black Lives Matter activist after he posts racist email', *Guardian*, 12 September 2016; Issie Lapowsky, 'It's Too Easy for Trolls to Game Twitter's Anti-Abuse Tools', *Wired*, 13 May 2016; Glenn Greenwald, 'Facebook Says It Is Deleting Accounts at the Direction of the U.S. and Israeli Governments', *The Intercept*, 30 December 2017; Russell Brandom, 'Facebook, Twitter, and Instagram surveillance tool was used to arrest Baltimore protestors', *The Verge*, 11 October 2016.

p. 126: **This meant, as Sarah Jeong pointed out . . .** Sarah Jeong, 'Turns out Facebook moderation sucks because its guidelines suck', *The Verge*, 24 April 2018.

p. 126: **Amanda Marcotte traces this to . . .** Amanda Marcotte, *Troll Nation: How the American Right Devolved Into a Clubhouse of Haters*, Hot Books Press: New York, 2018.

p. 126: **There is indeed some evidence that Russia uses trolls . . .** Thomas Ferguson, 'Paul Jorgensen, and Jie Chen, Industrial Structure and Party Competition in an Age of Hunger Games: Donald Trump and the 2016 Presidential Election', Institute for New Economic Thinking, Working Paper No. 66, January 2018.

p. 127: **The UK's Joint Threat Research Intelligence Group runs . . .** Samantha Bradshaw and Philip N. Howard, 'Troops, Trolls and Troublemakers: A Global Inventory of Organized Social Media Manipulation', Working Paper No. 2017.12 Computational Propaganda Research Project, University of Oxford, 2017; Nick Fielding and Iain Cobain, 'Revealed: US spy operation that manipulates social media', *Guardian*, 17 March 2011; Joel Gehrke, 'Pentagon, State Department launch $40 million counter-propaganda effort aimed at Russia', The *Washington Examiner*, 26 February 2018. The 'counter-propaganda' aimed at US citizens is so uncontroversial in US politics that it is openly vaunted. Nicole Gaouette, 'State Department touts counter-propaganda funds without mentioning Russia', CNN, 26 February 2018; Glenn Greenwald and Andrew Fishman, 'Controversial GCHQ Unit Engaged in Domestic Law Enforcement, Online Propaganda, Psychology Research', *The Intercept*, 22 June 2015.

p. 127: **As one activist told the *Guardian* . . .** Sanjiv Bhattacharya, '"Call me a racist, but don't say I'm a Buddhist": meet America's alt right', *Observer*, 9 October 2016.

p. 127: **More generally, trolling as a tactic of war suits the alt-right's agenda . . .** Quoted in Aja Romano, 'How the alt-right uses internet trolling to confuse you into dismissing its ideology', *Vox*, 11 January 2017.

p. 127: **They have volatilized politics, as Bruce Sterling argues . . .** Social media 'destabilizes the stately process of democratic power struggle, in much the way that, say, digital finance disrupts heavy industry. Bursts of popular viral fever appear, but very little statecraft gets accomplished. Old institutions are corroded or abandoned, yet no new ones are built.' Bruce Sterling, 'Notes on the 2106 US election', *Texte zur Kunst*, 11 November 2016.

p. 128: **He was kicked off Twitter for . . .** Elle Hunt, 'Milo Yiannopoulos, rightwing writer, permanently banned from Twitter', *Guardian*, 20 July 2016.

p. 128: **The comedian Bill Maher even invited Yiannopoulos on to his late-night chat show . . .** Maya Oppenheim, 'Bill Maher invites Milo Yiannopoulos back on show', *Independent*, 7 June 2017.

p. 128: **Likewise, when challenged about sexist statements by Cathy Newman . . .** Milo Yiannopoulos, 'Twitter's Post-Milo Depression', Breitbart (www.breitbart.com), 12 August 2016; Claudia Romeo and Joe Daunt, 'Milo Yiannopoulos defends his Leslie Jones tweets: All I did was crack a few jokes about a Hollywood star', *Business Insider* (www.businessinsider.com), 1 August 2016; 'Milo Yiannopoulos' fiery interview with Channel 4 News', Channel 4 News, 18 November 2016 (www.youtube.com).

p. 128: **The far-right troll 'weev' takes a similar approach . . .** The far-right troll Andrew Auernheimer, 'Statement on Sarah Jeong', weev.net, 2 August 2018.

p. 129: **In both cases, the liberal establishment was . . .** 'Timeline of Breitbart's Sherrod smear', Media Matters for America (mediamatters.org), 22 July 2010; Mark Jurkowitz, 'The Reconstruction of a Media Mess', Pew Research Center, Project for Excellence in Journalism, 26 July 2010; Chris Rovzar, 'Just How Heavily Edited Was the ACORN-Sting Video?', New York, 2 April 2010; on the astonishing gullibility of the liberal media in the ACORN case, see 'NYT and the ACORN Hoax', Fairness and Accuracy in Reporting (fair.org), 11 March 2010; Rick Ungar, 'James O'Keefe Pays $100,000 To ACORN Employee He Smeared – Conservative Media Yawns', Forbes, 8 March 2013; John Atlas, 'ACORN Vindicated of Wrongdoing by the Congressional Watchdog Office', *Huffington Post*, 5 May 2015.

p. 129: **In a vivid and telling stroke . . .** James O'Keefe, 'Chaos for Glory: My Time With Acorn', *Breitbart*, 10 September 2009.

p. 130: **When an insider described Andrew Breitbart as . . .** Lloyd Grove, 'How Breitbart Unleashes Hate Mobs to Threaten, Dox, and Troll Trump Critics', the *Daily Beast*, 1 March 2016.

p. 130: **It was, ostensibly, performance art . . .** Aja Romano makes the 'performance art' analogy in 'How the alt-right uses internet trolling to confuse you into dismissing its ideology', *Vox*, 11 January 2017.

p. 131: **As Sarah Jeong points out . . .** Jeong, *The Internet of Garbage*, pp. 22–5; Keith Stuart, 'Zoe Quinn: "All Gamergate has done is ruin people's lives"', *Guardian*, 3 December 2014; Zachary Jason, 'Game of Fear', *Boston* Magazine, 28 April 2015; Alex Hern, 'Gamergate hits new low with attempts to send Swat teams to critics', *Guardian*, 13 January 2015.

p. 132: **Before his attack, Minassian had declared on Facebook . . .** Jason Wilson, 'Toronto van attack: Facebook post may link suspect to misogynist "incel" subculture', *Guardian*, 25 April 2018; 'Elliot Rodger: How misogynist killer became "incel hero"', BBC News, 26 April 2018; David Futrelle, 'When a Mass Murderer Has a Cult Following', The Cut (www.thecut.com), 27 April 2018; Justin Ling, '"Not as ironic as I imagined": the incels spokesman on why he is renouncing them', *Guardian*, 19 June 2018.

p. 133: **During the rampage by former student Nikolas Cruz . . .** David Futrelle, 'Incels hail "our savior St. Nikolas Cruz" for Valentine's Day school shooting', We Hunted the Mammoth, 14 February 2018; Anna North, 'Men's Rights Activists Come Out In Support Of Salon Killer', *Jezebel* (www.jezebel.com), 14 October 2011.

CHAPTER FIVE

p. 137: **After about twenty minutes . . .** Matthew Haag and Maya Salam, 'Gunman in "Pizzagate" Shooting is Sentenced to 4 Years in Prison', *New York Times*, 23 June 2017; 'The saga of "Pizzagate": The fake story that shows how conspiracy theories spread', BBC Trending, 2 December 2016; Amanda Robb, 'Anatomy of a Fake News Scandal', *Rolling Stone*, 16 November 2017; Mark Segraves, 'Charging documents for Edgar Welch', Twitter.com, 5 December 2016; Andrew Kaczynski, 'Michael Flynn quietly deletes fake news tweet about Hillary Clinton's involvement in sex crimes', CNN, 14 December 2016.

p. 138: **In Giorgio De Maria's cult horror novel . . .** Giorgio De Maria, *The Twenty Days of Turin*, W. W. Norton & Company Ltd: London, 2017.

p. 139 **The social industry platform is one powerful faction . . .** Nick Srnicek, *Platform Capitalism*, Polity Press: Cambridge, 2016.

p. 140: **In the UK, print circulation is heading for a cliff fall . . .** 'World Press Trends 2017: The audience-focused era arrives', World News Publishing Focus, 6 August 2017; 'Newspapers Fact Sheet', Pew Research Center, 13 June 2018; Roy Greenslade, 'Suddenly, national newspapers are heading for that print cliff fall', *Guardian*, 27 May 2016.

p. 140: **British press barons are discussing . . .** Robert Cookson, 'UK publishers look to consolidate in print battle', *Financial Times*, 10 April 2016; Anna Nicolaou, 'Advertising revenues on US digital platforms set to surpass TV', *Financial Times*, 8 June 2016.

p. 140: **Most of it came from smartphone users . . .** Matthew Ingram, 'Google and Facebook Account For Nearly All Growth in Digital Ads', *Fortune*, 26 April 2017; John Koetsier, 'Mobile Advertising Will Drive 75% Of All Digital Ad Spend In 2018: Here's What's Changing', *Forbes*, 23 February 2018.

p. 141: **Already in 2016, 62 per cent of Americans . . .** Jeffrey Gottfried and Elisa Shearer, 'News Use Across Social Media Platforms 2016', Pew Research Center, 26 May 2016.

p. 141: **YouTube ranks second . . .** Geoff Colvin, 'Why Facebook and Google Still Resist Calling Themselves Media Companies', *Fortune*, 16 November 2016.

p. 142: **They are leaders of the pack among . . .** Simon Bowers, 'Google expected to reveal growth of offshore cash funds to $43bn', *Guardian*, 26 January 2016; Alanna Petroff, 'Top 50 U.S. companies hold $1.4 trillion in cash offshore', CNN, 14 April 2016.

p. 142: **The project proposes . . .** Hannah Kuchler, 'Facebook launches journalism project', *Financial Times*, 11 January 2017.

p. 142: **When Mark Zuckerberg writes . . .** Jeff John Roberts, 'Why Facebook Won't Admit It's a Media Company', Fortune, 14 November 2016; Karissa Bell, 'Facebook: We're not a media company. Also Facebook: Watch our news shows', Mashable, 8 June 2018.

p. 142: **Mark Zuckerberg's extreme agnosticism . . .** Kara Swisher, 'Full transcript: Facebook CEO Mark Zuckerberg on Recode Decode', Recode (www.recode.net), 18 July 2018; Alex Hern, 'Mark Zuckerberg's remarks on Holocaust denial "irresponsible"', *Guardian*, 19 July 2018.

p. 142: **Facebook's old media competitors miss the mark . . .** Sam Thielman, 'Facebook news selection is in hands of editors not algorithms, documents show', *Guardian*, 12 May 2016.

p. 143: **Google reacted as any good monopolist would . . .** Oscar Williams, 'Google News Spain to be shut down: what does it mean?', *Guardian*, 12 December 2014.

p. 144: **After all, Trump's candidacy was supposed to . . .** Ben Norton, 'How the Hillary Clinton campaign deliberately "elevated" Donald Trump with its "pied piper" strategy', *Salon*, 10 November 2016.

p. 144: **This false claim was shared . . .** Sapna Maheshwari, 'How Fake News Goes Viral: A Case Study', *New York Times*, 20 November 2016.

p. 144: **As Martin Baron, executive editor of the *Washington Post*, complained . . .** Jim Rutenberg, 'Media's Next Challenge: Overcoming the Threat of Fake News', *New York Times*, 6 November 2016.

p. 145: **For example, a study by researchers at Ohio State University looked at . . .** Richard Gunther, Paul A. Beck and Erik C. Nisbet, 'Fake News Did Have a Significant Impact on the Vote in the 2016 Election', Ohio State University, February 2018.

p. 145: **These other factors might include . . .** Thomas Ferguson, Paul Jorgensen and Jie Chen, 'Industrial Structure and Party Competition in an Age of Hunger Games: Donald Trump and the 2016 Presidential Election', Institute for New Economic Thinking, Working Paper No. 66, January 2018.

p. 145: **In another, Democratic National Committee chair Donna Brazile said . . .** Jordan Weissman, 'Hillary Clinton's Wall Street Speeches Have Leaked. No Wonder She Didn't Want Them to Get Out', *Slate*, 7 October 2016; Rachel Revesz, 'CNN fires Donna Brazile for allegedly giving debate questions to Hillary Clinton in advance', *Independent*, 31 October 2016; David A. Graham, 'Russian Trolls and the Trump Campaign Both Tried to Depress Black Turnout', *The Atlantic*, 17 December 2016.

p. 145: **Trump's claim that she lied . . .** Jon Greenberg and Angie Drobnic Holan, 'Trump right that Clinton made up story about Bosnia sniper fire', *PolitiFact*, 22 June 2016.

p. 146: **Both stories, aggressively promoted by the Post . . .** Glenn Greenwald, 'Russia Hysteria Infects WashPost Again: False Story About Hacking U.S. Electric Grid', *The Intercept*, 31 December 2016.

p. 146: **It is child's play to list a century of official hoaxes . . .** Phillip Knightley, *The*

First Casualty: The War Correspondent as Hero and Myth-Maker from the Crimea to Iraq, Johns Hopkins University Press: Baltimore, MA, 2004.

p. 146: **These include not just the usual run of . . .** Paul Lewis, 'Churnalism or news? How PRs have taken over the media', *Guardian*, 23 February 2011.

p. 146: **For example, the satirical claim that the US would . . .** Nicky Woolf, 'As fake news takes over Facebook feeds, many are taking satire as fact', *Guardian*, 17 November 2016.

p. 147: **The *Toronto Sun*'s false story . . .** Ishmael N. Daro, 'A Fake Online Review Claimed Refugees "Slaughtered Goats" In a Hotel. This Newspaper Helped it Go Viral', BuzzFeed News, 11 October 2018.

p. 147: **The baser truth is that Facebook profited . . .** Judd Legum, 'Facebook's pledge to eliminate misinformation is itself fake news', *Guardian*, 20 July 2018.

p. 147: **In 2017, Facebook launched a 'war on fake news' . . .** Dave Lee, 'Facebook's fake news crisis deepens', BBC News, 15 November 2016; 'Facebook fake news: Zuckerberg details plans to combat problem', BBC News, 19 November 2016; Mark Molloy, 'Facebook just made it harder for you to share fake news', *Daily Telegraph*, 20 March 2017.

p. 147: **Zuckerberg admitted that the problem was . . .** 'Facebook publishes fake news ads in UK papers', BBC News, 8 May 2017.

p. 147: **Subsequently, following Zuckerberg's appearance before Congress . . .** John Hegeman, 'Facing Facts: Facebook's Fight Against Misinformation', Facebook Newsroom, 23 May 2018.

p. 148: **Hardly anyone is susceptible to 'fact-checking' . . .** Aniko Hannak, Drew Margolin, Brian Keegan and Ingmar Weber, 'Get Back! You Don't Know Me Like That: The Social Mediation of Fact Checking Interventions in Twitter Conversations', Proceedings of the Eighth International AAAI Conference on Weblogs and Social Media, 2014; see also Alice E. Marwick, 'Why Do People Share Fake News? A Sociotechnical Model of Media Effects', *Georgetown Law Technology Review*, 424, July 2018.

p. 149: **For the philosopher Steve Fuller . . .** Steve Fuller, *Post-Truth: Knowledge as a Power Game*, Anthem Press: London, 2018, p. 1.

p. 149: **Michiko Kakutani, the esteemed journalist . . .** Michiko Kakutani, *The Death of Truth*, William Collins: London, 2018, p. 40.

p. 149: **This reflects the spontaneous ideology of professionals . . .** Matt Huber, 'The Politics of Truth/Facts', *Medium*, 25 January 2017.

p. 149: **Indeed, the *New York Times* has reported . . .** David Adler, 'Centrists Are the Most Hostile to Democracy, Not Extremists', *New York Times*, 23 May 2018.

p. 150: **The journalist Peter Pomerantsev . . .** Carole Cadwalladr, 'Daniel Dennett: "I begrudge every hour I have to spend worrying about politics"', *Observer*, 12 February 2017; Peter Pomerantsev, 'The rise of the postmodern politician', BBC Newsnight, 16 March 2017.

p. 150: **The theory that postmodernism has promoted . . .** Lee McIntyre, *Post-Truth*, MIT Press: Cambridge, MA, 2018, pp. 200–45; Matthew D'Ancona, *Post Truth: The New War on Truth and How to Fight Back*, Penguin Random House: London, 2017, pp. 89–110; C. G. Prado, *America's Post-Truth Phenomenon: When Feelings and Opinions Trump Facts and Evidence*, Praeger: London, 2018, pp. 5, 9, 21–2 and 110.

p. 150: **For example, Kakutani cites without apparent irony a preening comment . . .** Alan Jay Levinovitz, 'It's Not All Relative', *The Chronicle of Higher Education*, 5 March 2017.

p. 150: **For British journalist Matthew D'Ancona . . .** D'Ancona, *Post Truth*, p. 91.

p. 151: **According to philosopher Lee McIntyre . . .** McIntyre, *Post-Truth*, p. 202.

p. 151: **For Kakutani . . .** Kakutani, *The Death of Truth*, p. 56.

p. 151: **So is the motif of 'construction' . . .** Ian Hacking, *The Social Construction of What?*, Harvard University Press: Cambridge, MA, 1999, p. 41.

p. 152: **As Karl Rove put it, 'we create our own reality'.** Ron Suskind, 'Faith, Certainty and the Presidency of George W. Bush', *New York Times Magazine*, 17 October 2004.

p. 153: **The sacked National Security Council officer Rich Higgins . . .** Jeet Heer, 'Trump's Racism and the Myth of "Cultural Marxism"', *New Republic*, 15 August 2017.

p. 153: **The anti-Trump conservative Australian television news anchor . . .** Jason Wilson, 'Chris Uhlmann should mind his language on "cultural Marxism"', *Guardian*, 22 February 2016.

p. 153: **Their 'Enlightenment' is . . .** Dan Hind, *The Threat to Reason: How the Enlightenment Was Hijacked and How We Can Reclaim it*, Verso: London and New York, 2008.

p. 153: **Now a similar rhetorical move . . .** Kakutani, *The Death of Truth*, p. 45.

p. 154: **In surprise bestsellers . . .** David Ray Griffin, *The New Pearl Harbor: Disturbing Questions About the Bush Administration and 9/11*, Arris Books: Devon, 2004; Nafeez Mosaddeq Ahmed, War on Truth: Disinformation and the Anatomy of Terrorism, Olive Branch Press: Ithaca, NY, 2005; Nafeez Mosaddeq Ahmed, *The London Bombings: An Independent Inquiry, The Overlook Press*: London, 2006.

p. 154: **As Emma Jane and Chris Fleming's analysis . . .** Emma A. Jane and Chris Fleming, *Modern Conspiracy: The Importance of Being Paranoid*, Bloomsbury: New York and London, 2014 pp. 4–5. Devorah Baum notices a similar pattern. *Feeling Jewish: (A Book for Just About Anyone)*, Yale University Press: New Haven and London, 2017, pp. 53–5.

p. 155: **In a survey of 1,500 scientists . . .** Monya Baker, '1,500 scientists lift the lid on reproducibility', *Nature*, 25 May 2016. On the replication crisis, see Nature's special online report, 'Challenges in irreproducible research', *Nature*, 18 October 2018.

p. 155: **According to the historian of ideas Philip Mirowski . . .** Philip Mirowski, *Science-Mart: Privatizing American Science*, Harvard University Press: Cambridge, MA, 2011.

p. 156: **Among the worst examples of this degradation . . .** C. G. Begley and L. M. Ellis, 'Raise standards for preclinical cancer research', *Nature*, 483, 2012, pp. 531–3; C. G. Begley, 'Reproducibility: Six red flags for suspect work', *Nature*, 497, 2013, pp. 433–4.

p. 156: **The industry is riddled with . . .** Ben Goldacre, 'Foreword', *Bad Pharma: How Medicine is Broken, and How We Can Fix it* Fourth Estate: London, 2013.

p. 156: **When a peer-reviewed survey of scientists . . .** Daniele Fanelli, 'How Many Scientists Fabricate and Falsify Research? A Systematic Review and Meta-Analysis of Survey Data', *PLOS One*, 29 May 2009.

p. 156: **Data was hailed as . . .** 'The world's most valuable resource is no longer oil, but data', the *Economist*, 6 May 2017; Andrew McAfee and Erik Brynjolfsson, 'Big Data: The Management Revolution', *Harvard Business Review*, October 2012.

p. 156: **In an excitable piece for *Wired* . . .** Chris Anderson, 'The End of Theory: the Data Deluge Makes the Scientific Method Obsolete', *Wired*, 23 June 2008.

p. 157: **The bonus of big data is . . .** Carlo Ratti and Dirk Helbing, 'The Hidden

Danger of Big Data', in Dirk Helbing, ed., *Towards Digital Enlightenment: Essays on the Dark and Light Sides of the Digital Revolution*, Springer: New York, 2019, p. 22.

p. 157: **In 1948, 125 million telephone conversations . . .** James Gleick, *The Information: A History, a Theory, a Flood*, Pantheon Books, New York: 2011, p. 13.

p. 157: **Already by 2003, more data had been . . .** Paul Stephens, *The Poetics of Information Overload: From Gertrude Stein to Conceptual Writing*, University of Minnesota Press: Minneapolis, MN, 2015, Kindle loc. 83.

p. 157: **By 2016, 90 per cent of the entire . . .** Bernard Marr, 'How Much Data Do We Create Every Day? The Mind-Blowing Stats Everyone Should Read', *Forbes*, 21 May 2018.

p. 157: **In the same year, Google was . . .** 'There are over 3.5 billion searches per day on Google alone', *PRWeb*, 20 December 2017.

p. 157: **Google's estimates overstated . . .** Tim Harford, 'Big data: are we making a big mistake?', *Financial Times*, 28 March 2014.

p. 157: **The volume of data is not . . .** H. V. Jagadish, 'Big Data and Science', *Big Data Research*, Vol. 2, No. 2, June 2015, pp. 49–52.

p. 159: **Capitalism encounters . . .** David Harvey, *The Condition of Postmodernity: An Enquiry into the Origins of Cultural Change*, Blackwell: Cambridge, MA, 1989, pp. 284–307.

p. 159: **The development of information technologies . . .** 'Time and Space died yesterday. We are already living in the absolute, since we have already created eternal, omnipresent speed', Filippo Tommaso Marinetti, *The Futurist Manifesto*, 1909.

p. 159: **By 2008, the average American consumed . . .** Stephens, *The Poetics of Information Overload*, Kindle loc. 83.

p. 159: **When engineer Claude Shannon declared . . .** Gleick, *The Information: A History, A Theory,* A Flood, pp. 251–9.

p. 160: **Moreover, this production is taking place in a . . .** Jean Baudrillard, *Simulacra and Simulation*, University of Michigan Press: Ann Arbor, MI, 1994.

p. 160: **What seems like a device . . .** Ian Hamilton, 'Jaron Lanier Explains What Could Make VR "A Device Of Nightmares"', *Upload* (www.uploadvr.com), 8 June 2018.

p. 161: **For example, the BBC alleges . . .** Joel Gunter and Olga Robinson, 'Sergei Skripal and the Russian disinformation game', BBC News, 9 September 2018.

p. 161: **In 2016, a team of researchers published . . .** Michelle Drouin, Daniel Miller, Shaun M. J. Wehle and Elisa Hernandez, 'Why do people lie online? "Because everyone lies on the internet"', *Computers in Human Behavior*, Vol. 64, November 2016, pp. 126–33.

p. 161: **Averse to public ownership and regulation . . .** Richard Barbrook and Andy Cameron, The Internet Revolution: From Dot-com Capitalism to Cybernetic Communism, Institute of Network Cultures: Amsterdam, 2015.

p. 162: **Milan Kundera, reflecting on Stalinist tyranny, argued . . .** Quoted in John Forrester, *Truth Games: Lies, Money and Psychoanalysis*, Harvard University Press: Cambridge, MA, 1997, p. 81.

p. 162: **This, the 'sour grapes' theory of communications . . .** Evgeny Morozov, 'Moral panic over fake news hides the real enemy – the digital giants', *Guardian*, 8 January 2017.

CHAPTER SIX

p. 165: **In the moment of his supposed triumph . . .** 'Finsbury Park: Man "wanted to kill Muslims in van attack"', BBC News, 22 January 2018; Lizzie Dearden, 'Finsbury

Park attack trial: Darren Osborne was "smiling" after running over Muslims with van, court hears', *Independent*, 24 January 2018; Vikram Dodd, 'How London mosque attacker became a terrorist in three weeks', *Guardian*, 1 February 2018; Lizzie Dearden, 'Darren Osborne: How Finsbury Park terror attacker became "obsessed" with Muslims in less than a month', *Independent*, 2 February 2018; Nico Hines, 'Neighbor of Terror Suspect Darren Osborne: "He's Always Been a Complete C**t"', *Daily Beast*, 19 June 2017.

p. 166: **He wouldn't even know who . . .** 'London Muslim attack suspect Darren Osborne: Pub fights and anti-Muslim rants', Agence France-Presse, 20 June 2017.

p. 167: **The psychoanalyst Octave Mannoni once remarked . . .** '[I]t is only necessary to remember how often the negro figures in the dreams of Europeans who have quite probably never even seen a negro', Octave Mannoni, *Prospero and Caliban: The Psychology of Colonization*, Methuen & Co. Ltd: London, 1956, p. 19.

p. 167: **In cyberspace, the great 'consensual hallucination' . . .** William Gibson, *Neuromancer*, Berkley Publishing Group: New York, 1989, p. 128.

p. 168: **Throughout the early 1990s, far-right, Holocaust-denying groups . . .** Les Back, Michael Keith and John Solomos, 'Technology, Race and Neo-fascism in a Digital Age: The New Modalities of Racist Culture', *Patterns of Prejudice*, Vol. 30, 1996, pp. 3–27.

p. 168: **This is despite the fact that . . .** Tara McKelvey, 'Father and Son Team on Hate Site', USA Today, 16 July 2001; David Schwab Abel, 'The Racist Next Door', *New York Times*, 19 April 1998; 'World's oldest neo-Nazi website Stormfront shut down', Associated Press, 29 August 2017; Eric Saslow, 'The White Flight of Derek Black', *Washington Post*, 15 October 2016.

p. 168: **Journalist Paul Lewis and academic Zeynep Tufekci have . . .** Paul Lewis, '"Fiction is outperforming reality": how YouTube's algorithm distorts truth', *Guardian*, 2 February 2018; Zeynep Tufekci, 'YouTube, the Great Radicalizer', *New York Times*, 10 March 2018.

p. 169: **Part of the answer is . . .** Guillaume Chaslot, 'YouTube's A.I. was divisive in the US presidential election', *Medium*, 27 November 2016.

p. 169: **Zeynep Tufekci argues . . .** Zeynep Tufekci, 'YouTube, the Great Radicalizer', *New York Times*, 10 March 2018.

p. 169: **Nowadays all you have to do is . . .** John Naughton, 'Extremism pays. That's why Silicon Valley isn't shutting it down', *Guardian*, 18 March 2018.

p. 170: **As former Google engineer Guillaume Chaslot put it . . .** Paul Lewis, '"Fiction is outperforming reality": how YouTube's algorithm distorts truth', *Guardian*, 2 February 2018.

p. 170: **The artist James Bridle has written . . .** James Bridle, 'Something is wrong on the internet', *Medium*, 6 November 2017.

p. 170: **It reflected data coming from . . .** Tracy McVeigh, 'Amazon acts to halt sales of "Keep Calm and Rape" T-shirts', *Guardian*, 2 March 2013; Colin Lecher, '"Keep Calm And Rape", Plus 5 More Awful/Offensive/Hilarious Algorithm-Created Shirts', Popular Science, 6 March 2013.

p. 170: **And platform behaviour obeys . . .** Jeffrey S. Juris, 'Reflections on #Occupy Everywhere: Social media, public space, and emerging logics of aggregation', *American Ethnologist*, Vol. 39, No. 2, May 2012, pp. 259–79.

p. 171: **Alice Marwick, an academic and former Microsoft researcher . . .** Alice Marwick, *Status Update: Celebrity, Publicity, and Branding in the Social Media Age*, Yale University Press: New Haven and London, 2013.

p. 172: **This is one of the things that cultural critic Jonathan Beller is getting at . . .** Jonathan Beller, *The Message is Murder: Substrates of Computational Capital*, Pluto Press: London, 2018, p. 1.

p. 172: **The 'if . . . then' logic of algorithms . . .** Taina Bucher, *If . . . Then: Algorithmic Power and Politics*, Oxford University Press: New York, 2018.

p. 173: **As the political scientist Colin Crouch defines it . . .** Colin Crouch, *Post-Democracy*, Polity Press: Cambridge, 2004.

p. 173: **And, as the Italian anarchist Errico Malatesta once put it . . .** Errico Malatesta, *The Method of Freedom: An Errico Malatesta Reader*, AK Press: Chico, CA, 2014, p. 488.

p. 174: **The first mass market created by print . . .** Zeynep Tufekci, *Twitter and Tear Gas: The Power and Fragility of Networked Protest*, Yale University Press: New Haven and London, 2017, p. 641.

p. 174: **It helped create, as Justin Joque put it . . .** Justin Joque, *Deconstruction Machines: Writing in the Age of Cyberwar*, University of Minnesota Press: Minneapolis, MN, 2018, Kindle loc. 2941.

p. 175: **This is the context in which, Devorah Baum argues . . .** Devorah Baum, *Feeling Jewish: (A Book for Just About Anyone)*, Yale University Press: New Haven and London, 2017, p. 97.

p. 177: **She milked the last dismal vestiges . . .** Hillary Clinton, 'Secretary Clinton Speaks on Internet Freedom', US Department of State, 22 January 2010 www.youtube.com. Brand's full statement was: 'On the one hand information wants to be expensive, because it's so valuable. The right information in the right place just changes your life. On the other hand, information wants to be free, because the cost of getting it out is getting lower and lower all the time.' See '"Information Wants to be Free": The history of that quote', *Digitopoly* (www.digitopoly.org) 25 October 2015.

p. 177: **The wave of monopolization taking place . . .** Michael Corcoran, 'Democracy in Peril: Twenty Years of Media Consolidation Under the Telecommunications Act', *Truthout* (www.truthout.org), 11 February 2016.

p. 177: **It was easy for the State Department to lobby Twitter . . .** Nick Bilton, Hatching *Twitter: A True Story of Money, Power, Friendship, and Betrayal*, Penguin: New York, 2013, p. 327.

p. 178: **The Justice Department demanded access. . .** Kevin Poulsen, 'Prosecutors Defend Probe of WikiLeaks-related Twitter Accounts', *Wired*, 8 April 2011.

p. 178: **The security state's ancient dream had been . . .** David Sanger, *The Perfect Weapon: War, Sabotage, and Fear in the Cyber* Age, Penguin Random House: New York, 2018, pp. 227–8.

p. 178: **Twitter fought the Justice Department on its demands . . .** Kevin Poulsen, 'Judge Rules Feds Can Have WikiLeaks Associates' Twitter Data', *Wired*, 10 November 2011; 'You Don't Sacrifice Your Privacy Rights When You Use Twitter', ACLU, 6 March 2013.

p. 179: **FBI director James Comey complained that Apple . . .** Sanger, *The Perfect Weapon*, p. 227.

p. 179: **He said that such secretive, counter-security measures . . .** 'Mark Zuckerberg "confused and frustrated" by US spying', BBC News, 14 March 2014.

p. 180: **And yet, as the philosopher Gilbert Simondon pointed out . . .** See also Heidegger on the broken hammer: only when technology breaks down are we forced to reflect on the network of purposes to which it belongs. Gilbert Simondon, *On the*

Mode of Existence of Technical Objects, University of Minnesota Press: Minneapolis, MN, 2017.

p. 181: **Facebook's already much larger user base had increased . . .** 'Number of monthly active Twitter users worldwide from 1st quarter 2010 to 3rd quarter 2018 (in millions)', Statista, 2019; 'Number of monthly active Facebook users worldwide as of 3rd quarter 2018 (in millions)', *Statista*, 2019.

p. 181: **Most social industry users, still a minority . . .** Peter Beaumont, 'The truth about Twitter, Facebook and the uprisings in the Arab world', *Guardian*, 25 February 2011.

p. 181: **The infamous Facebook experiment, published in 2014 . . .** Adam D. I. Kramer, Jamie E. Guillory and Jeffrey T. Hancock, 'Experimental evidence of massive-scale emotional contagion through social networks', PNAS, 111 (24), 2014, pp. 8788–8790.

p. 182: **In Tahrir Square, a coalition of Islamists, liberals and Nasserists had built . . .** Atef Shahat Said, 'The Tahrir Effect: History, Space, and Protest in the Egyptian Revolution of 2011', University of Michigan, 2014.

p. 184: **The reduced costs of organizing also reduced the costs of quitting . . .** Thomas Rid, *Cyber War Will Not Take Place*, Oxford University Press: New York, 2013, p. 28.

p. 184: **And, as Paolo Gerbaudo's analysis in his book . . .** Paolo Gerbaudo, *The Digital Party*, Pluto Press: London, 2019, pp. 25–6.

p. 185: **On Ask.fm, another recruiter answered questions about . . .** Laurie Segall, 'ISIS recruiting tactics: Apple pie and video games', CNN, 30 September 2014; Wendy Andhika Prajuli, 'On social media, ISIS uses fantastical propaganda to recruit members', The Conversation (www.theconversation.com), 4 December 2017.

p. 185: **By 2014, as the Iraqi government suppressed Sunni protests against their political exclusion . . .** Martin Chulov, 'Isis: the inside story', *Guardian*, 11 December 2014; Michael Weiss and Hassan Hassan, *ISIS: Inside the Army of Terror*, Regan Arts: New York, 2016; Patrick Cockburn, *The Rise of the Islamic State: ISIS and the New Sunni Revolution*, Verso: London and New York, 2016, pp. 42–5.

p. 186: **By February 2015, it was estimated that . . .** James P. Farwell, 'The Media Strategy of ISIS', *Survival: Global Politics and Strategy*, 56:6, 2014, pp. 49–5; Ben Makuch, 'ISIS's Favorite Hashtag Is a Weapon of War', Motherboard (www.motherboard.vice.com), 27 June 2014; Emerson T. Brooking and P. W. Singer, 'War Goes Viral', *The Atlantic*, November 2016; Emerson T. Brooking and P. W. Singer, *LikeWar: The Weaponization of Social Media*, Houghton Mifflin Harcourt: Boston, MA, 2018.

p. 186: **They shared slick videos aimed at Western millennials . . .** Majid Alfifi, Parisa Kaghazgaran, James Caverlee and Fred Morstatter, 'Measuring the Impact of ISIS Social Media Strategy', MIS2: Misinformation and Misbehavior Mining on the Web (workshop), Los Angeles, CA, 2018; Matt Broomfield, 'Twitter Shuts Down 125,000 Isis-Linked Accounts', *Independent*, 6 February 2016; Lisa Blaker, 'The Islamic State's Use of Online Social Media', Military Cyber Affairs: The Journal of the Military Cyber Professionals Association, Vol. 1, No. 1, 2015; Jason Burke, '"Gangsta jihadi" Denis Cuspert killed fighting in Syria', *Guardian*, 19 January 2018.

p. 186: **If anything, ISIS became known for the extravagance of its displays of violence . . .** Laura Ryan, 'Al-Qaida and ISIS Use Twitter Differently. Here's How and Why', National Journal (wwwnationaljournal.com), 9 October 2014; Kyle J. Greene, 'ISIS: Trends in Terrorist Media and Propaganda', International Studies Capstone Research Papers, 3, 2015.

p. 186: **In the first six months of the US-led bombing campaign to oust ISIS . . .** ISIS drawing steady stream of recruits, despite bombings', Associated Press, 11 February 2015; Aya Batrawy, Paisley Dodds and Lori Hinnant, 'Leaked Isis documents reveal recruits have poor grasp of Islamic faith', *Independent*, 16 August 2016.

p. 187: **Polling controversially suggested that 7 per cent of British citizens . . .** Madeline Grant, '16% of French Citizens Support Isis, Poll Finds', *Newsweek*, 26 August 2014.

p. 187: **Nor did it build the torture chambers during the anti-occupation insurgency in Iraq . . .** 'Iraq torture "worse after Saddam"', BBC News, 21 September 2006; Terrence McCoy, 'Camp Bucca: The US prison that became the birthplace of Isis', *Independent*, 4 November 2014; Neal McDonald, 'Iraqi reality-TV hit takes fear factor to another level', *Christian Science Monitor*, 7 June 2005.

p. 187: **In fact, the invasion forces consisted of just two thousand jihadists . . .** Ned Parker, Isabel Coles and Raheem Salman, 'Special Report: How Mosul fell – An Iraqi general disputes Baghdad's story', Reuters, 14 October 2014; Matt Sienkiewicz, 'Arguing with ISIS: web 2.0, open source journalism, and narrative disruption', *Critical Studies in Media Communication*, 35:1, 2018, pp. 122–35; Steve Rose, 'The Isis propaganda war: a hi-tech media jihad', *Guardian*, 7 October 2014.

p. 188: **At one stage, ISIS accounts asked followers to video themselves waving the ISIS flag . . .** Greene, 'ISIS: Trends in Terrorist Media and Propaganda'.

p. 189: **Alberto Fernandez argued that the US . . .** Alberto M. Fernandez, 'Here to stay and growing: Combating ISIS propaganda networks', The Brookings Project on U.S. Relations with the Islamic World, U.S.-Islamic World Forum Papers 2015, October 2015; Richard Forno and Arnupam Joshi, 'How U.S. "Cyber Bombs" against Terrorists Really Work', The Conversation, 13 May 2016.

p. 189: **By 2016, they were vaunting their ability to use 'cyberbombs' . . .** Brian Ross and James Gordon Meek, 'ISIS Threat at Home: FBI Warns US Military About Social Media Vulnerabilities', ABC News, 1 December 2014; '"ISIS hackers" threats against U.S. military wives actually came from Russian trolls', Associated Press, 8 May 2018.

p. 190: **Another study by George Washington University . . .** 'Enhancing the Understanding of the Foreign Terrorist Fighters Phenomenon in Syria', United Nations Office of Counter-Terrorism, July 2017; Lizzie Dearden, 'Isis: UN study finds foreign fighters in Syria "lack basic understanding of Islam"', *Independent*, 4 August 2017; Christal Hayes, 'Study: ISIS has lost territory but could still pose long-term threat', *USA Today*, 6 February 2018.

p. 190: **Its use of the platforms shows us something . . .** Jonathan Beller, *The Message is Murder: Substrates of Computational Capital*, Pluto Press: London, 2018, p. 5.

p. 190: **If the spectacle is a social relationship mediated by images . . .** Guy Debord, *The Society of the Spectacle*, Rebel Press: London, 1994, 2014.

p. 191: **As a presidential campaigner . . .** Samuel C. Woolley and Douglas Guilbeault, 'United States: Manufacturing Consensus Online', in Samuel C. Woolley and Philip N. Howard, eds, *Computational Propaganda: Political Parties, Politicians, and Political Manipulation on Social Media*, Oxford University Press: New York, 2019, p. 187.

p. 191: **An analysis of Trump's tweets during the election . . .** Cora Lacatus, 'For Donald Trump, campaigning by Twitter limited the public's access to his policy positions and strategies', LSE Blogs, 21 January 2018.

p. 192: **Historically, the far right has succeeded by building roots . . .**Dylan Riley, *The*

Civic Foundations of Fascism in Europe: Italy, Spain, and Romania, 1870–1945, Verso: London and New York, 2019.

p. 193: **Rather, far more lethally, it may be indicated by the phenomenon . . .** For an explanation of this concept, see Heather Timmons, 'Stochastic terror and the cycle of hate that pushes unstable Americans to violence', *Quartz* (www.qz.com), 26 October 2018.

p. 194: **In the decade from 2008 to 2017, according to the Anti-Defamation League . . .** Aamna Mohdin, 'The far-right was responsible for the majority of America's extremist killings in 2017', *Quartz*, 18 January 2018.

p. 194: **Media commentary has begun to argue that the internet . . .** For examples of this style of coverage, see Amanda Coletta, 'Quebec City Mosque shooter scoured Twitter for Trump, right-wing figures before attack', *Washington Post*, 18 April 2018; Kevin Roose, 'The far-right was responsible for the majority of America's extremist killings in 2017', *New York Times*, 28 October 2018.

CONCLUSION

p. 200: **The average global internet user now spends . . .** 'Daily time spent on social networking by internet users worldwide from 2012 to 2017', *Statista*, 2019; 'People spend most of their waking hours staring at screens', *MarketWatch*, 4 August 2018.

p.200: **In the Latinized Christian use propagated by Evagrius of Pontus . . .** Jean-Charles Nault, OSB, *The Noonday Devil: Acedia, The Unnamed Evil of Our Times*, Ignatius Press: San Francisco, CA, 2015.

p.201: **As the historian of writing Barry Powell argues . . .** Barry B. Powell, *Writing: Theory and History of the Technology of Civilization*, Wiley-Blackwell: Malden, MA, 2012, p. 12.

p.202: **The ease of associative linking with hypertext . . .** Marshall McLuhan, *The Gutenberg Galaxy: The Making of Typographic Man*, University of Toronto Press: Toronto, 2011, p. 455.

p. 202: **It shows us how much our inherited standards of punctuation . . .** Marshall McLuhan, *The Gutenberg Galaxy: The Making of Typographic Man*, University of Toronto Press: Toronto, 2011, p. 455.

p. 203: **'The subject cries out,' Lacan exclaimed . . .** Jacques Lacan, 'Response to Jean Hyppolite's Commentary on Freud's "Verneinung", in *Écrits: The First Complete Edition in English*, W. W. Norton & Company: New York, 2006, p. 322.

p. 203: **'The more I read,' Frederick Douglass wrote in 1845 . . .** *Frederick Douglass, Narrative of the Life of Frederick Douglass, an American Slave, Literary Classics of the United States*: New York, 1994, p. 42.

p. 203: **Where it was taught, penmanship was indexed . . .** Tamara Thornton, *Handwriting in America: A Cultural History*, Yale University Press: New Haven and London, 1996.

p. 204: **The characteristic experience of literacy prior to the Internet . . .** Deborah Brandt, *The Rise of Writing: Redefining Mass Literacy*, Cambridge University Press: Cambridge, 2015.

p. 205: **As Colette Soler put it. . .** Colette Soler, Lacan: *The Unconscious Reinvented*, Karnac Books, London: 2014, Kindle loc. 3239.

p. 205: **An alluring myth of the internet's origins has it . . .** Cade Metz, 'Paul Baran, the link between nuclear war and the internet', *Wired*, 4 September 2012;

p. 206: **The underlying idea for a 'distributed network' of writing . . .** Paul Baran,

'On Distributed Communications: I. Introduction to Distributed Communications Networks', United States Air Force Project RAND, RAND Corporation, August 1964.

p. 206: **As Sandy Baldwin puts it . . .**Sandy Baldwin, *The Internet Unconscious: On the Subject of Electronic Literature*, Bloomsbury: New York, 2015, pp. 33–7.

p. 206: **It was desperate to outdo Britain and Germany . . .** Antonio Gonzales and Emmanuelle Jouve, 'Minitel: histoire du réseau télématique français', *Flux: Cahiers scientifiques internationaux Réseaux et territoires*, 2002, Vol. 1, No. 47, pp. 84–9.

p. 206: **Gérard Théry, the French director general of telecommunications . . .** Julien Mailland and Kevin Driscoll, *Minitel: Welcome to the Internet*, MIT Press: Cambridge, MA, 2017; Gonzales and Jouve, 'Minitel: histoire du réseau télématique français', *Flux: Cahiers scientifiques internationaux Réseaux et territoires*, pp. 84–9.

p. 207: **'I am dreaming,' wrote artist Ben Vautier . . .** Vautier quoted in Annick Bureaud, 'Art and Minitel in France in the 1980s', in Judy Malloy, ed., *Social Media Archeology and Poetics*, MIT Press: Cambridge, MA, 2016, p. 144; Emmanuel Videcoq and Bernard Prince, 'Félix Guattari et les agencements post-média: L'expérience de radio Tomate et du minitel Alter', *Multitudes*, Vol. 2, No. 21, 2005, pp. 23–30; Félix Guattari, 'Toward a Post-Media Era', *Mute* Magazine, 1 February 2012.

p. 208: **The 'machines of information, communication, intelligence, art . . .** Mailland and Driscoll, *Minitel: Welcome to the Internet*, pp. 289–90; Videcoq and Prince, 'Félix Guattari et les agencements post-média: L'expérience de radio Tomate et du minitel Alter', pp. 23–30.

p. 208: **During the strike, they forged a new union . . .** Danièle Kergoat, 'De la jubilation à la déreliction, l'utilization du minitel dans les luttes infirmières (1988–1989)', in *Les coordinations de travailleurs dans la confrontation sociale*, Futur antérieur, Paris: 1994.

p. 208: **Among other things, it was a state-maintained free market . . .** Mailland and Driscoll, *Minitel: Welcome to the Internet*; 'The French Connection', Reply All, Gimlet Media, 21 January 2015.

p. 208: **The telecom entrepreneur Xavier Niel made his fortune . . .**Mailland and Driscoll, *Minitel: Welcome to the Internet*; 'The French Connection', Reply All.

p. 209: **There was a chance that French technique . . .** Julien Mailland, '101 Online: American Minitel Network and Lessons from Its Failure', *IEEE Annals of the History of Computing*, Vol. 38, No. 01, January/March 2016.

p. 210: **As Julien Mailland points out, however, both Minitel and the internet . . .** Mailland and Driscoll, *Minitel: Welcome to the Internet*, pp. 18–19; Julien Mailland, 'Minitel, the Open Network Before the Internet', *The Atlantic*, 16 June 2017.

p. 211: **While the regime harnesses computerization and big data to state surveillance . . .** Jack Lingchuan Qiu, *Working-Class Network Society: Communication Technology and the Information Have-Less in Urban China*, MIT Press: Cambridge, MA, 2009.

p. 212: **A tour of a brewery won't explain why somebody became . . .** Francis Spufford, *The Child That Books Built*, Faber & Faber, London: 2010, Kindle loc. 120.

p. 212: **To break an addiction, the neuroscientist Marc Lewis has argued**, Marc Lewis, *The Biology of Desire: Why Addiction Is Not a Disease*, Scribe: London, 2015.

p. 213: **The whole earth, according to this dispensation . .** Kevin Kelly, *What Technology Wants*, Viking: New York, 2010, pp. 26 and 515.

p. 213: **The technium was 'actually a divine phenomenon . . .** Kevin Kelly, 'How Computer Nerds Describe God', *Christianity Today*, 1 November 2002.

p. 213: **From Manuel Castells' celebration of online 'creative autonomy . . .** Manuel

Castells, *Communication Power*, Oxford University Press: Oxford, 2009; Clay Shirky, *Here Comes Everybody: The Power of Organizing Without Organizations*, Allen Lane: London, 2008.

p. 213: **The openness and indeterminacy of the network seemingly permitted what John Stuart Mill would have called 'experiments of living'.** John Stuart Mill, 'On Liberty' in *The Basic Writings of John Stuart Mill*, The Modern Library: New York, 2002, p. 174.

p. 214: **. . . as the historian Enzo Traverso writes . . .** Enzo Traverso, *Left-Wing Melancholia: Marxism, History, and Memory*, Columbia University Press: New York, 2016, p. 9.

p. 215: **They cross-dressed and marched . . .** Katrina Navickas, 'The Search for "General Ludd": The Mythology of Luddism', *Social History*, Vol. 30, No. 3, August 2005, pp. 281–95; Richard Conniff, 'What the Luddites Really Fought Against', *Smithsonian Magazine*, March 2011.

p. 215: **We need the 'intercalary gush' of Catholic poet Charles Péguy . . .** Traverso, *Left-Wing Melancholia*, p. 226.

ACKNOWLEDGEMENTS

This book was written in a state of near-monastic isolation. Even so, it couldn't have been finished without some invaluable assistance.

First of all, I'd particularly like to thank China Miéville and Davinia Hamilton, both of whom reviewed the drafts closely and offered tonnes of suggestions, ideas and challenges. Thanks also to Rosie Warren for her thoughtful feedback. I also benefited from conversations with Sam Kriss, who knows the Twittering Machine quite well.

I'd like to extend immense thanks to Susie Nicklin for seeing potential in the book, my agent Karolina Sutton for her support and my editor, Ellah Wakatama Allfrey, for her sharp-eyed guidance. And thanks to everyone at The Indigo Press and Curtis Brown for their patient help.

ABOUT THE AUTHOR

Richard Seymour is a writer and broadcaster and the author of numerous books about politics including *The Liberal Defence of Murder* (Verso, 2008), *Against Austerity* (Pluto, 2014) and *Corbyn: The Strange Rebirth of Radical Politics* (Verso, 2016). His writing appears in the *Guardian*, *Jacobin*, *London Review of Books*, *New York Times* and *Prospect*. He lives in London.

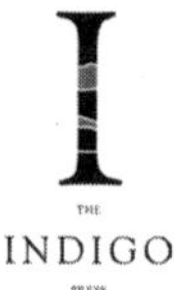

Sign up for our newsletter and receive exclusive updates, including extracts, podcasts, event notifications, competitions and more.

www.theindigopress.com/newsletter

Follow The Indigo Press:

Subscribe to the Mood Indigo podcast:

www.theindigopress.com/podcast